LIBRARIANSHIP AND LIBRARY SCIENCE IN INDIA

CONCEPTS IN COMMUNICATION
INFORMATICS & LIBRARIANSHIP
(CICIL)

For a list of titles in this series
see pp. 237 at the end of the book

Concepts in Communication
Informatics & Librarianship-60
General Editor : **S.P. Agrawal**

LIBRARIANSHIP AND LIBRARY SCIENCE IN INDIA

An Outline of Historical Perspectives

MOHAMED TAHER
Deputy Librarian
American Studies Research Centre
Hyderabad, India

and

DONALD GORDON DAVIS, JR.
Professor
Graduate School of Library & Information Studies
University of Texas
Austin, TX, USA

CONCEPT PUBLISHING COMPANY, NEW DELHI-110059

ISBN 81-7022-524-8

First Published 1994

Published and Printed by
Ashok Kumar Mittal
Concept Publishing Company
A/15-16, Commercial Block
Mohan Garden, New Delhi-110059 (India)

Lasertypeset by
Printing Express
H-13, Bali Nagar
New Delhi-110015

Dedicated to

Prof. DARA N MARSHALL (1906-1993)
who has long encouraged scholarship
in library history

LIBRARY HISTORY

"An account of the libraries in the first four periods (the Vedic, the Buddhistic, the Medieval, and the Muslim) must necessarily depend upon the historical research. This has not yet been done. The library profession is too small in India to spare a person to fill up this antiquarian gap. Those trained in the scientific method of tracing history are too preoccupied with dynastic and political history to spare sufficient time for cultural history in general and library history in particular". – *Dr. S R Ranganathan, the father of Indian Library science, in his radio talk in April 1956.*

Bibliophile

"The pride of the bibliophile in Asia has been his collection of manuscripts. Every manuscript, in the strict sense, is unique–being a hand-written text of hand-written copy of a text. Every manuscript, though unique, is not perfect. Its perfection depends entirely upon the writer's absolutely flawless writing of the words and symbols from the original. Being human, and many of these writers being quite illiterate, calligraphers seem to have been masters of inexactitude. Nevertheless, the biliophile's pride has been his manuscript collecting" (Diehl:1973:122).

Libraries of My Concept

"Knowledge cannot be attained without self sacrifice. India is poor and its wants are many; but this is a condition to be resolutely faced, as other nations have faced it in the past and as many others must face it in the future. The people must rise superior to their circumstances and realise that more knowledge is their greatest need, their greatest want. They must be brought up to love books, not simply attractive bindings or pretty pictures, but their contents. They must be taught to regard books as a part of their lives. Libraries will not then appear a luxury, but a necessity of existence".

"For the want of mental sustenance we lose many of the pleasures and opportunities that God has placed at our disposal. All our faculties are not developed. We must educate them and teach others to do the same, that is what libraries are for. The numbers who avail themselves of the opportunities offered may be few, but that should not discourage those who, like many of you are workers in libraries. Your duties and responsibilities are great, greater even than those of magistrates and Subas. You are the servants of the whole community. You must induce them to read more and more books. Particularly the children - who are the hope of the future generations. Mr. Borden realises the importance of this phase of the work as well as I do, and I have no doubt that his idea will be well carried our by his staff. I have no desire, therefore, to labour the point. One other thing however I would urge upon you the importance of the sympathetic and polite treatment of all readers, whatever their condition. I advise library workers to bear this continually in mind, and on this depends the complete success of the library work". – *Sir Sayajirao Gaekwad - At a meeting of the Baroda Central Library Club on October 29th, 1912.*

GENERAL EDITOR'S INTRODUCTION

As yet Library history has not received the attention it deserves. Library Schools in India especially, do not seem to have recognised the importance of the study of Library history, although the professionals do feel that the students of Library and Information Science (LIS) should have a sound knowledge of the library development in their own country as well as abroad. A result of this neglect is that LIS students, more often than not, betray an utter ignorance about the growth of Indian libraries in different periods of history.

Nonetheless, it does not imply dearth of literature on this area of study. We have appreciable number of standard monographs and articles detailing study of libraries in three well-known periods of Indian-history – the ancient (Aryan phase depicted by the Vedas forming the basis of modern Hinduism, the phase of Jainism and that of Buddhism), the medieval (Sultanate and Mughal Period) and the modern (British and Post-Independence period). These historical surveys, by and large, however, have limited coverage. While some are restricted to one period of history and only a few devoted to two periods, none seems to have covered all the periods taking an all-India comprehensive view of the library development.

The present Volume in CICIL series attempts a perceptive study of the library development in India as a whole from ancient times to the present day fulfilling the long-felt need of the researchers the LIS educators, the professional and the serious students of library history. It is reliable as Taher and Davis have extensively and critically used both primary and secondary sources (mostly in English though) available on the subject. It is comprehensive since it embraces almost all phases of Indian history in all regions of the country. Wherever other historical development studies during the medieval period are generally confined to Northern India, this publication has the distinction of presenting LIS scene both in Northern and Southern India. Moreover, in the context of library development in post-Independent India it records the growth of libraries and LIS in all important Indian States. Another noteworthy feature of the volume is that not only does it survey, but does also detail useful information on different types of Libraries, their Administration and Management, Professional Associations, Leaders in Profession, LIS Literature, and LIS Education (LISE) in modern India – both British and Post-Independence period.

To quote Taher and Davis: The idea of this work emerged because of : (a) the large number of gaps in available resources, (b) the lack of single work, brief but exhaustive in coverage, and (c) the neglect of vast resources in the area of study' we believe it so; but for this, user will be the judge to tell us as to how far the target goes and how much the task has succeeded.

S.P. AGRAWAL

CONTENTS

PREFACE

Students of history in general and the library world in particular have recognised a continuous need to study Indian Librarianship and Library Science. The few attempts to satisfy this need have limited coverage; there remains no single source that comprehensively covers the topics–comprehensive, that is, in the sense that it treats all developments of theory and practice throughout the ages.

The idea of this work emerged because of : a) the large number of gaps in available sources, b) the lack of a single work, brief but exhaustive in coverage, and c) the neglect of vast resources in the area of study.

The present work spans the historical periods from ancient through medieval and modern India,thus covering the development in the field comprehensively. This brief, but complete history, is based on primary and secondary sources available in English and other languages. The bibliography appended, attests to this fact. This work would not have been completed if the historians of past and present had not already begun the task of writing India's library history. They deserve all due praise and acknowledgement.

Although this work will fill a great void in the world history of librarianship and library science, it too is only a beginning. As an outline, it serves as a kind of synthesis and bibliographic essay that ties together the long story of libraries in India and points the reader to the existing literature. Students of library science in South Asia and elsewhere, will benefit the most from this effort. However, as a contribution to the study of international and comparative librarianship, the work should initiate and facilitate indepth research in areas which are identified as understudied and in areas which are still unexplored.

We wish to acknowledge with particular gratitude the assistance of the following persons: Dr. S.D. Vyas (University Librarian, Banasthali), Prof. Sayed Mohammed (Tirunelveli), Dr. M.A. Dalvi (former Librarian, British Library, Pune), Dr. M.A.K. Fatimy (former Asst. Librarian, Osmania University, Hyderabad), Mr. Nasrullah Khan

(Asst. Librarian, Osmania University), Prof. N.B. Inamdar (former Librarian, Osmania University), Dr. Masood Ali Khan (Deputy Director, ICSSR, Hyderabad), Mr. Muhammed Burhanuddin (University of Hyderabad, Library), Dr. C.P. Ramashesh (Asst. Librarian, Mysore University), Prof. M. Bavakutty, Chairman, Dept. of Library Science (Calicut University), Prof. S.G. Mahajan, Chairman Dept. of Library Science (Poona University), Prof. H.A. Khan, Dept. of Library Science (Mysore University) and Dr. N.G. Satish (Deputy Librarian, American Studies Research Centre, Hyderabad). Dr. P.S.G. Kumar, Chairman, Dept. of Library Science (Nagpur University), and Dr. M.B. Konnur, Reader, Dept. of Library Science (Poona University), deserve special thanks for the permission granted to use material from their scholarly and historical works. Fulbright scholars Prof. K. Ranveer, Dr. A.K. Panda, Mrs. Rukmini Sanjeev Mitra, and Mr. R.L. Raina also deserve a word of thanks for their cooperation and suggestions. Professors Betty Turrock, James Anderson, Henrick Edelman, And Norman Horrocks too deserve a word of appreciation for the encouragement and generous advises.

MOHAMED TAHER
DONALD GORDON DAVIS, JR.

1

INTRODUCTION

1.1 Sources

For an understanding of the history of libraries in India one must understand the nature of the existing sources. These sources are in Pali, Sanskrit, Chinese, Arabic, Persian and European Languages, most of which have been translated into English. These exists in various formats, such as Manuscripts (mss.), inscriptions, copper plates, etc. The sources are either indigenous or foreign. Foreign sources emerged from the travelogues of Tibetan, Chinese, Muslim (Arabic, Persian, etc), Portuguese, English and other Europeans. Prominent among the Chinese, are Itsing, Fahien, Hieun Tsang; among Muslims are Alberuni, Ibn Batuta, Minhaj, Firishta, Badauni, and Afif; of the Europeans, prominent writers include Bernier, Mandelso, Manrique de Lara, Martin, and Count Noer. Historians who have largely contributed on these libraries are Henry M. Eliot, John Dawson, Stanley Lane-Pool, Ishwari Prasad, R C Majumdar, Jadunath Sarkar, V D Mahajan, Mohammed Mujeeb, Khan Bahadur Zafar Hasan, Abu Zafar Nadvi, D N Marshall, Muhammed Zubair, and J S Sharma.

There has been a major problem in ascertaining facts in the ancient Indian history. For any historic facet, entity, process, there have been divergent opinions in the ancient history of India. For instance: "With the literary sources there is not only the problem that the Puranic texts were compiled centuries after the events referred to, and even in the most meticulously maintained oral tradition chronological discrepancies are bound to enter thereby changing the concordance of the event and its record; there is also the problem that the Vedic and Puranic texts are sometimes in serious disagreement even with regard to order of succession of the various descent groups" (Thapar:1978: 261). The sad state of affairs is that even the leading personalities and fathers of the ancient Indian history and culture can't be precisely located, nor exactly placed in a chronological order. In this context aptly remarks Nirad Chaudhuri, "Even the date of the greatest Sanskrit poet, Kalidas, remains wholly speculative" (Chaudhuri:1965:198).

What sense of historicity prevailed, in one of the oldest civilizations of the world ? Says Chopra, "Hindus were not interested in recording events, because they 'despised this world and its ephemeral occurrences'. Only four biographies are said to have been preserved in Sanskrit and in all of them 'facts lie buried under a mass of flowers of rhetoric, tricks of style and round-about expressions'. Dates are completely ignored. The dry, methodical and matter-of-fact Muslims, on the other hand, kept a regular record of their campaigns and achievements in whatever part of the world they went to. Their advent in India led to the production of a large number of chronicles and autobiographies, which serve as source material for the history of the period. Hindu writers naturally imitated their style, and thus was introduced, as Sir Jadunath Sarkar writes, 'a new and very useful element into Indian literature" (Chopra, 1976. p. xvi).

Further,"In societies where the oral tradition rather than the use of literature is the more functional means of communication on a large scale, myths become one of the means of passing on information" (Thapar:1978:297). This ancient Indian period apart, the periods of medieval and modern are less problematic, and there has been a lot of historical research, which enables us to find out facts and information in a far better manner. This is what proved to be the result of Muslim rule in Medieval India, and some feel otherwise, that the Muslim rule extinguished the existing sources: "The Turkish conquests of more than half India between 900 and 1300 were perhaps the most destructive in human history. As Muslims, the conquerors aimed not only to destroy all other religions but also to abolish secular culture. Their burning of libraries explains the large gaps in our knowledge of earlier literature" (Basham:1975:193).

Can Someone ask, with all respect and regards to the age old oral tradition of India, which was the culture Muslims destroyed, and which was the cultural heritage Muslims preserved, translated and passed to the West, through Arabic, Persian, Turkish and Urdu, not to mention that –whole world of ancient Indian literature– which Max Muller could generate along with other Orientalists. Or, the sole reason for the extinction of the literature was the oral tradition itself (Ramakrishna Rao:1961:151).

There is a school of thought represented by Rhys Davids, who feels that with the shift of political power in India, the linguistic predominance has been also effected. At first it was in Punjab; then in Kosala; then in Magadha; and finally, when Sanskrit had become the lingua franca, it was in Western India that the most important vernacular was reportedly found, ultimately effecting the present picture of the Dravidian and Aryan dialects and language history of India. Davids is also of the opinion that there has been always a contest between Guelph and Ghibelin, priest and noble, rajput and brahmin, i.e., to say the contest between the spiritual and the temporal powers (Davids:1903:158). The sum total of this seems to be the existence of a lay movement, (or the non-priestly sources which did have their position in the development of the society) before the rise of the Buddhists, that also needs to be considered in writing the history of the great land India. Allowing us to think of non-spiritual literature and sources that existed for the study of the past, have these words any sense? "And we shall continue to have but a blurred and confused idea of Indian history unless, and until, the priestly views are checked and supplemented throughout by a just and proportionate use of the other views now open to research". (Davids:1903:157-158).

In the present monograph, for the sake of convenience and clarity, the standard pattern of classifying history by four major periods, viz., ancient, medieval, modern (or British) and independent India, has been followed. This is the pattern which James Mill used in writing Indian history and has been followed since then. However, the contention is not in any way to show that each has a distinct and separate entity. Professor Humayun Kabir rightly says "When two powerful currents meet, there is no question of the absorption of the one in the other. The two streams join to create a new form. There separate contributions can hardly be distinguished" (Kabir: 1955:89). The other preferable alternate could have been a dynastic history and this has not been attempted here. Since there is a lack of single comprehensive work, the present work limits itself to an outline, and leaves much to be worked in future to establish causal relationships.

1.2 **Art of Writing**

There has been no agreement among historians about the period when writing began in India. One school of thought holds that writing was originally imported. However, the seals discovered during excavation of Harappa and Mohenjodaro provide some indications of indigenous written traditions. Resolution of this issue awaits the completion of the deciphering process. Asoka's inscriptions (of third century BC) are considered the earliest hitherto known written documents, according to some historians. Others, however, claim that the origin of classical Indian literature occurred as early as the 6th century BC with the compilation of Vedas. Panini's grammatical sutras (4th century BC) reveal that the words akshara (or alphabet) and granthas (or mss.) were used in those days. Similarly, Buddhist texts, of about 6th century BC, have used the words Lekha (writing) and Lekhaka (writer). The Greek traveler Nearchus (Admiral of Alexander the Great), wrote in 4th century AD, that ink was used to write on wood or cloth. Puranas too have references to the word ink, as a writing material, implying from both the sources that writing existed in those early periods.

Concerning the language of thought content there has been interesting debates among scholars, and some have conclusively opined that "Sanskrit was, and is written in India in various alphabets, a scribe in the north using that form of the Brahmi alphabet current in the district in which he wrote, and a scribe in the south using the corresponding form of the Dravidian alphabet. The particular one of these many alphabets usually selected for use in Europe is an alphabet from Western India of the ninth century AD, and it is, therefore, often called the Sanskrit alphabet" (Davids:1903:155).

Interestingly, Indian literary tradition progressed quite slowly, as against other aspects of the history. The main reason for this is the all pervasive oral tradition. This pre-inscriptional period ended in the encouragement of learning and literature given by the Buddhist and Jains - rather than by Hindu/Brahminical culture. This culture supplied the people who established library traditions in India. In this context we find, Sanskrit was promoted in the Brahminical culture, Pali by Buddhists and Ardhamagdhi by Jains. Despite this seeming imbalance, Sanskrit has been a leading language of the land. One reason for predomination of Sanskrit was the fact that it alone came into common use, being the language of religion and learning of the majority community of India, from about the 2nd century AD to the advent of Persian during the Muslim rule in India. Persian became the successor, by the 13th century.

1.3 **Writing Material**

In that paperless-age writing was on skin, rocks, boulders, pillars, palm leaves (*tala patra*), metal plates, silver plates, wooden boards or birch bark (also called Bhoj patra and called Tuz in the Mughal tradition) and cloth. According to Abul Fazal's evidence ancient manuscripts were written on this material, which he refers to as Tuz. Babur refers to Paper made of Tar (Chopra:1976:166). Inscriptions on stones, metallic items, etc., were also common. Writing, which was commemorative and dedicative, for instance, found its place on stones, whereas religious and secular writings appeared mainly on copper. Literature found its place on palm leaves, birch bark and cotton cloth. Dhammapada, is found on Birch Bark, and serves as an example of its use. Wooden boards were used by Buddhist monks to write their sacred literature. Leaves of fibrous material formed the most important medium of writing. Regarding Papyrus, while was in Indian use as early as the 4th century BC, shows no trace of its existence today.

Paper, although invented in the 2nd century AD in China, was not used in India before the 11th century. There is a strong difference of opinion again on the exact date of its introduction as a writing medium. According to D N Marshall it was in 1089 AD but according to Ramakrishna Rao paper was used only from the year 1310. Itsing, the Chinese traveler in India (672 AD) bears testimony to the fact that fine and costly paper was occasionally, used for some religious purpose. Its quality improved in the medieval period. Most of the manuscripts of the Mughal period were on good quality paper. Sialkot (now in Pakistan), was famous for paper - Man Singhi and Silk quality; so also was Shahzudpur. Kashmir was famous for ink in this period. Despite the availability of paper, inscriptions of grants of land and some other official business were still found on metal plates, presumably for permanent preservation.

The ink and pen used for writing are also of interest. Two ink pots were discovered at Mohenjodaro. The vessel was in the form of a couchant run (Kumar:1977:1). The quality of ink depended on the economic situation of the user. The rich used golden ink and ink-pots, or brass ink stands and a reed mended like a quill. The poor used iron pens. The rich used silk and higher quality paper, while the poor used palm-leaves, cocoa-leaves, etc. Writing was manual throughout centuries in India. Copying flourished as a profession to bring out multiple copies. The profession was supported by patronage throughout the ancient, medieval and early modern periods in Indian history. "It is amazing that the Chinese knowledge of wooden-block printing did not evoke even a ripple of response in India... in spite of frequent communication between the two countries in the past" (Qaiser:1982:58).

Printing with moveable type came to India in 1556 when the book was first printed in Goa. It was in Portuguese and consisted of religious material published for the Jesuits. The first Indian book in Tamil, appeared in 1578, and was also on religion. While Akbar (1543-1605) did not officially endorse or promote printing, he was not even hostile to this art. Europeans presented printed books to Akbar and Jahangir, and these did become a part of the Imperial Library. This attitude of Akbar has been compared to that of Federigo, Duke of Urbino, who a century earlier in Italy proved to be a patron of books and libraries, though he neither owned printed books nor had them in his collection (Suend Dahl:109). However, the Mughal Period did not evince any major development in the field of printing history. In the words of Jadunath Sarkar, "Ever since the middle of the 17th century there had been close commercial exchange between India and England, but our royalty and ruling classes imported only European articles of luxury; none cared for European knowledge; no printing press, nor even the cheapest and small lithographic stone..." (Sarkar:1950:Vol IV 345).

As the rulers so the ruled, says an Arabic proverb. "What perturbs us is the total indifference of Indians in Goa in this matter. This lack of interest had gone to such a length that in the entire range of literature printed at Goa in the Portuguese or Indian languages... not a single contribution came from Indians, not even from the converts" (Qaiser, 1982. p. 59). In every dark world there is some light, and hence we find a significant exception to this attitude: a merchant (chief broker) of the English company at Surat, Bhimji Parak, wrote to the Company Officers, who in turn forwarded with their comments to the East India Company, in 1671:

> "Bhimji Parak makes his humble request to you: that you would please send out an able printer to Bombay for that he hath a curiosity and earnest inclination to have some of the ancient Braminy writings in print and for the said printers encouragement he is willing to allow him 501 sterling a year for three years, and also to bear the charges of tools and instruments necessary for him, and in case that will not be sufficient he humbly refers it to your Prudence to agree with the said printers according as you shall see good; and promises to allow what you shall enorder. It is not improbable that this curiosity of his may tend to a common good; and by the Industry of some searching spirits produce discoveries out of those or other Ancient manuscripts of those parts which may be

useful or atleast grateful to posterity. We recommend his request to you and interest your pardon for his and our boldness therein" (quoted by Qaiser:1982:61).

It is reported that Shivaji, the Maratha ruler, acquired a printing press in 1674, but he sold it to Bhimjee. There are evidences that Bhimjee did receive support from the British in this regard (Kumar: 1977:28-29).

In addition to this attitude toward imports, even the Portuguese, the first great political power to emerge in India, exported none of the advancements in science and technology, to India. The chief exports included missionaries and these came with books. These books were mainly theological and missionary literature. What is more, in the early years instead of printing this literature for the use of Indians, they wrote on palm-leaves with iron styles (Strickland and Marshall:1865: 140). Interestingly, the Romish mission enterprise adapted its evangelistic practice to the practices and communication formats of the native culture folkways (Richer:1908:60). It was rightly felt by the Portuguese that the most effective way of winning converts, particularly among the literates, would be through the native tongue. For the same reason we find that even what emerged as printed work dealt with religion, and these were in Marathi and Konkani. It was in Roman script than in the Devanagari or Marathi scripts (Qaiser:1982:58).

Even in modern India the factor responsible for the continuation of the non-print age was the fear of unemployment. Introduction of any other means of copying, and calligraphy, would dislocate these people. Ovington remarks "Neither have they endeavored to transcribe the art of printing, that would diminish the repute and livelihood of scribes who maintain numerous families by their pen" (Ovington:1869). Apart from Portuguese, none of the other foreign forces present in the country established a press in India. "Without going into the political motives of the use of the Roman script, it could be said that the technical difficulties of type-casting (in the native languages and dialects), at any rate, in the sixteenth century, might have been one of the reasons for not printing books in Goa in the Konkani and Marathi script (Qaiser:1982:58-59). Evidently, circumstances and forces - political, social, cultural, or religious - did not stimulate any interest in the improved ways of document delivery or in adopting advanced means of reproduction of the written word.

1.4 Growth of Subjects

In terms of content, in the earliest times whatever was produced was limited to religious lore, literary progress was confined to the priests and aristocrats (i.e, the Brahmins) who then constituted the sole group of intelligentsia. This limitation of the art of writing to one class and the then rigid caste organization made the art an exclusive one and its development was exceedingly slow. This state of affairs was limited to the Hindus, but other communities like the Buddhists and Jains did flourish. The literary contributions experienced greater diversification with the growth of Jains who gloried in having beautiful copies not only of sacred books but also of other works of merit. The available evidence in this regard is a reference of a later date which indicates a period (by 12th century AD) when the secular powers of the Jains reached its zenith. The oral tradition gradually gave way to the written. The Gupta dynasty (AD 320-540) heralded a new era in this regard, and what emerged was the renaissance of Brahmanical culture. Harsha Vardhana (606-647) was famous for patronizing language and literature. Sanskrit received greater popularity during this period. Even Buddhists wrote in this language. Again, in the 9th and 10th centuries, literary activity gained impetus in another period of Brahminical renaissance.

A number of factors supported the growth of new subjects. Notable is the growth of erotic theme in literature. "The introduction of the erotic theme in Hinduism was closely connected with fertility cult and Tantrism". Similarly, "The local nucleus of the new culture led to a large range of religious expression, from the powerful temple religion of Brahminism to a widespread popular Bhakti religion and even more widely spread fertility cult". Again, "The conscious reference to being Kshatriya, a characteristic group among Rajputs, is a noticeable feature in post-Gupta politics". Furthermore "Fundamental changes took place around the 8th century, when the medieval ethos was introduced" (Thapar:1988:49-50).

Philosophers like Sankaracharya (9th century), Ramanuja (11th century), and Madhava (13th century) carried philosophical debates on knowledge, salvation by devotion, problems of metaphysics and nature of reality. The emergence of Arabs as traders, Sufis, and warriors on this soil "changed Indian society at all levels" (Thapar:1988:50). There emerged as a result many new subjects, themes and areas in the literature. The age of Reformation in India started in the growth and rise of the preachers of Bhakti movement, of whom Kabir stands as leading pillar. The sum total of literature produced in Persian and Arabic, in the medieval India excelled all the past records. In the same time the growth of regional or local languages added a further boost to the country's total literature output. The latter reduced the productivity of Sanskrit literature. India was fortunate to have its Reformation (Bhakti movement) and Renaissance (in literary achievements) at a time when Europe was awaking, but its industrial revolution was the only thing which delayed its modernization. In addition to the above-mentioned subjects, political matters lie buried in various sources including *Arthashastra*, chronicles of kings, travellers, accounts of battles, etc.

1.5 **Literacy**

To understand the status of literacy there is a need to rewrite the intellectual history of India, from the point of our context. In the absence of any specific relevant record about information literacy one fact, however, is evidently proved: this relates to the reading habits of the few elites, such as nobles, royal family members, Brahmins, and Kshatriyas. Although members of these groups did not read personally, the historical record reveals that the ancient and medieval people availed the services of one of the limited number of readers. In this context, it can be implied, reading became a profession. This was clearly evident in the rule of Kanishka, Akbar and Shah Jahan. The history of this profession needs to be written separately. But the general concern is the question of literacy. With the presence of the professional readers, the idea whether the audience, such as, Akbar can or should be called literate or not has been highly debated by historians. Literacy for the Brahmins was the preserve of the socially-determined few which in any case laid greater stress on oral tradition (Thapar:1978:58-59). And the extension of literacy, that was symbolic of the golden age of Buddhists, was an action of individuals, not institutions.

Taxila, a leading centre of education had received an international reputation by 6th century BC. Nalanda and Vallabhi reached remarkable heights during the age of Gupta's, i.e., in between 4th and 8th century AD. Nalanda was world famous, and attracted foreign students. Its admission test was so strict that only 20-30 per cent of the applicants attained admission. Gupta kings patronised learning and this led to Brahminical Renaissance. The students must have been from the upper castes (Brahmins and Kshatriyas). Indian education had its impact on its neighbourhood, and more so on Southeast Asia from 2nd century AD to 15th century. These educational currents lead us to infer that there was pattern of elementary and secondary education all over the country. But its classification by such levels was not easy. The Buddhist centres of learning which attained prominence after the fall of Gupta's include Vikramasila, Odantapuri, and Jagaddala.

The Muslim rule brought a clear classification of educational levels, and we find the existence of *Maktab* (elementary) and *Madrasa* (higher) education. It was uniform throughout the country. Prof S N Mukerji indicates that the first and foremost distinction of the education offered by the Muslims, as against the past was that "...education was democratic. As in Mosques, so in a *Maktab* or *Madrasah*, all were equal and the principle was established that the poor should be educated" (Mukerji:1988:35). Secondly, this rule influenced the system of education of the Hindus too, by way of patronizing institutions, by establishing academies, and by setting up translation bureaus.

Further, in the medieval period, we find some reference to the state of literacy among the masses, "There is no evidence to show that women belonging to the lower ranks of society, such as housemaids, were illiterate, but there is nothing to discountenance female education" (Chopra:1976:149), Chopra states further, that "There is, however, little doubt about the literacy of the average middle-class women who had sufficient knowledge of either Hindi, Persian or of the native provincial language to enable her to study scriptures". The fact is that literacy did exists among high born and well off women. It was irrespective of Muslim or Hindu or Rajput or Bengali zamindar society. A famous work of the medieval period, Mahila-mriduvani gives a list of (at least 35) women all of literary taste. For the same reasons works by Mughal princesses abound. On the whole women received a limited level of education. And so also is the case of the urban man in this period. Further,"Our knowledge of education in India during the periods of Hindu and Muslim supremacy is very imperfect, but it is sufficient to show that literacy was not regarded as a necessary training for life in general was either an accomplishment for the few, or a path to certain definite vocations, especially the priesthood, commerce and administrative employment" (Moreland and Chatterjee: 1957:340).

The year 1835 saw the introduction of English language as a medium of instruction. It saw the Macaulay's minutes for the

Anglicization of Indian Education. English literature injected into India has had effects oddly parallel to Latin for medieval Europe and Greek for the renaissance. Similarly is the feeling of Mathews "Again, the poetry of a Sir Muhammed Iqbal in the Islamic north or of a Rabindranath Tagore in Bengal, great as it is as a literary event, is still more potent as sounding a reveille". (Mathews:1937:50). There has been a general understanding that the British presence benefited the conquerors (English) alone. But contrary to this, there are some who feel otherwise, and historians like Jadunath Sarkar say that there have been many gifts of the Britishers and the greatest is the "Renaissance which marked our 19th century". (Sarkar:1957:62). The year 1835 also brought an end to the controversial debates between the Anglicists (or Occidentalists) and the Orientalists.

The Census of 1891 discloses the figures that nearly 11% males and less than 0.1% female were literate (Denning:1902:260). As compared to this the Parsi community had 12.2% males and 8.84% females (Karaka:1884:330). This was the beginning of the mass effect of British presence in the country. While it took Britishers a period of over one hundred years to settle down and infuse their culture, the results of this appeared not very soon. According to 1941 census 12% of the entire population of sub-continent were literates. "Indian education is in fact unintelligible except through its history. The structure is top heavy. The lower classes who constitute the bulk are largely illiterate while the intelligentsia are in point of number at least educated to a pitch equal to that of countries whose economic conditions are more highly developed... The Report on the Post-War Educational Development in India had recommended the introduction, as speedily as possible, of a system of universal compulsory and free education for all boys and girls between the ages of 6 and 14. The plan outlined in this Report required 40 years to achieve cent per cent literacy" (The India and Pakistan Year Book:1949:49-50). This was probably one of the last developmental programmes of the British rule in India. The level of literacy in the country has had a very slow progress. Reading habits, nevertheless, need to be, inculcated; this is a continuing problem of all historical periods. One can note that in the recent past the U S Library of Congress declared 1989 as the Year of Reading, a thrust that was observed world wide. History, records that the Jain monks were supposed to 'read' scriptures at least three hours every day (Das Gupta:3), implying that those who have access to 'scriptures' will continue to be the only reading community !!!

1.6 Etymology of 'Book'/'Library'

Kautilya's *Arthashastra* mentions an officer "*adhyaksh*" as incharge of the manuscripts entitled *Nibhanda Pustaka-Sthana*. Another scholar of repute, Pandit Danasila (10th century) wrote a work and titled it "*Pustaka-Pathopaya*" (= reading a book). So also Telugu writers like Tenali Ramkrishna and Allasani Peddana (16th century), used the terms *Pust-Pusthaka Bhandagaramulu*–which also shows the possible existence of popular usage of the term (Kumar:1977:17, 24). Hence, the use of the term Pustaka, for books, is common in Indian regional languages - which have either Aryan or Dravidian roots. *Pust*, is probably/taken as the root of the word, meaning piled one above the other and sewn together. The Sanskrit '*knot grantha*' acquired the sense of book from the gathering of loose materials; *granth kuti*, too had the same usage. Libraries, were called *Jnana Bhandar* and *Saraswathi Bhandar*, literally these mean storehouse of knowledge. Another instance notable is of the Chalukya King Deva who had a library and named it *Bharati-Bhandar. Viniya pitika* and *Nikyas* mention a list of games one of which is called *Aksharika* (=lettering). In *Mahabharatha* we find the use of the word *Grantha* (=books) (Kumar:1977:3, 20). Interestingly, there emerged a class (in a society already full of classes) whose main profession was to write. These came to be known as Kayasthas in the eastern part of the country. Elsewhere they were called Divira or Divirapati. (Kumar:1977:13). In Jaipur the royal library which first appears during the rule of Maharaja Sawai Jai Singh II (1699-1743), was called *Potikhana* (or *Pothikhana*).

In the words of Max Muller, "If we take the ordinary modern words for book, paper, ink, writing, &c., not one of them has as yet been discovered in any Sanskrit work of genuine antiquity". Book, in the modern Sanskrit, is *Pustam* or *pustakam*, a word most likely of foreign origin. It (*pustak*) occurs in such works as the *Hitopadesa*, where we read of a person, 'Neither read in books nor taught by a tutor'. The *Hitopadesa* itself is said to be written (*Likhyate*) as an extract from the *Panchtantra* and another book. To write is *likh* and *lip*, the former originally used in the sense of scratching, whether on stone or leaves, the latter, in the sense of covering a surface with ink... The words for ink (*masi, kali, mela, gola*) and pen (*kalma*) have all a modern appearance; and as to Kayastha, the name of the writer-caste, proceeding from a Kshatriya father and a Sudra mother, it does not even occur in Manu" (Max Muller:1860:512-514). Of all these, *Kalama*, or *Khalam* (in Arabic and Quranic usage), is one single example of the Muslim contribution to the Indian culture.

Kitab has an Arabic origin and the Muslim rule in India found the use of the term *kitabkhana* (department of books). Hindu rulers of the medieval period did not like the Arabic word, *kitab*, and used *punti* for manuscripts (Dutta:1970:4). Thus, *puntikhana*, emerged as an alternate source, meaning department of manuscripts. In the historical sources one finds *vidyasala*, a term probably for the royal library, though *vidyasala* commonly connotes a school. *Darul Mutalia* was another term used for reading room, in the Muslim libraries. In the modern Bengali the term *Gata Ghar* is found, where *Gata* is from *Grantha* and ghar refers to a house/room. *Granthalya* is another common term in Indian libraries. Priolkar called the Indian Incunabula in Marathi as *Dolamudrise.* He preferred to classify all books printed in India up to 1867 as Indian Incunabula. The reason he felt was that books published from 1867 were systematically indexed, and the retrospective publications were not taken care. The year 1867 made some distinct impact on the library development with the 25th Press Act. From that year started a quarterly list of all publications in India, a landmark in India's bibliographic control.

1.7 **Historiography**

Writing this state-of-the-art and tracing the evolution of the field is a gigantic task, and ours is only a humble initiative attempt. Re-writing the library history, assessing the available facts (with limitations of historic and other types), and re-presenting these clearly without bias, is the purpose of this work. What we are presenting to the profession, to the historians and to all those concerned in this Outline is simply a framework for indepth, exhaustive and comprehensive works in the field.

In passing we have made references to religion, society, technology, etc., as well as forces and factors which probably went into shaping the Indian librarianship and library science. These we hope would become the source for inter- and multi-disciplinary studies.

As correctly mentioned by Raman Nair (1994:1) "In history of libraries we are concerned with the purpose and content of libraries and with the social background which produced them, in consequence we become involved in the history not only of scholarship in its narrower sense, but of human civilization, culture and literacy".

The Outline follows a chronological order in presenting the evolution of the field. The chapters follow the normal historical approach of periodisation, as ancient, medieval, modern and post-independent India. The appendices provide an historical map of activities and movements.

And again as Nair suggests in the application side, we too hope the same "Library history should enable those in the field to respect the antiquity of our calling, to appreciate the gradual advance and sometimes decline of various movements and systems and to base our future on sound foundations. We can take advantage of past experience and learn from the mistakes of others instead of repeating them" (Nair:1994:5).

2

ANCIENT INDIA (3000 BC-AD 1206)

The history of ancient India possesses certain periods of literary and cultural revivalism. This has been due probably to existence of various factors, notably, (1) political influence –Asoka's promotion of Buddhism, and Chandra Gupta's promotion of Hinduism); (2) assimilation of foreigners–Greeks and the Sakas called as fallen Kshatriyas); and (3) changes in the philosophies–in Buddhism emerged sects like Theravada and Saravastivada/Hinayana and Mahayana; Brahminism altered Vedic sacrifices and Vedic deities faded gradually; Jainism split into Digambara and Svetambara. The most significant periods of this revivalism for Jainism and Buddhism lasted till 340 AD. From 340 to 750 is a period in Indian Brahminical revivalism, and is also referred as Classical Age of India, by historians.

Historical record reveals three types of libraries in this ancient period, libraries attached to : (a) palace/court; (b) Centres of learning; and (c) Centres of religion (Brahmins had Matths, Buddhists had Viharas, and Jains had Upasarayas).

2.1 Palace/Court Libraries

Of these libraries we have a very scanty knowledge. History has left names of some kings who patronized learning and literature and who built a royal or court library. King Harsha Vardhana of Kanauj had a large library. This is derived from the report that Harsha gave several horse-loads of books to Hieun Tsang, the Chinese Buddhist Traveller (633-642 AD). The king only demonstrated his habit of generously granting the wishes of his guests. The original collection hence must have been quantitatively and qualitatively large. The imperial library of the Chalukyas was equally important. It was named Bharati Bhandagara. Hieun Tsang reports the existence of a palace library in a place near Kashmir (then called Gandhara) during the rule of Kanishka, the Kusana King.

Hieun Tsang was offered, here, the task of reading and giving commentary on the scriptures. For this he was given full access to the royal collection along with a band of copyists, attenders, etc. We also learn that Kanishka got transcribed the authorized Tripitaka texts on copper plates, placed these in stone boxes and had a stupa erected on it. It is also clear that everyday in his leisure time he studied the Buddhist scriptures, having a monk for instruction and reading.

Another royal library was in Kamarupa at Assam. Hieun Tsang describes King Bhaskaravarman's bibliophilic nature and his generous gift of manuscripts, among other gifts, to Harsha Vardhana, the King of Kanauj.

Royal libraries formed a part of loot; booty was at times transported *in toto*, including books. The royal library of Paramara Kings of Malwa, founded by King Bhoja in the early 10th century, was taken away by King Siddaraja Jayasimha (1094-1143), in and around 1140, to Anhilvad in Gujarat (Buhler, p.93). He is said to have employed 300 copyists. There are reports that this king had ordered 1,25,000 copies of a treatise to be made for the use of students. This collection formed thence a part of royal library of Chalukyas.

Yet another royal library must have been at Pattan, in Gujarat. This flourished during the rule of Sri Kumarapala Deva (1143-1174). He founded 21 big libraries. Sadly, his successor, Ajaypala destroyed all these libraries in a fanatic zeal to wipe out all traces of Jains. Hindu fanatics even joined hands, whenever time permitted, and burnt libraries and manuscripts of Jains. (Dutta, 1970.p.39). The Minister of Kumarapala, Udayana and few others, moved the collection from Pattan. Some of these went to Jaisalmer. Whatever was left in Pattan, either from royal collection or from private libraries, ultimately was sold and reached various libraries in the region, as well as foreign libraries. Another monarch Vikramaditya, is also mentioned to have had a royal library. Similarly, Visal Deva, a Chalukyan ruler, had a royal library and named it Bharati Bahandar.

2.2 **Centres' of Learning Libraries**

Of the educational centres known, in this early period, Taxila University is the oldest. Others included Kasi, Kuru, Panchala, Videha, Matsya, Usinara, and Naimisara (Kumar:1977:2). Taxila flourished for a thousand years in the city of Gandhara. The university must have had a large library. This library, probably, had its own classification scheme, given by an outstanding Sanskrit Grammarian Panini. The city, its university, as well as the library, were destroyed within a century during the Huna invasion. Evidences show that Panini and Kautiliya were products of this academia.

Nalanda, located near Patna, in Bihar, existed as a centre of learning for several centuries, but it is not probably as old as Taxila. As a leading university it flourished from 414 to 1205 AD, with a break when the Huns attacked. Huien Tsang gives a detailed account of this learning centre, and this same account with other evidences allows us to visualize various aspects of education in India. The curriculum probably included both Buddhist and Hindu literature (Devahuti:1970:144). Its large collection was stored, reportedly, in three buildings, viz., Ratnadadhi, Ratnasagara and Ratnaganjaka. The library complex was called Dharmaganja (mart of religion or piety mart). May be this name conveys the sense that the literature stored was all about religion and secular literature was almost absent. Ratnadadhi, or, probably, Ratnasagara as some varying reports state, was a nine storeyed building.

Many travellers/pilgrims hearing the fame visited this institution. These travellers came to procure Buddhist books in original language and to learn the true meaning of obscure doctrines from orthodox pundits in India. This was not only the purpose of Buddhist pilgrims from China, but it did characterize travellers from Tibet, Japan and Korea. About 57 pilgrims visited with the same purpose, between 629 and 671 AD (Saletore:319). A modern scholar of Chinese literature, Liang Chi-chao, identifies 162 visitors, between 5th and 8th centuries (quoted in Devahuti:1970:144). Fahien (also Fa hsien), who visited India, from 402 to 414, for instance stayed in Patliputra and Tamluk monasteries to learn the ancient languages–probably Sanskrit or Pali. During the Buddhist heyday, Patliputra was famous for its monasteries; it was a centre of attraction for Buddhist school of thought in India.

Itsing managed to get about 400 manuscripts in Sanskrit copied. This fact enables us to imply that Nalanda must have been very rich in its library collection. So much was its repute and standing that the King of Java managed to get a grant of five villages to keep up the University's finances. This grant given by Devapala, King of Bengal, had a separately headed provision for preparing copies of the Mss. available in the university. Sadly, Nalanda came to an end and final destruction by having living embers thrown into the establishment by two indignant Tirthaka mendicants, allegedly because they were insulted by some young novices at the university (Datta: 1970:28).

Another library of prominence was attached to Vikramshila monastery in Magadha in Bihar. This was founded by King Dharmapala of the Pala dynasty in 8th century A C. With the decline of Nalanda, this nearby Buddhist university came into prominence. The institution had 8000 students and 200 faculties. The academic council of this institution was in charge of the library. In this institution was Sri Jnana, who wrote nearly 200 works which must have required a large library. The Tibetian sources have recorded these details. A Persian source, *Tabaqate-i-Nasiri* by Minhajus Siraj corroborates this evidence. Incidentally, Bhaktiyar Khilji, a contemporary of Minhaj, who was on his conquests, crossed this centre of learning. Minhaj informs us that there were great number of books on the religion of Hindus (i.e., the Buddhists). By the time the conqueror's might could feel free, the conquered populace had fled and none could give the Mussalmans, information about the contents of these books. The conqueror had destroyed the library mistaking it for fort (Dutta:1970:29). Such is the historical report available even to this day, when it is emphatically claimed and repeatedly highlighted that the Muslims were always bent on the destruction of the Hindu identity, where as this is not true.

In the southern India under the Western Chalukyas there flourished an important academy for advanced education, known as Ghatikasala. It was at Nagai in Maharashtra. A prominent ruler of this dynasty was King Trailokyamalla. The existence of this centre has been traced in an inscription dated 1092 A C. The library reportedly had six people on its staff, who were called Saraswati-Bhandagarikas. These librarians received pay equal to the faculty, and whose responsibility included preservation, processing and guidance of students. This last function is one of the important sources as relevant to the present day, because it indicates that the library staff have been from an academic tradition and that they normally possessed some scholarly background. This academic character made them scholarly librarians rather than mechanical librarians. Further, this library, being attached to an advanced centre, gave its library staff the status and position of the teaching faculty.

The Jetawana Monastery, in Oudh, is another centre of learning which Hieun Tsang has recorded. The centre had a library and reading room. The reading material comprised of not only Buddhist literature, but also, Vedic and other non-Buddhist works. The original monastery was destroyed by fire in Buddha's time. Itsing informs us that in India there was a practice of selling non-Buddhist works, probably by the

Buddhists themselves. The money so earned was to be distributed among the resident priests. Also that the Buddhists Scriptures and their exegetical works were not be disposed off, but rather stored and read by the followers (Dutta;1970:24; Kumar:1977: 13). Hieun Tsang reports the off and on destruction and misuse of the Jetawana monastery by non-Buddhists. " At one time, the place was utterly abandoned by the Buddhists and was used as the royal stable for some time", by the Hindu King. Such instances of intolerance, refer to the unruly scenes when Brahmin and Buddhist rulers tried to destroy each other. Libraries and centres of learning were not spared either.

Maitraka monastery (of the Maitraka Dynasty of Gujarat), at Vallabhi–now Wala, also called Mahavihara–flourished from 5th to 12th century, under the Maitraka rulers. It is known from history that this monastery consisted of some hundred sangarams or schools. What is not clear is whether each had a library or whether the central library served all the needs of the 6000 priests and many thousand students. It had a library receiving royal grant to purchase manuscripts for the library. This level of funding is evident from the grant of King Guhasena I dated 559 A C. and is reported by Itsing (Joshi:1973:102).

At Pattan in Gujarat, was the first known library of Marathi manuscripts, an one man's lifetime contribution of a genius. The historical records of the twelfth century show the name of this Scholar and Librarian as Bhaskaracharya (d.1192-93) - he was a renowned personality of his age. Bhaskaracharya acquired so much of his scholarship from his own father, till finally "the scholar ran before the master" (Joshi:1973:99). He had collected all the available texts of ancient times, on astronomy, mathematics, science and religion. As his works speak of Buddhist and Jain ideas, it is imperative that he possessed even literature relating to these two communities. Bhaskara built a school, a laboratory, a research institute and a library. His grandson Changadeva developed these into an advanced research institute. In fact, while Bhaskara built the institution on his own funds, Changadeva sought the royal patronage and was generously granted. This support came from the Nikumbhas of Pattan. An inscription carries the date of the grant as 1207. It was a long standing commitment to support the great Acharya's work. The inscription enjoins that these grants "should be protected by future rulers for the great increase of [their] religious merit". Interestingly the inscription has made use of both Sanskrit and Marathi in its text. By implication India was heading towards a multiplicity of languages and further Sanskrit was used with restrictions. It was no more the single predominant language. The same inscription speaks of a tax levied to contribute for the recurring nature of the commitment (Joshi:1973:104).

Other centres of learning, traced in history, are found at Mithila and Odantapuri (in Bihar), Somnathpuri (or Sompura Mahavihara/ paharpura Jagaddala in Bengal), Sarnath (also in Bihar), etc. Of Mithila we learn that it prohibited its students from taking away from its school any of the books or even notes of the lessons taught there, for the simple reason of non availability of these reading materials in the market (Chopra:1976:152). In another instance, Vasudeva finding it impossible to find a copy of Tatta Chintamani and Kusumaanjali, memorized both while studying at Mithila, and then fleeing and reducing them to writing at Nadia. This case is very nicely recorded by Badaoni. In short, centres of learning in India did attract as much of interest as did the centres of trade and commerce. In the south at Palnadu by the side of Krishna River, Nagarjuna –a Buddhist –monk built a University. The five storeyed building on its top floor had a provision for the library (Kumar: 1977:8) These centres of learning were also the place for philosophical debates carried out by great Gurus. By implication the collection must have had impact of the changing philosophies and changing beliefs of the rulers and the elite.

We have in history evidence to show that Muhammed Ghori (d.1206) set up the first Madrasa at Ajmer in 1191. This opened up a new type of libraries in the Indian history.

2.3 **Centres' of Religion Libraries**

The centres of religion have different names in different communities. These have been generally called Temples. The existence of a prominent temple library with a reading room is recorded in art history. This refers to the Paramara's of Malwa, who build the Nilkanteswara Temple at Udaipur, in 1059 A C. Four small temples on each of the main temple along with four square vedis for reading Vedas, formed the corner stone of this library architecture (D C Ganguly:262).

Other Temple library, recorded in Muslim annals is the Jwala Mukhi Temple at Nagarkot. The library flourished and had a large collection in the 12th century. By the time Muslims reached and had access to this library, only 1300 volumes were traced. When Firuz Shah Tughluq conquered this place he invited scholars for translating the storehouses contained in the library. This is reported by Firishta (Kumar:1977).

According to Tamil inscription (dated 1251) found in the Temple of Jatavarman Sundara Pandya, Raja Raja Chola (985-1013) developed a special collection of Devaram Hymns of a seventh century saint.

The Jain Temples, called Upasaraya, also had reading material. As a tradition, mentioned earlier, writing (or reproducing existing works) formed a source of Divine Goodwill, and also daily reading was stressed as one of the duties of a layman. The library, also called Granth Bhandaras, was managed by priests. There are traces of such Bhandaras at South Kanara District (in Karnataka), Jaisalmer and Jaipur (in Rajasthan), Agra (in Utter Pradesh), Pattan and Khambhat (in Gujarat), Arrah (in Bihar) and Delhi, to name a few. Jains built numerous institutions, including libraries to preserve manuscripts, which was a trait "imitated by other Indian religious groups" (Basham:1975:109). Jainism through its literature, as did the Buddhist literature, contributed much towards the growth of libraries and reading materials. In the wake of revivalistic periods which Brahminical system faced, its impact was reflected even in the destruction of Jain and Buddhist libraries. Tirujnana Sambandar a Tamil Saivaite destroyed many Jain scriptures and murdered many monks (Kumar:1977:10).

The collection was extensive and huge. We find many travellers carrying books in hundreds. Fahien (also Fa hsien), visited most important centres of Buddhism at Udayana, Gandhara, Taxila, Patna, Nalanda, Varanasi and Ceylon. He returned to China by sea after spending over twelve years, in 414 AC . He deepened his knowledge of Sanskrit and collected major texts of Buddhist studies – those not in China - which must have been in hundreds. Hieun Tsang could collect 657 books in a period of eleven years. What were the sizes and dimensions of each of these books, we have no idea. But it is clear that he shipped the entire consignment to China in 520 cases. And in the remaining nine years of his life (d.664) he settled in China and translated only 73 titles, or one-tenth of this treasure island. Based on his extensive studies and research he established at home Buddhist Consciousness Holy School. Hieun Tsang stayed mostly at Nalanda where he perfected his knowledge of Sanskrit, Buddhism and Indian thought. Itsing (672 also I-Ching) was another prominent Buddhist Chinese Traveller who could get 400 books transcribed only from Nalanda. How many he could collect from other institutions we have no clear picture.

Private collections of nobles, elites, and the like is a topic for indepth search. A glance at the descriptive Mss. catalogue of Pattan Jain Bhandaras reveal that there was a practice of maintaining private libraries (Dutta:1970:39). The literary giants like Bana, Kautiliya, Patanjali, Panini, Bhasa, philosophers like Sankracharya, Ramanuja, etc., must have had personal collections. Itsing makes a mention in passing of private libraries of monks.

2.4 Administration and Management

There are indications in the excavation at Harappa and Mohenjodaro that there was a practice in libraries of maintaining records of administration and achievements (J S Sharma:1965:13-14; and P N Kaula:1958:58). While there are evidences of the preservation techniques used, there is not much on the care for the design of the building. Gordon Child is of the opinion that during the Indus Valley Civilization library buildings were well planned and built of bricks (Child:1952:225). The Nalanda library complex is another structure whose few details are available. One of these was a nine storeyed building, as described earlier.

Arthashastra is an important source which makes a mention about the personnel, that is the people responsible for maintenance of Mss. Regarding the personnel we have a reference of the academy at Nagai which had six staff and these were given pay and status of the faculty. Archivists and record-keepers were becoming common. History informs that Bhimadeva of Vikrama Sambat appointed a keeper of records (Kumar:1977:21). This description apart, there is hardly any other source to mention about the staffing pattern. Any such trace of staff could be more in the period after 10th century when the history is more clear and well documented, which means the beginning of Muslim period in India. The copyists and allied workers were probably regular part of the library staff.

The collection development was, probably, either by gifts, booty of war, or copying from the available texts. Purchase of books is not heard. The contents of the libraries probably included sacred texts. With the growth of lexicons a set of reference books must have also emerged as possible items for study and research. These lexicons and grammar books increased by about 8th century. The local populace as well as the non-Indian dynasties of the north and east used Sanskrit for literary works, and who must have been the primary users of these lexicons. From this period hymns were composed and congregations were addressed in the popular languages. It gradually led to breaking away from Sanskrit and Prakrit. And eventually emerged a series of local languages like Kannada, Telugu, Marathi, Malayalam, Gujarathi, Bengali and Oriya. The Bhakti movement which took momentum in this era popularised these languages. This must have started an era of more number of books in Sanskrit. But the thought content probably remained the same, as there was not much of social and scientific literature as yet. There were nevertheless a few scientific and technical books that were written and which were passed on to the west through the Muslims.

These books were arranged according to various classification schemes. There were variations from Buddhists to Brahminical and Jain libraries, and Muslim libraries had altogether different schemes. For instance, Buddhists literature had three main divisions, Jains had six groups, and the Brahminical classification had four divisions.

A survey of ancient Indian schemes reveal the existence of the idea and level of knowledge classification. Buddhists had three divisions for the Tripitaka's, viz., Vinaya, Sutra and Abhidamma. Jains made six groups of their canonical literature, and these were, 12 Angas, 12 Upangas, 10 Painnas, 6 Cheya-Sutras, 4 Mulla Sutras, and 2 individual texts. The Brahminical classification formed four categories, namely, *Dharma, Artha, Kama* and *Moksha.* Four are also the divisions which Kautiliya thought befitting: *Avikshaki, Trayi, Varta* and *Dandaniti* (Gowen:1975:93; Dutta:1970).

In ancient and medieval periods some crude form of listing prevailed all through the ages, as catalog. The earlier period had *Anukamanikas* (or Indianised bibliography) which consisted of a list of hymns, authors, form of sutras, number of verses, Rishi's name to whom hymn was described, and metre in which hymns were composed. Being dissatisfied with the Indian bibliographic tradition, Indologists, since over 150 years have been devoting their energies to bring out systematic catalogues of ancient works.

In successful preservation, probably, Jains took the lead. The library was normally in the basement to save the Mss. from the sunlight and dust. Leather and wooden boxes were also in use to store the Mss. A knot of cotton thread was used for the Mss. to protect from the changing atmospheric conditions and dust. Further, Birch Bark and palm leave Mss. were held together by a cord drawn together a single hole in the middle, and this was all, known as book binding. The cover would at times be of cloth. Generally outer covers were made of seasoned woods, rarely with skin and hide covers - as was introduced in India by the Muslims. Birch Bark often breaks, when folded, and hence large number of ancient Mss. on bark have been found in roll form.

Private funding for libraries is hardly traced in this period. Regarding the funds, we find a specific mention in *Mahabharata*, which enjoined every king to continue *Shiranivis*, or financial grant, for book activity. This grant was controlled by the courts for establishment and enrichment of libraries (Raghunanda Shastri:1951). Instances of royal funding are available from records, like, the grant of villages by King Guhasana of Vallabhi in the 6th century AC; grant of villages for Nalanda by King Devapala; similarly in the 11th century, King Trailokyamalla founded and maintained a school and a library with six librarians. The grant given by the Pattan rulers to Bhaskara's research institute and library and the tax it generated for continued support is a remarkable record. The Gupta dynasty committed financial support from many villages for the maintenance of Nalanda University.

To sum up this description of non-print culture, one can quote the opinion of a foremost historian of Indian books and libraries, Professor D N Marshall: "The theory of some scholars regarding the existence of many great libraries in pre-Muslim India is more patriotic than true" (Marshall:1983:79). One cannot simply insist that the library was a common institution in ancient India. The ancient period inaugurated an age of repositories, rather than libraries–an age of guarding and storing materials, and of a belief that it is "irreligious" to share information sources.

3

MEDIEVAL INDIA
(1206-1526 and 1526-1757)

This period is distinct in many ways, from the ancient period. The basic difference lies in the predominant position of Muslim rulers. This position enabled Muslims to import many cultural and literary activities: writing history, maintaining a record of minute details, maintaining libraries, manufacturing paper, tanning of leather for book binding, employing professional binders, caligraphers to make copies, proof readers (*musahib*), and others. The history of the library development of this period can be seen in three different perspectives, viz., (i) the continuation of the old Hindu traditions of library patronage: 1206-1707; (ii) the early period of Muslim rule (Sultanate Period 1206-1526 or pre-Mughal period); and (iii) the Moghul period (1526-1707). This period also witnessed the entry of Europeans as traders. They brought the library material for evangelizing. But the history of their libraries before 1750s, is either limited or it needs further research to find out the material.

3.1 Hindu Rule

The libraries of Buddhists gradually declined. Jain and Brahmanical libraries continued flourishing in their respective lands. The palace/court libraries of Kashmir, Jaipur, Bikaner, Mysore, and Tanjore, existed during this period.

3.1.1 *Palace/Court Libraries*

The Kashmiri library tradition of Kanishka was continued by his successors. A court library was founded by Maharaja Anup Sinhji in the late 17th century at Bikaner (in Rajasthan). It comprised of Mss. in Sanskrit, Rajasthani, and other scripts. Another court library in Rajasthan was "Potikhana" of Sawai Raja Jai Singh II (1699-1743) of Jaipur.

The library had many books and Mss. and hence it attracted scholars from distant regions. In 1716 he is said to have had 336 printed books. Its library benefited by the disintegration of Mughal Imperial library, as evidenced by seals of imperial collections. Apart from this, the library has traces of books being procured also from Europe. His successors were less scholarly. It is reported that, Jagat Singh, his successor, donated the library to a friend-courtier from which time it lost its value and was distributed among his poorer relations.

Apart from this royal collection, we find, historically traces of Anoop Sanskrit Library of Bikaner (it is difficult to identify this with the above-mentioned similar library at Bikaner), so also royal libraries of Jodhpur, Jhalawar, Bharatpur–all in Rajasthan. A court library of the ruling Telugu Nayaks of Tanjore was established in the 15th century. Its value and content enhanced greatly in the 19th century when the Marathas took over this collection.

At Mysore the ruler of the Wodeyar dynasty had a royal library. Its flourishing dates are in the 17th century during the period of Chikka Devaraya (1672-1704). This was the same collection which went to the Library of Tipu Sultan, and will be discussed in the next section. According to historical evidences, it had a collection of valuable Sanskrit books. Ahom Kings (15th to 17th century) of Assam are reported to have some out houses to preserve the collection of Mss. along with the records and other archival material.

3.1.2 *Centres of Learning Libraries*

Centres of traditional Hindu learning became popular in and around tenth century. In South India, there are very scanty and scattered reports about the libraries. In this period, probably in 13th century was established a Jain mutt library at Moodabidre (North Kanara Distt.). Much research is not done on its early history. But the glaring fact is that this survived the age old oppression of anti-Brahminical currents, and is still flourishing. We hear about a Brahminical school at Sringeri Mutt (in the present state of Karnataka) which had a library. An inscription of 1406 of the Vijayanagar Dynasty refers to a grant of villages. Kings Bukka and Devaraya have been reported to have given this grant. This grant was meant for maintenance and renovation of this library. The same inscription mentions that there was an office of a Librarian who received the grant in person. The name of this Librarian is mentioned as Narasimha Bharati Woodeyar. (*Annual Report of the South India Epigraphy*:1936-1937).

Another institution about which we have some information is the Mithila. This centre of learning represented the Brahminical culture. Its origin is unknown, but it did exist in the ancient India and definitely flourished between the 12th and 15th centuries, during the Karnataka and Kameswara Dynasties. Its Mss., collection multiplied by passage of time. One reason for growth of its collection was the practice of asking the students to compulsorily deposit all class notes after completion of their study. Another reason for this growth of Mss. was the need of the collection in the final examination. In this exam the student was to explain any page of a manuscript which was pierced last by the needle. (Vidyabhushan: 1921:523).

3.1.3 *Temple Libraries*

Libraries attached to Hindu and Jain centres of worship continued their tradition. At Daryabad in the Kingdom of Oudh a Library of Jains was established in 1744. Some two hundred years old, was another library for the Hindus. These are reported to have been destroyed in 1857.

Kavindracharya, who lived at Benaras (present Varanasi) was visited by Bernier, during his travels (in 1656-1668). Kavindra was a scholar of Sanskrit, and a contemporary of Shah Jahan and Aurengzeb, had a very good collection. Its manuscripts bear the seal "Sarvidyanidana Kavindracharya Saraswatinam Pustakam". Its collection must have been qualitatively valuable as its catalogue traced from a Mutt in Benaras was published in Gaikwad's Oriental Series. Bernier saw this library, and was amazed to see a large room "entirely filled with such scripts" (Bernier:1891:335; Dutta:87; Chopra:1976:155). Existence of other important collections is scattered in vast amount of resources. One such is the Travel notes of Fryer who substantially wrote down the minute details of his observations, and informs about existence of several libraries of Hindus which were a good place to find precious and valuable Mss. in Sanskrit, and each unfolding the mysteries of their religion (Fryer: 1873:392; Chopra:1976:154-155). According to another Persian source, *Iqbalnama-i-Jahangiri*, the Brahmins of Kashmir maintained libraries which they regularly used.

3.2 **Delhi Sultanate Period**

In the medieval period, under the Delhi Sultanate and under the provincial dynasties prominent types of libraries were palace/royal and court libraries, libraries attached to Madrasa, Mosque and Qanqah, and private library collections. Except the last type, the others normally received some or the other kind of royal patronage and support.

With the fall of Baghdad in 1258 Delhi became the most important centre of the Muslim world. The destruction of cultural centres in Central and Western Asia forced poets, scholars and learned to take refuge in India. The Delhi Sultanate and all the other Muslim rulers kept their doors open for these people. These people produced a lot of literature and despite the time that has passed much has been still preserved. "If the surviving poetry of Khusrau, the historical works of Barani, and table talk of Hazrat Nizamuddin Auliya are any indication of the cultural vitality and richness of the age, one can well understand why Amir Khusrau and others felt that Delhi was the metropolis of the Muslim East" (Ikram:114).

3.2.1 *Palace/Court Libraries*

Among palace libraries we hear the names of the libraries established or maintained by Mahmud Ghazni (998-1030), Balban, Jalaluddin Khilji (1290-1296), Allauddin Khilji (1296-1316), Firoz Shah Tughluq (1351-1388), etc. Sikendar Lodhi encouraged learning, translation projects and libraries. He brought books from Khursau and distributed free of cost (Jaffar:1972:122-23).

This period has a record of libraries and librarians in the literature. Annamerie Schimmel has been able to highlight, in the contemporary Persian sources, the emergence/use of the words relating to books, manuscripts, page, lines, etc. So also we find in this period the presence of a Librarian Amir Khusro (d.1325). He was a poet par excellence in the language called then Hindustani, and today called Urdu. He served as Librarian on the order of Jalaluddin Khilji (d. 1290). He is the first known librarian of this period, and is also carries the title of Prince of Poets.

Firuz Shah Tughluq's love of books avoided destruction of the Jwala Mukhi Temple Collection (Kumar:1977:21). He went on adding his collection. He was the author of *Futuhat-e-Firoz Shahi*, and employed a series of scholars to write books. The topics/themes which concentrated in this exercise included exegesis, law etc., For this work of research, there must have been an unmatchable royal library at the disposal of the king and the scholars. Scholarly collections varied in languages and subjects. At the palace library of Nawab Jalaluddin at

Lucknow, it is reported to have a book on astrology translated from Sanskrit into Persian in Firuz Shah's reign.

Even the nobles and courtiers tried to imitate this taste of literary merit. Tatar Khan, a courtier of this king, too had a personal library, and based on this collection he compiled an encyclopedic exegesis, called *Tafsir-e-Tatar Khan*, and also *Fatawa-e-Tatar Khan* in 30 volumes.

3.2.2 *Centres of Learning Libraries*

As per the tradition the centres of learning for Muslims were Madrasa (Muslim educational centre, used for school, college, University level of education), *Qanqah* (hermit) and the Mosque.

3.2.2.1 *Madrasa Libraries*

Education has been the only most emphasized, most meritorious, most important and of primary concern in Islam. Col. William Sleeman, an English officer observed: "Perhaps there are few communities in the world among whom education is more generally diffused than among Mohammedans in India" (Sleeman:1844:283). The concept of library has been an inherent component of the Muslim culture, wherever they lived. Muslim India was no exception to this rule. The Muslims imported their own system of education, and, Madrasa in India. Therefore, the library in India did not have any major deviation - in terms of subject approach, methodology, administration, terminology, arrangement and organization of books, and so on - from a Madrasa Library in any other part of the then known Muslim World. The details of the library system are however, buried deep, in records like travelogues, narratives, epithets, and so many other literary pieces. To bring out these requires a life of Noah. The description of few of these Madrasa Libraries will be made under the provincial histories.

3.2.2.2 *Qanqah Libraries*

This type of collection refers to a library of the Sufi saint, or a collection of reading material at the meeting place of these Sufis (or mystics), called *Qanqah*. About this type of library whose existence is undeniable, there is hardly any detail available even in the Sufi annals.

3.2.2.3 *Mosque Libraries*

The history of this library is again as old as the *madrasa* libraries. Its importance in the history of Muslim librarianship makes it necessary to place it under detailed analysis. This is however not attempted here. Many mosque libraries are reported to have been existing in India since the Muslim rule began (Zubair: 1961). "Agreement is almost unanimous amongst historians that mosque libraries are an important segment of Muslim Librarianship" (Sibai: 1987:39).

The concept of public libraries, in the true sense of the term emerges in these mosque libraries, in India and in the other parts of the then known Muslim world. Entrance to mosque was never limited to Muslims, and being openly accessible to all it attracted many a people. These libraries attached to mosque or were near the mosque and served as a public reading room. In the words of Marshall "Save for a few mosque collections, with their inherent limitations, there were no free public libraries in the modern sense of the term or even approximating thereto", in this period of Indian history (Marshall:1983:69).

3.2.3 *Private Libraries*

Personal collections of saints, nobles, elites, and landlords formed another type of library. These were open to the public either during their life time or were declared to such an effect, in their will.

Fazil Khan, a prime minister probably of the Tughluq dynasty, must have had a large collection of both Eastern and Western languages. Bernier says, he taught Fazil Khan "the principal languages of Europe, after he had translated for him the whole philosophy of Gassendi in Latin, and whose leave he could not obtain, until he had copied for him a select number of best European books, thereby to supply the loss he should suffer of his person" (Bernier:1895:352-353). Again, Bernier was also associated with another noble, Agha Danishmand Khan. He was a man of scholarly possession and found time to seek knowledge despite his official tasks. "My Nawab Agha Danishmand Khan, expects my arrival with much impatience. He can no more dispense with his philosophical studies in the afternoon than avoid devoting the morning to his weighty duties as Secretary of State for Foreign Affairs and Grand Master of the Horse. Astronomy, geography, and anatomy are his favourite pursuits, and he reads with avidity the works of Gassendy and Descartes" (Bernier:1895:352-353).

The saint-sufi Nizamuddin Auliya (d.1325 A C) lived in Delhi, and his collection was reportedly kept accessible to all. The library of this learned scholar was the property of the *waqf* (or endowment) after him. It was opened to every man of letters. Another private, but notable collection belonged to an Afghan noble, Ghazi Khan. It was the same collection which Babur could lay hands on when he became the ruler at Delhi.

3.3 **Provincial Muslim Rule**

Apart from the rule of the Delhi Sultanate there were principal provincial states, which were either independent because of their strength or because of the inability of the Delhi Sultans to control them directly. There were many such independent provincial states, or we can call them kingdoms, for instance at Gujarat, Deccan, and Bengal. Even if they were subdued, the control of the Emperor was nominal, or remained for a while.

3.3.1 *Gujarat*

Among the rulers of Gujarat Sultan Mahmud Begda (1458-1511 A C) had inherited a library. The Librarian was Syed Usman *alias* Shami Burhani - the librarian as a practice was a scholar of repute. The library was housed in Osmanpura Madrasa, near Ahmedabad, which gave it the character of palace-cum-academic library. After the conquest of Gujarat by Akbar, this collection was added to the imperial Mughal library.

A large number of personal/private libraries have been identified by historians, which were scattered at Ahmedabad, Pattan, Cambay, Champaner, Broach, and Surat. We find herein names of the people who owned these like, Maulana Yaqub's library in the Jamia Masjid, Maulana Ahmed's library and Maulana Muhammad Bin. Tahir's library, all at Pattan; Shaikh Ahmed Khattu's library and Shahia library (belonging to Shah Alam and Badr Alam), at Ahmedabad; Dewan Abdul Latif's Library at Cambay; and Alidarusia library and Shaikh Muhammad Fadil Shah's library at Surat. Specifically attached to the centres of learning were libraries like, Shah Wajihuddin's library, Shaikh Uthman's Library, Maulana Nuruddin's library, Waliullahi Library and Ismaili Libraries.

3.3.2 *Bahmani Kingdom*

The one time most powerful Deccan kingdom was that of Bahmanides, which later split into five separate dynasties with capitals at Golconda (Hyderabad), Bidar, Berar, Gulbarga and Bijapur. The Bahmanides too were patrons of education, libraries and culture. History has to this day the name of the College of Mahmud Gawan and its library (founded 1472) at Bidar, in Karnataka. This college of Mahmud Gawan had a significant style of architecture, and this feature made its library well documented in the history of the world. We find from historical records that this great Vazir-cum-scholar, left behind him a huge library of about 30,000 titles (Chopra:1976:154). But what happened to its collection and what was its content, is a part of imagination as we don't find much about it anywhere. A small portion of it which was left in Bidar, reached Delhi after the Mughal conquest during the reign of Aurangzeb. The Bahmani kings (1347-1527) maintained a royal library, details of which have again been lost.

3.3.3 *Bihar*

Madrasa of Azimabad, on the bank of Ganga, in present-day Patna had reportedly vast resources, and some traces of this still survive similar centres were at Phulwari Shariff in Patna, Khalibagh in Bhagalpur and Islampur.

3.4 **Mughals**

3.4.1 *The National Library or The Imperial Library of Mughals*

The coming of Mughals in India initiated yet another step in the progress of library development. Mongols and Tartars were notorious for destruction of civilization, but a soul from the same clan, Timur (d.1405), did devote his life to literary scholarship. He even found a royal library at Samarqand. The progeny of this Timur, the Indian Mughals, had a fine literary taste. They were well read and have been rightly called highly cultured men. Babur to Aurangzeb, the Mughal emperors, runs a continuous history of library tradition and patronage of libraries along with other cultural and literary activities. The Imperial Library grew leaps and bounds. By the time of Akbar and Jahangir it had collected printed and non-printed materials, in major languages of east and west. Printed books were brought in numerous quantities to the country. Akbar had added to the collection material in Indian languages for his comparative studies. And this Library was organized in the best known methods. Hence it deserves to be called the first National Library in India.

3.4.1.1 *Babur*

Zaheeruddin Muhammad Babur (1483-1530) was the founder of both the Mughal rule and the Mughal library tradition in India. The imperial library which he established was consolidated under Akbar, and to some extent under Jahangir, reached the height of its glory under Shah Jahan and Aurangzeb. He brought books from Fargahana and he acquired more after settling down in Delhi, as the emperor of India. This allowed him to develop both the imperial library and a personal library. In the personal library he went in for relaxation. Here he kept his selected books and he took rest when he was poisoned. His library must have been a major source for his famous historical/ autobiographical work "Baburnama".

His literary taste is more so evident from his disappointment at not getting proper selection to send to his sons Humayun and Kamran. This refers to Ghazi Khan's collection which Babur had access to. He says, "I did not on the whole find so many books of value as, from their appearance, I had expected'. His multi-lingual knowledge (of Arabic, Persian, Turkish and Hindustani) enabled him to develop a vast variety of reading material.

Babur encouraged calligraphy. He was the person who contributed to a new type of writing, which came to be known as 'Babri hand' (or *Khat-e-Baburi*). The idea his great grandson, Jahangir got of adding a gallery of painting and the art of book illustration originates from Babur.

Babur encouraged men of letters. Khwandmir, Librarian of the minister of Herat, when reached the court of Babur, Babur made him his confident. He even accompanied this Timooride tiger on an expedition to Bengal. After Babur, Khwandmir served Humayun in the latter's literary endeavors. And similarly achieved the status on the expedition to Gujarat. He accompanied Humayun along with the latter's personal library as the custodian of the collection. Very little reaches us about the actual administration of the library and its maintenance. His memoir refer to the name of librarian - Khwaja Muhammad Ali

Kitabdar (Aziz:59).

During Babur's rule, one of the duty of the Public Works Department (or *Shuhrat-e-am*) was building of maktabs and *Madrasas*. It is obvious that each Madrasa must have had a provision for a reading room and reading material, as Islamic tradition of teaching was no at any time totally oral, rather it was always with the books.

3.4.1.2 *Humayun*

The brief, but successful rule, of Babur ended and Nasir-ud-din Muhammad Humayun (1507-1556) took over as the ruler in 1530. Despite many ups and downs in this period of Indian history and in the life of Humayun, the imperial library continued its growth. He had a large number of chosen books in his library. According to Abul Fazl's *Akbarnama*, he had the practice to carry even to battle fields some of his choicest books. This cannot be surprising as the military camp of these rulers was a mobile city. "During his expedition to Gujarat, when he was camped at Cambay, some forest and hill tribes probably Kolis, made a noctural raid on his camp. In the resultant confusion many rare books which were his real companions and were always kept in his imperial Majesty's personal possessions were lost".

Humayun was a bibliophile like Babur. He is reported to have once said, though still in childhood, "Thank God, the treasure which cannot be got again is safe, other things are easy to obtain" (Ishwari Prasad:1955:364). This was his reaction when he found his lost books. Art historians tell that Humayun's *Khana-i-Tilsim* at Agra had three buildings and the central building (called *Khana-i-Sadat*) had the library.

Sher Shah Suri (d. 1545) the Afghan, defeated Humayun. This forced Humayun to run as a fugitive from Delhi in 1540. His companions included his book collection. This is recorded faithfully in Count Noer's *Akbar*. Humayun returned to Delhi as a victor in 1555. Sher Shah a great monarch, had taste of art equal to the Mughals. He has even been regarded as the most remarkable royal builder in the history of India (Asher:1984). He built in 1541 a pleasure house (Sher Mandal) in the old fort at Delhi. After resuming power, Humayun converted this into a library. Ironically enough, it was on the steps of this library that he tumbled. He sustained severe injuries and died later on. When he had heard the call (*Adhan*) for evening prayer he rushed out to pray and in his haste he slipped. He used this library for one year and he died in 1556.

Adding books to the library being a normal process, probably Humayun even purchased books. An inscription on *Tuhfat-us-Salatin* by Mir Ali, shows Humayun's name, and that it cost him Rs. 2,500/-. Apart from names of a few librarians of this period, we have no other information on the library administration and management. Nizam, styled Baz Bahadur, was his Librarian, according to *Tuzuk-i-Jahangiri,* Mulla Surkh is named as Librarian in *Humayunnama*. Lala Beg is also found in records. Historically it was one of his librarians who informed the treacherous design of Maldev and thereby saved Humayun from being conquered by Sher Shah.

3.4.1.3 *Akbar*

Jalalluddin Mohammed Akbar (1543-1605) after his ascension in 1556 emerged as one of the greatest rulers of the world. He took much delight in the collection of books in his library. A part of the books was kept in his *harem* and the rest in the Imperial Library. The personal collection was of those books which were read often. Some books were read many a times. One may pause here and question as to what sources are there to show the existence of an Imperial Library. The minute details of the collection, its structure, and of seals on the books it possessed in its holdings, are enough evidences to identify the Imperial Library - for its existence,and, its exemplary nature. Contemporary writers, both indigenous and foreign visitors bear testimony to it. We find in the *Ain-i-Akbari* the following:

> His majesty's library is divided into several parts; some of the books are kept within, and some without, the *Harem*. Each part of the library is sub-divided according to the value of the books. Prose books, poetical works, Hindi, Persian, Greek, Kashmiri and, Arabic are all separately placed. In this order they are also inspected. Experienced people bring them daily and read them before His Majesty, who hears every book from the beginning to the end (quoted in Ojha:1975:113).

Books belonging to Akbar's library bear the seal 'Muhammad Akbar, Padshah-i-Ghazi, 1013 A.H' (or 1603 A. D). Another source which indirectly hints at the existence of this Mughal Library is that Badayuni, a contemporary traveller and historian, borrowed books from this library. One of the books which he borrowed '*Khirad Afza*' was lost, and another book he borrowed was returned as over-due. These and similar instances make up the historical sources for the existence of such major libraries of the period.

To know how much of time Akbar devoted for study and research one instance would be sufficient. Abul Fazal (d.1602) in his *Ain-i-Akbari* mentions that Akbar would listen daily to the perusal of books by paid readers. Their remuneration depended on the number of leaves read; and that of the last of the leaves perused, Akbar wrote daily with his own pen in numerals the number of leaves gone through; on the basis of which the remuneration was calculated and paid in cash to the readers then and there.

It is reported that Akbar's Imperial Library expanded its size from the collections acquired from libraries of other rulers and nobles. For instance Itemad Khan Gujarati's collection, and Faizi's library (containing 4600 volumes), etc. Faizi's collection had multiple copies of some books, and so were also in Akbar's. The latter donated books to the learned from such duplicate sets.

Significantly the Imperial Library was catalogued and arranged in three different sections, viz., (i) poetry, medicine, astrology, and music, (ii) philology, philosophy, sufism, astronomy, geometry, and (iii) commentaries on Traditions and *Quran,* theology and law. These sections were primarily arranged by languages of the thought content, primary languages being Arabic, Hindi, Persian, Kashmiri, Greek, Latin, and English.

Akbar, also called Akbar the Great, was genius, and he organized all his departments. He created a separate department for libraries to look after the state library and other libraries located in the capital (R Das:1964). The officer incharge was called *Nazim* and *Muhtamim* or *Darogha* was the next officer. Abul Fazl's *Akbarnama* reports the name of Mulla Bilal and Badauni's *Muntakhabut Tawarikh* has recorded the name of Inayathullah, who was a *Katib* (calligraphist), as a librarian of Akbar's period. Mulla Pir Muhammad was one time Superintendent of the library, reports Qandhari's *Tarikh-i-Akbari.* The Nazim had under him assistants who were to "enter the books in the register and to keep separate registers for separate subjects and number the books" (Chopra:1976:153). In short he became the forerunner of Indian library organizers. He reformed the library from each and every angle: acquisition, processing, storage and even to some extent retrieval was systematized of the type that was found useful to recall the stored information.

He established and patronized many libraries in the kingdom. So much so was his zeal to popularize education and learning that Hindus, Muslims, and others received his favours in this regard. At Fatehpur Sikri he established a library to help education of women (A Prasad:1977).

The idea of esthetic outlook was seen in every part of Mughal constructions. The Imperial Library was located in the big hall, which was on the side of the octagonal tower in Agra fort. In the words of Howell "passing through these (i.e. rooms known as apartments of Akbar adjoining the Samman Burj) we enter a long room known as the library in which a not very small successful attempt was made some years ago to restore the painted decoration" (E B Howell:66; and Ojha:1975:113).

Akbar's reign provided a stable and peaceful environment by which art and literature received royal patronage. Akbar's reign paved the way for emergence of translations, compilations, calligraphic illustrations, and other literary works. The spirit of tolerance and a desire to understand other religions made necessary for Akbar to set up a bureau of translations. This bureau rendered prominent works of Sanskrit, Arabic, Turkish into Persian. Interestingly, a voluminous amount of the sacred literature in Sanskrit was translated, so also was the translation of *Bible*. The Persian version of *Bible* was named *Dastan-i- Masih*. The collection inherited by Akbar expanded by additions (from conquests in Bengal, Gujarat, Jaunpur, Kashmir, Bihar, Deccan, etc.), original compilations, translations and books received as presents from nobles and western scholar-cum-traders.

According to Smith, the Imperial Library of Akbar, located in the Agra fort was so rich in its thought content, "to which probably no parallel existed, or even has existed in the world". This library had 24,000 rare Mss., reports, *Manrique de lara*, costing Rs 64,63,731. It had laid the foundation for a national library, representing different languages and subjects. The Jesuits and others who brought books made it the first national repository of European printed books. Whether this Imperial Library was used at all by others ? We have one instance of a scholar citing from this collection in the Imperial Library. *The Diwan of Humayun Shah* available in Akbar's collection is cited by Abul Fazal in the *Akbarnama*, while the latter borrowed a few couplets from the *Diwan*.

What was Akbar's greatness, is visual item in the world of Indian cinematography. In the 1940s and 1950s many films were made depicting his royal personality and the grandeur that was this great Moghul. Historians of yester-years had only books to read and spread the history of culture of the past, but today we are in possession of a variety of media to re-read and re-pack this history of India which Jawaharlal Nehru (prime minister of India), wrote as '*Discovery of India*'.

3.4.1.4 *Jahangir*

Nooruddin Jahangir (originally named Muhammad Sultan Saleem, 1569-1627) was famous for his rule of justice. He continued the literary tradition and library tradition of Timur. Himself a poet he was a great patron of learning. Though literary endeavors were not totally inherited from his ancestors, yet Jahangir was a chip of the old block. He, like Babur, wrote an autobiography, entitled *Tuzuk-i-Jahangiri*, proving his literary attainments (Barua:1972-73).

The library went on expanding both in quality and quantity. Jahangir paid exorbitant prices to purchase rare Mss. He paid 10,000 pounds for one such Ms. entitled *Yusuf-Zulekha* a book which is full of illustrations and paintings. Whether the sum was worth or not, Martin tells us that it would not fetch 2000 pounds even in Paris. "From notes and calculations I have made, miniatures by Bihzad were worth hundreds of pounds each and certain of his manuscripts were worth ten times than now" (Martin:58). Like Humayun, he had a library collection which was always on the move along with him. So informs his autobiography. When he visited Cambay in Gujarat, he autographed and presented several books to Ulema (Tuzuk:218). However, it is not sure whether he distributed multiple copies of same title, or he had procured enough of titles (which were duplicates in the Imperial Library).

Jahangir not only added books, as was the practice in the Imperial Library acquisitions till then, he also added a picture or art gallery to the Imperial Library (Barua:1972-73). Albums belonging to his period are often regarded as the golden age of Mughal painting, (Devapriam:1972). Art historians derive the degree and level of influence of Western art on Mughal paintings. Jahangir's collection as reported by them contained copies and adaptations of European prints in the Mughal style.

He made a law that when a wealthy man died without a heir, the property had to be used for building and repairing educational institutions, and library was not outside this target (Anirudhi Prasad:1977). We have only one name of the Librarian, who was Maktub Khan said to be Librarian and Superintendent.

3.4.1.5 *Shahjahan*

Shahabuddin Muhammad Shahjahan (1592-1666) was another great builder of Mughal art and lover of learning and scholarship. The size of the library further grew in this period. This is evident from Mandelso-Harris, the German traveller, who reports, that the Imperial Library had "well-bound 24,000 books. This was in 1638 (Mandelso-Harris:118). Strangely, these figures are same as those at Akbar's death. That was reported by other sources. Either there is a difference in counting, or, because of the policy of donating, books have been gifted, or there must have been much more 'unbound' of which Mandelso could not get an account.

Shahjahan, reportedly took active interests in the establishment of libraries and other educational institutions in the empire. His literary taste is evident from his daily schedule. He spent the earlier portion of the night in his personal library attached to his sleeping chamber. Sir Jadunath Sarkar writes, "At about 8.30 p.m. he returned to *harem*. Good (male) readers sat behind a *purdah* which separated them from the royal bed chamber and read aloud books on travel, lives of saints and prophets, and histories of former kings - all rich in instruction" (J Sarkar:174).

Printed books had entered the Imperial Library, as stated above, and these went on increasing from time to time. Persian and Arabic books were printed in this period in Europe, more so in Leyden, after 1630s. The visits by the missionaries to the courts of Akbar and Jahangir continued even to the time of Shah Jahan. Therefore, it is in all probability that the Imperial Library and the other leading libraries of this period had such books, particularly the contemporary Persian works of Fr. Jerome Xavier. Another book (printed in 1649) in Arabic entered the country and the Wazir of Shahjahan, Sadullah Khan refused to accept it, as it dealt with theological refutation of an Islamic work (Qaiser:1982:61).

Regarding the library staff we have a few names of the some senior personnel, such as Sayyid Ali ibn Sayyid Jalal was Nazim, who succeeded Itemad Khan and Inayet Khan ibn Zafar Khan. The *Darogha* or *Muhtamim* was Abdur Rahman Khushnavis, and was succeeded by Muhammad Salih ibn Abdullah Miskin Raqam, and Mohammed Shafi. The name of the latter is revealed by a seal on a copy of the *Quran* which is in the possession of Royal Asiatic Society, Calcutta. There is another name of a *Darogha* given in Mulla Abdul Hamid Lahori's *Badshah Nama*, and that is Rashid Ali, the calligraphist.

3.4.1.6 *Aurangzeb*

The Imperial Library was greatly improved, before its final decay, by the last great Mughal Muhiyuddin Muhammad Aurangzeb Alamgir (1618-1707). He knew apart from other languages Hindustani too well, and his popular sayings in that language are recorded in history. On this period of Aurangzeb, interestingly, we have two experts in history, viz., Sir Jadunath Sarkar and Allama Shibli Nomani. Sarkar informs us that Aurangzeb patronized Hindi poets and scholars such as, Birdad, Bhushan and Brinda (Ojha:1975:112). Hence the Imperial Library collection must have had a variety much larger than that of Akbar in major languages of the east and the west. Is Aurangzeb still a bigot and destroyer of every thing named with Hind? Further, it was the same Aurangzeb who patronized Hindu scholars of Persian literature, like Sujan Rai Khatri, Wamat Khatri, Rai Brindaban, Ishwardas Nagar, Bhim Sen, etc. Which library other than the Imperial Library these scholars had access too, if they were really patronized and supported by the Emperor of Mughal India.

The library added its collection and became the basis for the emperor's literary activities. *Fatwa-i-Alamgiri*, the greatest digest of Muslim law in India, was compiled by a board of eminent jurists under his personal supervision. This compilation would have necessarily required accumulation of various books relating to law in the primary Islamic languages - Arabic, Persian, Turkish and Hindustani. In the Deccan trips, the Mughal armies could find the library of Mahmud Gawan. This was transferred to Delhi and added to the imperial collection on the order of Aurangzeb. His reading tastes were a replica of his own ancestors, and it is reported that his reading hour stated at 2 p.m. every day. This literary taste and culture could not be continued by his successors, and whatever was collected by the great Mughals was lost in a number of ways.

The Nazims of the Imperial Library who have been mentioned in the history included, Muhammad Salih ibn Isa khan, Syed Ali Tabrizi (the tutor of Aurangzeb in the art of calligraphy), and the *Muhtamims* are named as Muhammad Mansur, Sayyid Ali al-Hussaini (identified from a seal on the copy of *Quran*), and Kabir Khan (mentioned in *Maathir-i-Alamgiri*, and *Jawahar Raqam*) (Dalvi:1989:253).

3.4.2 *Libraries of Nobles/Elites*

The Mughal era saw an increase in the number of libraries developed by nobles/elites. The development of libraries by this class of the society was a fashion and a challenging one. Each wished to out beat the other in building the library and in increasing the size of the collection.

In Delhi, under the Moghuls Abdur Rahim Khan-i-Khanan, developed a library which was marvelous. Being a son of Akbar's guardian - Bairam Khan - he had the privilege of having access to large collections in and outside the kingdom. This collection was not a closed personalized one, rather it was used by many scholars and learned men. Strangely, this bibliophile, didn't equal his contemporaries in rearing scholarly accomplishments, but he did excel them in patronage of literature. In travel and in toilet, he is said to have read books.

Much research is in progress on the life and contributions of the Khan Khanan. There is a reference in literature to the type of paper Khanan had access to for the purpose of caligraphy. "As Khan Khanan was very fond of tracing-paper, he invented for him a tracing paper of seven colours, and developed this art to a high degree. For this he received many favours and rewards. He was the inventor of variegated paper also" (Khan, Rahmat Ali:31-31).

The worth of this library of Abdur Rahim Khanan is evident from the fact that books from this library have been preserved. Raza Library, Rampur has a book on sufism by Khwaja Abdullah Ansari and this bears also autographs of Jahangir and Shahjahan. The Andhra Pradesh Oriental Manuscript Library, Hyderabad has Tabir roya, a book gifted by Akbar. There are other libraries which stock books from his collection, and the list includes Khuda Baksh Library, Patna, Asiatic Society Library, Calcutta, etc.

The *Nazim* or Director (or as commonly called then Superintendent) of this library, is reported in the, sources as Mir Baqi, and the *Kitabdar* or Librarian as Maulana Ibrahim Naqqash. Mir Baqi was appointed and trained by Khanan, while this noble was in Gujarat. Whereas Maulan Ibrahim was Librarian at a time when Khanan started Ahmednagar campaign. Another Librarian was Niamathulah who authored *Makzan-i-Afghan* (or History of the Afghans), and was a historian of Jahangir's period. This library is reported to have had 95 men on its staff (Datta:68). The famous book-binder of Mashhad (in Iran) and the inventor of Abri paper, Muhammed Ameen Khurasani, was a regular staff of this library, and was employed on a salary of Rs. 500 per month. Books were illuminated by Muslim and Hindu artists (Nadvi: 426). According to *Maasir-i-Rahimi*, scholars used this library for "study and self-improvement".

Shaikh Barhami of Bahraich, basically à Bhaka poet, was a librarian. His son Shaikh Abdus Salam was trained by Khan-i-Khanan and was appointed as Darogha. Shuja of Shiraz was appointed as one of the officers (scribe or *Katib*) of the library in 1590 (Nazir Ahmed:1927:58). Shuja was soon promoted to the highest post of superintendent. We also hear of the name of an expert binder, in this library, Mullah Muhammad Hussain.

Similarly Nawab Ibrahim Khan had a rich library. He was counted among the influential nobles of Delhi. Interestingly, each book had the seal of its library owner "This book is entered in the Library of Sirkar Nawab Ibrahim Khan Bahadur Hazabar Jung". This library had many invaluable collections. Innumerable books from this library went to the royal library at Oudh, after this owner's death.

Shaikh Faizi (d. 1595; an eminent Persian poet and scholar and brother of Abul Fazal) was another Mughal noble who had a prestigious collection. (According to R Das the collection was 4600, and Pulin Barua reports as 4800, and the original sources of Badaoni support it to be 4,600). As per the tradition of his age he had books on poetry, medicine, philosophy, etc. As was the medieval tradition, Which was lived even by Aurangzeb, some of the books in Faizi's collection were his own writings. This valuable collection was taken over by Akbar, after the death of Faizi.

A famous Saint of Gujarat, Sayyid Muhammad Shah Alam had a personal library. He was very fond of reading. Both his hands, are reported, to have marks which were caused by leaning during deep excessive study. There is another noble who must have had a precious collection. He is reported to be a favourite courtier of Jahangir. A few literary master pieces of his library (including a copy of the *Diwan* of Hassan Dehlavi, which Shaikh Farid had bought) are today available in the Khuda Bhaksh Oriental Public Library, Patna. One may see a lot more in the published catalogue of Khuda Baksh Library.

Khusro (d. 1622) son of Jahangir, was a bibliophile. He is reported to have made a regular purchase of books. At a later stage, books were read to him by his wife, due to his blindness.

Dara Shikhu, son of Shahjahan, was an accomplished scholar. A scholar of comparative religion, mysticism, etc., a translator of about ten Sanskrit books into Persian, he was also an author of many scholarly works. His library must have been larger in terms of collection on the subject of Indo-Muslim studies, compared to his contemporaries. The preciousness of the collection is evident from the fact that the album of Dara Shikhu's Library is also available in the India Office Library (Devapriam:1972:90).

He collected rare books for his library. When *Tuzuk-e-Jahangiri* became rare, it is reported that, this rich man however procured a copy. So much was this library famous for its rare collection that Prince Muhammad Sultan, son of Alamgir, got his own book from this library. In the last days of the Mughal empire this Nawab, kept up the torch of learning. His personal library had books worth at least Rs. 25,000. This library was destroyed in the war of 1857.

Keeping in line with this practice of maintaining private libraries, the elite too did not sit quite, they rather developed their own collections. This was an ubiquitous feature.

The elite/learned of Daryabad, Bilgram, Lucknow, Murshidabad, etc. had large library collections. One of these elites, Syed Abdul Jalil (d.1725), wrote to his son, " My boy, the book... is put in that trunk which was brought from Gujarat. What should I write to you about the care and precaution to be taken for the books. You know well how much I love my books, and after how much labour and search I have collected them... Air the books in the sun as often as possible". Another scholar Shah Tayyib (d. 1739), had a fine collection. Azad Bilgrami informs us in *Maathir-ul-Kiram* that he left to his memory a big library with fine specimens of calligraphy. Yet another Bibliophile Nawab Shaikh Mir Alamgiri of Bilgram, willed that the Mosque should be completed after the sale of his books, which he loved very dearly. So informs *Maathir-ul-Kiram*.

Maulvi Mashuq Ali (d.1845) of Jaunpur, had 5000 books in his collection. Another scholar, Mufti Syed Abdul Raza had a library and he memorized contents of his collection. Shah Jahan is reported to have used his services, due to his strong memory. Nawab Muinuddaula of Bengal, a bibliophile and a scholar of repute, must have had a systematic library. We find that he had a Darogha named Mir Ahmadullah in this library. Tahwildar, Hafiz Asadullah, was another staff of this library. From historical records we gather the information that a scholar Mir Muhammad Ali possessed a personal library of thousands of books. He was patronized by the Nawab of Murshidabad, Ali Wardi

Khan. The Shia Mujtahids had libraries of their own in Lucknow and at other places. About Nawab Munim Khan we are told that he was fond of purchasing rare books and for which he paid enormous amount. For instance, he paid Rs. 500 for the *Kulliyat of Sadi* (d. 976).

3.4.3 *Centres of Learning/Religion*

Madrasa libraries, and, *qanqah* (spelled also as *Khanqah*) libraries, did find their role in this society. Moghuls and the provincial rulers patronized learning, as they did in art and architectural fields. Wherever *Madrasa* was established the library automatically emerged. The syllabus and the curriculum had a system to provide both oral and written education. Shaikh Ahmed Khattawi's contributions included among other institutions, the establishment of a *Madrasa* and its library in one of the apartments of the *Madrasa*. The library users being basically students and faculty, the community of the learned did have access to the collection, and in this sense, Chopra rightly says these academic libraries, to be worth being called public libraries. And the biggest in size was the Imperial Library (Chopra:1978:152-153).

The Sufi tradition so strong in India in this period, did have learned men and learning resource centres in their *qanqahs* and there were such sufi residencies at various places. Worth mentioning *qanqah* libraries were of Shaikh Ahmed Khattawi (d.1445), in Ahmedabad, *Qanqah Abbasi* in Bhagalpur, *Qanqah* in Phulwari Sharieff, and *Qanqah Madrasa Arabia* in Sahsaram, etc.

The libraries at Fort St. George, Madras (1663) and Fort St. David, Cuddalore (1707), basically contained theological materials. And, while these were meant for Europeans, the large number of native (Indian) employees must have had some access to these collections. As per the order of the East India Company, books were sorted into subjects, listed (or catalogued), and an annual inventory was started (Kumar:1977:33). It was the same missionary zeal which worked for the printing of the first book in India in 1556 by movable types. It was a sole venture of the Jesuits. These Jesuits apart, there soon developed printed book collections in many corners. This was evident in the schools and colleges that emerged in the next century. Instances of these are in Calcutta's Hindoo College, and Calcutta School Society. Calcutta was the centre of earlier European activities, and hence its prominence in this regard.

As in Islamic tradition, so in the Indian history, there was a regular cultural activity and religious education in its premises. People donated their books to the Mosque and thereby evolved a large collection in these places. In fact these Mosque libraries became the hub of public library activity in these days, and even to this day there are Mosques where the reading room is open to all and the collection includes a variety of reading resources (Taher and Fatimy:1984).

Christians found time appropriate in 1498 to start their trade/missionary activities, when Vasco da Gama entered the Indian soil. These European missionaries earlier established libraries at propagation centres. Examples of these are in Tranquebar, Trichnopoly, Bengal, and wherever they had possibility of doing so. It originally started with Catholic missionaries and later the Protestants continued the tradition. Each centre had some reading material available for propagation.

Church (Chapels) housed libraries. Church Library tradition in the West progressed as any other type of library (Harvey and Musavi, 1981). But in India Church libraries arose and never came into prominence, except for some seminary libraries. Nevertheless, the English factories had church libraries at Surat which housed many books in a variety of languages. Visitors to these factories must have been also taken round this library collection. So also is the record of another Church Library which existed at Masulipatnam (Andhra Pradesh) even before 1671. Tranquebar (Tamil Nadu) is probably another place where a library was set by a missionary, by name Ziegenbalg who had according to his inventory in 1715 the following books: 119 by Hindu authors, 21 by Roman Catholics and 14 works which he himself had generated (Qaiser:1982: 61; Kumar:1977:30-33).

3.4.4 *Libraries of Queen-Consorts*

As was the male tradition of patronage and developing the library culture, so also women in this society did share the area of activity. We know from the Muslim history that there were many women teachers whose male students became jurists. This is only to mention one highly specialized field of the times (Dalvi, 1989). In the Mogul household, we find there were women authors, writers, poets, and bibliophiles.

The Mogul history includes names of Gul Badan Begum (the daughter of Babur), Salima Sultana Begum (Akbar's queen), Moham Anang (the nurse of Akbar), Nurjahan (Jahangir's queen and an indirect ruler of the Mughal India), Mumtaz Mahal (Shahjahan's queen and the inspirational source for the existence of Taj Mahal), Jahanara Begum (the daughter of Shahjahan), Zebunnissa Begum (the daughter of Aurangzeb), and others.

Gul Badan must have had a large library as she herself wrote the famous *Humyunnama*. Salima Sultana, possessed large and valuable personal treasure of books. It is reported that once when her original copy of '*Thirty Two Thrones*' was lost, which she was studying at that time, many of her fiends and book borrowers, including the historian Badauni, were embarrassed. Moham Anang, founded a college in Delhi in 1561, and she too had a personal collection. This college either was *Khair-ul-Manazil*, or, *Madrasa-i-Begum*, situated opposite the western gate of Purana Qila. (=old fort) (Carr:1876:139-140; Chopra:1978:139). This same nurse of Akbar, was controlling even state affairs, between 1560 and 1564.

Nurjahan had a personal library and she multiplied her books by purchase. Probably she maintained record of each book purchased. A book '*Diwan of Kamran*' has on it 'Three Muhar the price of this treasure: Nawab Mehrunnissa Begum' (Dutta, 1970, p.72). Mehrunnissa Begum is her earlier name before she became the beloved of Jahangir. Hence it is easy to understand that after entering into the royal household she became the Noor (=light, beauty, literary giant, knowledgeable) of Jahan (=world; and Jahan is the first part of Jahangir's name, where 'gir' means seizer) and where Jahangir was seized by her beauty and knowledge (Devapriam:1972:13). Zaibunnissa is reported to be a "sedulous collector of books and a large library for the use of scholars was available (Dutta:1970:74). Another name recorded in history is worth mentioning here. Gulrukh Begum, sister of Humayun, had a daughter Salima Sultana (153-1612). It is likely that she is the same lady of Akbar's household, but we have no direct evidence to relate these two personalities. Jahangir in his *Tuzuk* spoke high about her abilities (Devapriam:1972:181). She was very fond of reading books and had a personal library of her own (Nadvi:1946:336).

3.5 Provincial Dynasties

The provincial rulers or provincial governors have themselves made a history in the development and patronage of libraries and librarianship.

3.5.1 *Bihar*

The Moghul Governors or *Nazims* of Bihar like Raja Ram Narain,

Raja Kalian, and Raja Shitab Ray, had their personal libraries. Abu Zafar Nadvi, reported in the 1940s that some of their descendants continued to maintain these rare books (Nadvi:1946:5). Whether this stock was ever used by the successors, is difficult to comment, but what is worth is they were bibliophiles and had taken some care to maintain their family collection–as a source of prestige and pride.

3.5.2 *Oudh*

The Governors of Oudh, emerged as independent rulers, as soon as they found the decline of their Moghul masters. These rulers founded academies and established libraries. The site of the once prestigious royal library of the Kingdom of Oudh, was probably now in the vacant land in Lucknow, between iron bridge and Qaiser Bagh. It was in the old Daulat Khana. It had over 10,000 books and Mss. Ghaziuddin Haider had improved this library greatly (Nadvi:1946:7).

Apart form this royal library, there were other libraries in the Palace of Moti Garden, another in Farrukh Baksh Mahal, and at other places. Moti Garden on River Gomti, but away from Qaiser Bagh, is now called Moti Mahal. It is said to have in its collection over three thousand books. The library was specially collected by the orders of Nawab Wajid Ali Shah.

The Oudh Nawab, Shuja-ud-Dawla also annexed the neighbouring Rohilkhand. The treasures that came as booty included a library of the conquered. Shuja-ud-Dawla preserved this collection in the Top Khana building. This gave the library the name Top Khana Library. The books were dumped in trunks. Sprenger, an Englishman, visited Lucknow in 1848. He witnessed the decaying of this collection (Nadvi:1946:7).

Sprenger found that a Nazim of the library sold books worth Rs. 10,000 and got his sons married on the proceeds. Sprengers' narratives of the ruins of this city of Lucknow has also many interesting details of the environment and culture of the society of Oudh. This city is today a centre of many libraries with an admixture of both traditional and, modern libraries.

3.5.3 *Jaunpur*

Among the libraries set up by the Governors, Munim Khan had yet another example. This Governor of Jaunpur, during the rule of Akbar, had advised his friends to send him books, which they considered rare. In return he enriched them with precious and costly presents.

3.5.4 *Gujarat*

Sultan Mahmud Shah II (1538-1554), was a bibliophile. The courtiers imitated his life style. Asif Khan, his chief Minister, while returning from Mecca lost his precious collection of books due to shipwreck.

3.5.5 *Khandesh*

After the death of Feroz Shah Tughluq the Nazims of Burhanpur had become independent. Malik Raja hence founded the Faruqi Sultanate, till Akbar annexed it to the empire in 1601. Firishta visited their royal library in 1604. From one of the books in the library he copied the history of Faruqi's. The British Museum has a letter of one Malik-ush Shura Faizi written to Raja Ali Khan, a Faruqi Sultan, requesting for some pages of the *Tughluq Nama* available in this library (Nadvi:1946:6). This resource sharing request is not of the post-modern age. It is the pre-industrial revolutionary era. Despite the absence of a union catalogue, the communication links were strong, and oral communication about locational information worked to some level efficiently.

3.5.6 *Bijapur*

The offshoot of the Bahmani Dynasty, the Adil Shahis of Bijapur, too had a royal library in the Asari Mahal. Adil Shah II (1558-1580) was fond of books. *Tazkirat-ul-Muluk* has the following about him "He had a great inclination towards the study of books and he had procured many books connected with every kind of knowledge, so that a coloured library had become full" (quoted in Dutta:1970:80). Once it so happened that on way back home, there was heavy rain and the troops dispersed in different directions. The books that he carried went in some other camp. A special Amir was deputed to go and fetch the books and the king was restless until he saw those returned. This is reported in *Basatin-us-Salatin*. Its value enhanced when it was taken to the Mughal Imperial Library. This transfer took place at the time of Aurangzeb's expeditions to the Deccan, and they were in hundreds and thousands. Firishta reports about the existence of another royal library at Ahmednagar, a principal town in the Bahmani Kingdom.

"Nearly sixty men, calligraphers, gilders, binders, and illuminators, were busy doing their work whole day in the library" (Dutta:1970:80). The royal library had a gem in the person of Librarian, named, Waman Pandit bin Anant of Shesh family hailing from Bijapur itself. Naro bin Gangadhar and Hussain Khan in 1567 and Manjan Khan in 1575 supervised the library (Dutta:1970:81)

3.6 Administration and Management

The knowledge about administration and management of the Muslim period is more complete, than the ancient period of Indian Library history. In the Muslim period, as a part of the general administration each department was called *Karkhana*, and *Kitab khana* was one such example. When Akbar organized all departments, he created a separate department for libraries to look after the state library and other libraries located in the capital.

In the Moghul period the administration became largely systematic in character. The efficiency of the Imperial Library, with its then known librarianship, was remarkable. Babur laid the foundations of the empire and the Imperial Library, and Akbar the Great consolidated the same.

The in-charge officer of the library during the Sultanate period was called, as Afif reports, *Mushafbardar*. *Mushaf* has been used at times for collection of scriptures. And in this sense, literal meaning is keeper of scriptures. But in the history of Islamic librarianship none segregated mundane and spiritual materials, and this term must have been used therefore for librarian. This title seems to have been popular in the Delhi Sultanate period. So also, the keeper of pens was *Khiratdar*, keeper of inkpot was *Dawatdar*, and these later two were more so identified in the period of Muhammad bin Tughluq. The period of Delhi Sultanate is also important in the context of having the first Muslim Librarian, Amir Khusro, the Prince of Poets. Amir Khusro served as Librarian for three consecutive rulers of this period.

There is some definite information on the personnel of the imperial library. The senior most staff member was the Nazim or Mutamid. He was responsible for staff and finance. Generally, this post was for nobles of the Court. Seals on the books of this library, now scattered, reveal this fact. *Darogha* or *Muhtamim* was the next position. This was a supervisory post, but at times he was supposed to function as acquisition-cum-processing librarian. Under the *Darogha* were many assistants: Clerks, *Sahhaf, Warraq*, etc. The latter two specifically were concerned with care of the physical book and checking each book page by page, primarily for ascertaining the originality of the sources.

The other library staff included *Jildsaz* (binders), *Naqqash* (painters), *Kushnavis* (penmanship/calligraphers), *Katib* (scribes), *Muqabila Navis* (comparing scribes), *Musahhih* (corrector/proof readers), *Jadwalsaz* (Marginal drawers in papers), etc. The copyists copied, *Muqabila Navis* compared it, the correctors corrected, and the process continued in a chain and link form. One single library with this staffing pattern was that of Khan-i-Khanan's library. In the Bengal's library tradition we find a different title used for the librarian, i.e., *Tahwildar* (=custodian). This is found in the history of the Library of Nawab Muniruddaula of Murshidabad.

Book collection in the early period expanded by gifts and as war booty. Purchase must have come in later, when peaceful atmosphere was available to a few of the rulers of Delhi Sultanate, like Allauddin Khilji. It became a practice only in the Moghul rule. The profession of copyists/scribes was considered of prime importance. Muslims believed in receiving favours if they transcribed the *Quran* and the *Hadith*. And in keeping up with this tradition, they even went on transcribing all books, and were sure of rewards from *Allah*. In the Moghul period book acquisition by purchase became a normal routine, and some instances have been described in the earlier pages. To mention a few these were by Noorjahan, Khusro the son of Jahangir, and others. Jahangir's Imperial Library and the Art Gallery must have been a better example–see the exorbitant price he paid, also mentioned above, about which Martin tells us that such a book of illustrations and paintings even today would not fetch one-fifth of the cost paid – in this process of collection development. Further, "Travellers and traders, simultaneously introduced material of a profane nature. There are current sources which bear witness to the fact that European pictures were present in great numbers in India during the period of Akbar and Jahangir. The importation of prints by the Jesuits is well documented" (Devapriam:1972:41).

As for who classified the books, what classification schemes were used, what catalogues were compiled, and how user-friendly were the medieval librarians, consciously or unconsciously–these are some questions that can be discussed here. Classification of books was apparently the responsibility of academicians and not left solely to those with primarily technical skills. Down to the present day, the Oriental libraries employ scholars as Librarians–people who know, classify, and interpret the content of materials, as well as run the institution.

The use of classification schemes is another topic of interest to library historians, as well as intellectual historians. What has become increasingly clear is that systems employed for the organization of knowledge used by Muslims like Al-Kindi, Al-Farabi, Al-Ghazali, Ibn Rushd, and so many others is very scientific and logical; these became the basis for arranging the books on the shelves. The Muslim period in India used a syllabus imported from citadels of education like Cairo and Baghdad–Not Saddam's, but of Abbasids.

The library had similar subjects for classificatory purpose, viz., *Quran* (Study of Scripture and exegesis), *Hadith* (study of the Prophet's Traditions), *Adab* (Literature), *Tarikh* (History and Historiography), *Seerah* (Biography of the Prophet), *Ulum-i-Nujum* (Astronomy), *Mantiq* (Logic), etc. This pattern of classification, which synchronized with the educational pattern, was worth being called User-friendly scheme where the user knew the subjects and the classificatory order and hence needed no User Education on how to access the shelves.

The Imperial Library had thirteen subject categories for classification of books, broadly under three groups, as following: i) poetry, medicine, astrology and music; ii) philology, philosophy, sufism, astronomy and geometry; iii) commentaries on *Quran* and Traditions, theology, and, law. The shelf arrangement was broadly by languages, and within each language the thought content was arranged. This arrangement and classification is a good example of Indo-Islamic literatures; and Prof. Schimmel has a bibliographic description of these literary trends in the Muslim India (Schimmel:1973).

Muslims did have bibliographic heritage and they imported even this in India, enabling compilation of many catalogues. It remained though in a crude form from our contemporary standards, nevertheless, served the purpose to tell the user what information is stored. Ram Sharma's *Bibliography of Mughal India* and *Marshall's Mughals in India: A Bibliographical Survey* provide ample of source material on this theme. We have also seen an instance of inter-library exchange of resources: Firishta's use of Faruqi Sultan's collection and the authorization letter he carried for availing the library facility. Is this not user-friendly attitude, is this worth being recorded as one of the earliest evidence of Resource Sharing and existence of user-friendly librarians ?

There is much difficulty in tracing the storage information of this period. There is a stray trace of the College of Mahmud Gawan and its Library. The art historians have identified it to be a good academic structure, and the remnants of this in Bidar are still a testimony of this fact. Similarly, we know of the library in the remaining structure of Asari Mahal of the Adil Shahis of Bijapur.

Beginning from the Lodi Dynasty, we have some information which allows us to infer that there was a separate building, or separate annex for the library. Babur found the Ghazi Khan's library in the Delhi Fort. He must have retained it there, as we don't hear of his shifting it from the place where he found it. Humayun had the advantage of using Sher Shah's Sher Mandal, which the latter built probably for recreation. The building was made of granite and red sand stone. Akbar developed the Imperial Library in Agra Fort. Probably it was situated in the Jahangir Mahal, where a hall is now identified as Library hall. This hall is a representative of the Mughal architectural style with decorated wall paintings.

Regarding the library meant for women at Fatehpur Sikri, art historians have given an idea of the library, its wall space, book shelves, etc. (Smith).

These extraordinary details apart, we don't have any knowledge of the library buildings of later Mughals. It is possible that Jahangir must have erected a special building for the library and art collection, but further records need to be scanned to substantiate this idea.

Muslims excelled in calligraphy, illustrations and binding. These arts were their own, and none was their competitor. Of these, book-binding alone continued to this day with their own binders. Indian book binding owes much to this art of Muslims, and is well stated by Dutta, "The story of migration of the art of book binding from Ethiopia to India is highly interesting. Moreover, it is important to note that, with the increasing power of the Muslim empire the art flourished, as it was they who built tanneries and produced excellent raw materials (Dutta:1970:140). Paper usage changed the methods of binding and the Muslim binders introduced thin boards to hold the sections together.

The Moghuls produced leather for binding. Book-binding was recognized as an art, and a department specifically for this job was always an essential component of the library. Decorative book binding was yet another contribution of Muslims in India for aesthetic outlook. In fact the Muslim rule in India gave an opportunity to open the industries relating to calligraphy, illustrations, and, binding. For instance binding requires leather, cloth, paper, and many more things, and these were generated in large quantities to meet the demands. Economic historians can probably provide facts and figures on how useful these industries were to an agricultural society, and how these industries later enabled the industrialization process in India.

Another progress made in this period related to the field of book illustrations. "From the early medieval period we find a good number of illustrated manuscripts preserved in a fairly good condition (Dutta:1970:148).

In this period there emerged much larger class of library benefactors (or friends of libraries). Apart from the continued tradition of royal funding, there were now, philonthrophists, elites, and nobles. Instances of royal funding and support are available in records of private and public institutions. A Tamil inscription of 1251 found in the Temple of Jetavarman Sundara Pandya mentions of allotment of sites to men of various occupations including Pandaraputtakamudayar. This referred to men of Pandaram community who were custodians of books in village libraries. In the Muslim period Mosques received funds and the library was managed in this fund. Jahangir had made a public call for handing over that property to which their was no heir after the decease of its owner when none inherited in the family of the deceased - for maintenance of institutions, including libraries.

Public support came in the form of the foundations, or *Wakf* (literally translated as trust, or endowment) and each well-to-do created a trust for the benefit of the populace. Such trusts are even today a source for libraries and educational institutions, throughout the country. Of late many studies have been carried on to find out how these voluntary organizations are functioning, and the results of the study are encouraging, i.e., encouraging others to follow the same line of action.

The Europeans funded and supported the libraries. They in return required accounting/auditing. The first of these is found in the case of Fort St. George Library. An annual inventory was desired of the stocks. This practice of stock taking continued.

To sum up, this discussion on the medieval Muslim India, one can conclude by saying that the primary purpose of this age was to build a storehouse of knowledge. It brought a sense of library culture among the reading public. The emergence of a public library with its foundation in popular literacy and mass education awaited a later time.

While the royal libraries of this period can well be compared with their counterparts in contemporary West and even while it attracted scholars for study and research, the benefits from these rare collections, was really speaking, too limited. The level of its use was not commensurate with the amount of cost it involved in maintenance and care. With the end of Aurangzeb, and the emergence of certain unfavourable circumstances, like lack of peace, and lack of public initiative in promoting the spread of library culture in its entirety, many libraries closed down and a considerable number was totally disrupted.

And what level of achievements were made by this age has been very aptly said "Yet despite the cultural eminence of the capital (Delhi, during periods of Sultanate rule), it cannot be claimed that the Sultanate is a period marked by that solid scholarship and study of sciences which distinguished Baghdad and Cordova. The reason is obvious. Learned and gifted men had come to India, but without their libraries. Those who were escaping with their lives could not be expected to carry loads of books over long distances. We get a glimpse of this in the case of Fakhr-i-Mudabbir, who fled from Ghazni without his family papers, and had to wait for an opportunity to go back to reclaim them. The result was that only those cultural activities gained prominence which, like poetry, belles letters, local history, architecture, and music, were not dependent on accumulated stores of knowledge. Probably for the same reason–the lack of libraries–great educational institutions of the kind found in Baghdad and Cairo did not develop in India, There were, however, schools and colleges, in Delhi and all important provincial capitals" (Ikram:114-115). This is also true of the Mughals who despite all the wealth of the world and glory and grandeur could not develop another Baghdad.

The degree to which private collections were accessible to persons other than owners is difficult to determine. We are not in position to say; but on the strength of information available we can say that in those days every well provided lover of learning had in his/her house a modest library which was enough for the immediate requirements. People gave books to or borrowed books from one another and made copies in an ornamental hand for preserving in their own collections (Jaffar:1972). "On the whole, however, it can be mentioned that the general principles regarding the management of the libraries were considerably well-developed. The libraries, with their rich collection and under stable management, served as great centres of knowledge. True, their number was not very large, and since they were almost invariably located in the urban areas, the teeming millions inhabiting the rural areas could get practically no advantage from them. In spite of all these shortcomings, caused chiefly by the limitations of that age, the progress made in this field was considerable" (Ojha:1975:117).

Books were as precious in the history of libraries as any other bounty of war and battlefield. This was more so evident in the history of medieval India. Babur brought not much of his family wealth, but he did carry among the few valuables a collection of his favourite books. The libraries of the kings and emperors of this period find a point of mention in each expedition. Akbar could enhance his Imperial Library by many thousands of books from different expeditions of the country. Nadir Shah carried away many precious and valuable manuscripts and printed books from the Imperial library. Books moved with the camp and in the case of the defeat of the enemy the war bounty did include books, and the occupied lands too provided a scope to annex the library of the conquered. In the words of Ohdedar "So libraries, the storehouses of the fruits of intellectual labour, were to the Muslim conquerors things worth plundering. Libraries were thus considered rich possessions in Muslim India" (Ohdedar:1945:59).

4

MODERN (BRITISH) INDIA (1757-1947)

This period, in comparison to the one that followed, does not seem to be characterized by startlingly new developments. Most of the obvious changes in the system of libraries and librarianship began in the early twentieth century. Yet important movements began in this period, first in the academic libraries, and then, public and special libraries. In the academic librarianship the most distinctive impact appeared with the starting of English higher education (Bose:1971:2).

4.1 **Academic Libraries**

With a modest, but a continued academic tradition, India entered the modern period. The decline of the Mughals by 1750 paved way for the rise of the East India company. The sponsoring agencies for educational and related activities, till this time were Mughals, provincial Muslim and Hindu rulers, nobles, and elite. The British took up the sponsorship and became the major force in the this area of education as in politics. The other indigenous forces now became complimentary or supplementary.

4.1.1 *College Libraries*

The British power beginning from 1750s did perform certain welfare functions. In 1781, Warren Hastings a master of Bengali, Persian and who also knew Urdu, founded the Calcutta Madrasah for cultivation of Arabic and Persian studies. In this context, Warren Hastings is rightly considered as the introducer of higher education in India (Bose:1971:5). In 1792, Lord Cornwalis, founded the Sanskrit College at Benaras (now called Varanasi). These two institutions inaugurated a new era in the field of academic studies. It also gave vent to introducing an official support for the promotion of Oriental learning in the country. Says Anima Bose "Taken together, the Muhammedan

Madrasa and the Benaras Sanskrit College mark the beginning of the Oriental School of thought which played a role in the educational policy of the country" (Bose:1972:5). The purpose of starting these was "to recover and collect books" of the ancient learning.

Indian leaders like Raja Ram Mohan Roy who were representatives of progressive popular opinion favoured western education. He even protested in 1823 against the establishment of Calcutta Sanskrit College. Despite the protests this college and its library started functioning from 1824 (Bose:1972:23).

The founders had a provision in the planning for a library at each of the two colleges, which included the appointment of native librarians whose salary was to be the same as that of a teacher; and that the libraries would extend services to people other than the teachers and the students.

The opening of Fort William College at Calcutta in 1800 was another milestone in collecting all Oriental Mss. and books at one place. Instruction was given in Arabic, Persian and Hindustani, the library collection included materials in all these three languages. The Western (Occidental) collection had 5224 books; and Eastern (Oriental) 11,718 books and 4253 Mss.

The College lost its popularity soon, and so also was the case with the other two above-mentioned institutions. By 1835 the Fort William College Library was closed and later in 1854 the college was also closed. The decline in the library budget is one fact available to us - from Rs. 41,011 in 1815 to Rs. 6,611 in 1830 - suggesting the attitude of its sponsors towards the library. Its oriental collection was transferred to Asiatic Society. Significantly, in 1811 Lord Minto ordered public libraries in Bengal to serve the area colleges. Added to this the Presidency (Hindu) College Library, was opened to the non-Hindu public around 1835. This library became famous all over, which led to the increase in the number of users, and only for this reason authorities had to appoint a librarian.

Opening of college by rulers and elite started becoming a normal practice. Nawab Itmad-ud-daula the prime minister of Oudh opened the Delhi College in 1829. The college, which closed in 1858 when the district of Delhi was transferred to the Punjab, was revived in Lahore in 1864, by the Punjab Government. The rationale to revive the college was that it would provide scope for higher education and for the spread of the English language (Bose:1971:132). Similar institutions in the country were founded by Maharaja Ranjit Singh of Punjab, Sir Syed

Ahmed Khan at Aligarh, and others. It was the aftermath of 1857 which gave rise to nationalism and in the educational field led the Indians to build their own institutions. The emerging political elite felt a nation wide need for education and literacy. Prominent were Anglo-Mohammedan Oriental College, Aligarh (1875), D A V College, Lahore (1816) and Central Hindu College, Benaras (1898). Libraries were a luxury earlier but became gradually a necessity due to various rules and regulations of the academic set up.

The British and American missionaries opened many colleges. While the first missionaries from America came in 1813 they did not do much in the area of higher education. It started only after three quarters of the century. The most distinct was the Lucknow Christian College, Lucknow (f. 1888). It was an American involvement with the support of the Methodists missionaries. In 1892 appeared the provision of library in the new building and the Annual Report of 1893, "the college made an appeal for newspaper and magazine subscriptions and introduced the practice of library fees. From the meagre place devoted to the library, it may be concluded that in the beginning building up the library did not take the top priority in the college. The Presbyterians, on the other hand, were concerned about the library from the very beginning and considered it as an important educational tool in Forman College at Lahore" (Bose:1971:231). Similarly, in 1886 was founded the Lahore Christian College, later named Forman Christian College. It was by the efforts of the American Presbyterians. With the idea of social concern the founder of the College, established the Social Service League, in 1888. This was later called League of Service Library. The members of this League conducted extension activities and included literacy campaigns too. They made use of slides (also known as magic lantern slides). This social involvement of library and college was a new notion in India. It altered the past tradition, and limited notion of education for acquiring knowledge (Bose:1971:160-161).

4.1.2 *University Libraries*

The establishment of a system of higher education in British India in 1857 was a major achievement. On the recommendation of Woods Educational Commission three modern universities were established in 1857 in Bombay, Calcutta, and Madras. Libraries were opened a little later in 1880, 1873 and 1904 respectively. The first professional librarian was appointed in 1915 in Bombay University. Dr. Nihar Ranjan Ray, was the first professional Librarian of Calcutta University appointed in 1937; Dr.S R Ranganathan was similarly the first professional Librarian of Madras in 1924.

Among other prominent university libraries, Punjab deserves a high rank. Its collection had originated in the University College, Lahore, and with the generous gift of Sir Donald Mcleod in 1873. The services of Dickenson at this university, in 1915-16, opened a new age of university librarianship in India. He heralded a thorough and systematic revitalization of the university library. He set a pace to the development of the university libraries in the country. Not only the country had his presence felt–by organizing professional meetings, by encouraging professional spirit on an all round basis–even the host Library did lead the country for a while. He imported such ideas and notions which made the Indian library users–the focal point of western librarianship–feel at home. It was he who for the first time introduced the Dewey Decimal Classification scheme in the country. This was the first university in the country to adopt open access system. He took all pains to organize and modernize the library and with in a period of just one year he surmounted unimaginable heights.

As a consultant he worked in a holistic way. He did not only concentrate on the development of the library, he also had eyes on an developing other areas of university librarianship. He initiated a training programme – the first library school at the university level. He published a guiding manual of library organization and management, entitled "Library Primer" (or Panjab Library Primer). This manual was a handy source for any one interested in organizing the library. This publication was made possible by the assistance of Lal Mukund Lal Bhatia.

To promote professionalism among the librarians Dickenson's foresight prompted him to bring together librarians. It was the formation of the Punjab Library Association. These contributions to the development of university librarianship in India–initiating training, literature and professional spirit–had a magical impact in kindling a sound professionalism and a systems approach in theory and practice. Apart from his contributions and effort, the University Library had no person of that stature and his impact was felt even after thirty years of his departure. In the words of Flora B Ludington, "the results of the work of William A Borden in Baroda and Asa Don Dickinson in Lahore were still apparent after thirty years when I visited libraries in India" (Ludington:1954).

The Indian University Act passed in 1904 empowered universities to insist on colleges seeking affiliation for "maintenance of a library and lending of appropriate books (not only text books) for the use of pupils." Interestingly, from 1857 to 1947 a total of over 20 universities opened in the country. Libraries did appear sooner or later. Prominent Universities in this long list also include name of Allahabad University.

Centres of Oriental library patronized once by royal families were getting a set back. By introduction of Oriental languages and literatures in University curriculum the use of oriental libraries received a great momentum.

4.1.3 *School Libraries*

School libraries remained a dream and this was a general feature. Only schools run by missionaries–in this period–aimed at inculcating the use of books. This was more clear from the Danish Missionaries who laid great stress on well conducted schools and the education of the young. These schools paved the way for the convents and similar British patronized centres of learning in due course. The British Government had suggested to the local bodies, in the 1930s to open the doors of school libraries to the public to enhance its use...That the success in this method of spreading knowledge would be in proportion to the amount of public cooperation and support which school authorities are able to enlist. The Government desired to have honorary services on the days when the library is open to the public. It wished that these libraries should add on by public donation and the resident officials to propagate for such donations. There was a request made to the Director of Public Instruction to implement these. A departmental meeting was held on this issue at Ranchi under the Chairmanship of Dr Syed Mahmud, the then Minister of Education, Development and Employment. This body decided to open 4000 Hindustani and 200 Bengali school libraries in the province. This decision of special concentration for Bengal was a consequence of the already conducted literacy programme in this area. Further, each library was to receive 200 books and one weekly newspaper (Kumar:1977:139-140). Probably the first book in India on school libraries was written by Ranganathan himself in 1942, Schools and College Libraries.

The British rule in India had another interesting feature, namely the availability of library resource persons, (today called consultants), from Great Britain and America. In the academic libraries one thinks immediately of Asa Don Dickinson, but there were others.

4.2 **Public Libraries**

An import of the idea of western public library was wilfully done in 1804 in Bombay. It was the opening of the library, which later became the Bombay Branch of the Royal Asiatic Society. It was "Public" in its function, from the first day of its inception. It did not opt at any time to be with a restricted category of users. Rather this restriction did occur in the case of the Calcutta 's Library of the Royal Asiatic Society. This came into being much earlier, in 1784. Only members of the latter were allowed to borrow books and no book was to be issued out of Calcutta. Another point of interest among the two was the former received valuable collections of Medical and Literary Society of Bombay (founded 1789), and the latter received, many rare and valuable books from the Tipu Sultan's library. The Bombay Branch slowly grew into a free public library. By 1818 a similar public library emerged under the Madras Literary Society. Both of these found a mention in the media - Calcutta Journal. Of these two, the Bombay Branch and the Madras Library, the latter could maintain its existence and today it is the oldest public library in the country (Ohdedar:1966:129).

This period gave rise to many attempts to establish some kind of a public library. History records that about 1818 a group of people of Calcutta joined hands and established the Calcutta Library Society. Of particular interest is the fact that this society had its primary concern as the library; the library was the centre of all activities. This was an independent body formed by a group of proprietors based on whose investments the library was established. It was available to use by the public on the basis of membership fees. The 1819 report of the library reveals that the collection, housed in the Town Hall, consisted of 27,000 volumes with the additions from England on a monthly basis. Alas, it closed in 1831.

Since it must have created some public support and have stimulated some enthusiasm for libraries, its seemingly premature closing is perplexing. The *Calcutta Journal* noted its appearance to the impulse of the library movement in the west, it did have a sense of public libraries in the nineteenth century itself. What made its progress slow (or rather stagnated the developmental process) was the level of literacy and financial support. There were even other factors, but these were detrimental.

Bhatia, took pains to highlight the situation in each type of library and the required strategy to make the library a user-oriented centre: He very rightly commented on the position of the college librarian, stating that he "is still backward, still not fully trained to be a guide to the teacher and the taught". To the school librarians, he advised "You have in your hands a nation to build. Build it well", so that the citizens of tomorrow will be aware of the national interests and help the growth and development of the country. This he emphasized could be possible only if the student is provided with a wide background of unbiased information.

To build a better India of tomorrow Bhatia was equally conscious of the rural–the majority–population. He went to the extent of stressing the importance of this user and mixed no words in putting straight the idea that "Unless you start good library centres in every nook and corner of your rural area the country will remain steeped in poverty and ignorance". He included the special librarians in his review of the situation and even added the training aspect of the professionals. His last lines were addressing the library authorities, the planners of the future of India: "When there is nationalization of libraries in our country–which I hope will be soon if we are able to get a national Government at the centre–he is to be the leader of the community, the book producer and publisher: let the Institute of Library Studies train him for the future: Let educationists, in their plan, realize that without the aid of a good librarian and library their scheme will not make any strides. For the key of India's future progress lies in the hands of the Indian Librarian" (Bhatia:1945:47-51).

Bengal Haraku, Calcutta's first daily, informed its closure. In short it did receive a good media coverage. Public opinion has been a good source of motivating people and movements in Calcutta. Perhaps this has been the direct impact of being the capital city of British India. Moreover, the presence of British for a very long time in this city must have created an elite who responded to Western methods of thinking and assimilated faster than others, the basics of western liberalism, modernism and an appreciation for the value of public opinion.

In 1817 was founded the another important institution, Calcutta School Book Society. Its need was basically to supply printed books for the growing number of modern schools. The other presidencies, namely, Bombay, and Madras too established branches of the Society, in the same direction. Elementary text book literature on Christianity, and some books useful for adults formed the collection of its library. Its second annual report of 1819 gave a call for book donations. It also mentioned that its books are separated under three categories: 1) publications of the parent body, 2) elementary works, and 3) miscellaneous. The Bombay General Library was opened in 1830 as subscribing public library. In 1845 it was named Bombay National General Library. Today it is called People's Free Reading Room and Library.

The history of circulating libraries finds its place before 1770s. This was John Andrews Circulating Library in Old Fort premises at Calcutta. It survived for a shortwhile and by 1780s it closed. Not only did this library circulate books to subscribers it also allowed its members to take home its catalog for consultation. What more user-friendly librarians did the people need? Why did this library so nice and so kind, close down? Perhaps people did not know the value of such a friendly situation. This was also a book selling store. During this period we have historical evidences of existence of other similar circulating libraries.

Another type of public lending libraries emerged for missionary reasons. This was founded by the Society for Promotion of Christian Knowledge. Many such lending libraries were opened within a short period, beginning the one at Calcutta in 1709.

4.3 National Library

The year 1835 was remarkable in the history of libraries. First of all, it marked the opening of the Calcutta Public Library. This same library merged with other libraries in the city to form Imperial Library in 1903. This institution in turn became the basis for the National Library, that emerged in 1948. Its collection was built basically from a book donations, which began with a gift of 1,500 books. More important than this, however, was the addition of the 5000 books from Fort William College Library. The College had closed in the same year and its collection formed a good base for the future National Library.

The year 1835 was also important in other respects as it witnessed two major documents relating to libraries–the Macaulay's minutes for the Anglicization of Indian Education and the Freedom of Indian Press Enactment. The former found an expression in the form of opening of a free and open public library.The latter in the form of providing of reading facilities to the public at large and making freedom of expression possible, and a freedom to establish Indian printing presses. Funds were raised in this year for a separate building for the Calcutta Public Library, to an extent of Rs. 45,000 as donations both from proprietor's and private persons. The library started functioning in 1836 and its own building was ready in 1844. The year 1903 saw the amalgamation of the various libraries, including the Secretariat Library, into the Calcutta Public Library. The Imperial Library Act, 1903 made it Imperial Library.

The first Librarian was W H Stacy and Sub (Asst.) Librarian was Peary Chand Mitra. The latter succeeded and was Librarian from 1848 to 1866.The first Librarian who had a regular pay scale was Bipin Chandra Pal in 1890. Radha Raman Mitra served as Librarian in 1891; Harinath De from 1907 to 1911; J A Chapman from 1911 to 1930; and Khan Bahadur K.M. Asadullah from 1930 to 1947.

The collection at the National Library expanded due to purchases, gifts and compulsory deposit programmes. The Library received enormous material as gifts. Some major gifts received include: over 5000 Asutosh collection; 3500 Ramdas Sen Collection; 2500 Sir Jadunath Sarkar Collection; around 14000 from Buhar Library of Munshi Sayyid Sadruddin and others; Sapru Papers; 2943 Prof Vajpuri Pillai Collection; 2736 Dr. S N Sen Collection; 3000 DR Baird Barun Mukherjee Collection; etc.

The acquisition of books in this Library also occurred by purchase or by the compulsory deposit of one copy. This deposit achieved legal status by the Registration of Books Act of 1867, and its amendment of 1890. Whatever was received before 1903, were deposited in the Bengal Library. In 1903, all the deposited material was shifted to the Imperial Library. As per the Act, publishers were to deliver three copies of every printed or lithographed book. The three copies which were received as compulsory deposit, were distributed to India Office Library, British Museum Library and the third for a public library or disposed off as the local government found appropriate. In 1926 the Imperial Library became the copyright depository library. (A very lengthy note on its historical development appears in *India and Pakistan Year Book*:1949:537).

In the year 1948 the National Library was declared as Indian National Library. Its collection building was strengthened by Delivery of Books Act, 1954. Its status and working conditions were reviewed in National Library of Indian Act, 1976. Its bibliographic service was facilitated by shifting the Central Reference Library to Calcutta (from Delhi) in 1959.

4.4 Other Efforts for Public Library Development

The spirit of a free and open public library system saw its roots in the soil during the late 19th century, and was a result of efforts of many since about fifty years. One can trace this with the emergence of libraries like: Bibliotheca Publica, Goa (f.1832), Bhagalpur Institute Library, Bhagalpur (f.1834), Hemabhai Institute Library, Ahmedabad (f.1849), Gaya Public Library, Gaya (f.1855), Hardayal Municipal Public Library, Delhi (f.1862), Government Public Library, Allahabad (f.1863), Hardinge Municipal Library, Delhi (1886), Sri Saraswathi Nilayam, Visakhapatnam (1886), Khuda Bakhsh Oriental Library, Patna (f.1888), Rampur Raza Library, Rampur (f.1889), Asafiya Library, Hyderabad (f.1891), Sri Gautami Library, Rajamundry (f.1898), and Sri Krishna Devaraya Andhra Bhasha Nilayam, Hyderabad (f. 1901). Of these Asafiya and the Rampur, for instance, received state patronage and the third (Khuda Bakhsh) was a one man's life-long devotion to build library of Orientalia. This pattern of state support indicated that the states which had some autonomy promoted the public library development. And a major development in this regard, of state sponsored public library movement, can be seen at Baroda.

In 1910, William Alanson Borden was given an appointment to advise, plan and implement a state library and a statewide library development programme. This appointment was done by Maharaja Sayaji Rao of Baroda. Borden's tenure in office was from 1910-1913.

Borden, a pioneer of library movement in India, introduced many distinct features in the professional scenario. His contributions to the development of public libraries and more specifically in making public libraries accessible to masses was the most innovative. This innovation he introduced at a time when even 'literates' in India had no idea of using libraries. He brought in the concept of free and open access public libraries. He must have inspired Ranganathan's first three laws by this achievement. Similarly another distinct work of Borden was developing the country's first state level network of libraries. He added to this the notion of children library and mobile library. For providing access to the collection he introduced a scheme of classification called "Baroda Classification", and modernized the cataloguing practice. He demonstrated for the first time the practicability of extension services like mobile libraries (or book mobiles), and visual instruction branch.

His ideas must have been a source even to the Andhra Desa which followed some of these in its region in a short while. Borden has the honor of opening the first regular school to train library staff. For continuing education purpose he founded the Baroda Central Library Club and started a journal "*Library Miscellany*". Borden's name can be erased from the history, but his plans, patterns and programmes were used on and often in different settings. A lot of research work has been done to find out his innovations and to keep the posterity informed of his achievements.

He became the father of Indian Public Librarianship. He was a man of foresight and insight and his experience in different positions in US could be guessed from his own words: "I determined to introduce into Baroda what we in the United States have recognized as a goal to be ultimately attained but which we have not yet reached. I mean a system of centrally located book storehouses, each surrounded by a network of small, inter-depending libraries. These small libraries to have the books commonly called for and the storehouses to supplement these small collections. This has been done and the result is now known in India as the Baroda System... If there is any value in this library cooperation throughout a large state let it be remembered that it as first introduced, not in the home of the modern library movement, our own country, but way down in India, 10,000 miles from here" (Borden:1913).

The programme went on well and by 1926 the state provided library services to 100 per cent of the residents of town and from 50 to 65 per cent of village residents. There was one central library working as a network. It controlled all libraries of towns and villages. But with the death of the royal patron (1926) the spirit of the movement ended.

For a several decades after this experiment, effective public libraries in India did not exist. Apart from opening of a few public libraries, in different cities and states, like that of public library of Social Science League, in 1911 in Bombay by Chandavarkar (Basham:1975:380), for few decades after this public libraries in India had no significant history to make. Only after independence, library legislation heralded a new era. Even funding was not systematized for the existing public libraries in this period.

An exception to the bleak picture was the Government in Bombay Province which appointed a Committee in 1939 under the chairmanship of A.A.A. Fyzee to report on Library Development in this area. The aim was to investigate the possibilities of setting up central and regional libraries. It probably generated some heat and the Government of Bombay implemented the recommendations, by establishing copyright libraries in Dharwar, Poona and Ahmedabad (Kumar:1977: 174). The Government also adopted these recommendations by appointing a Curator of Libraries for library service in the Province. These worked, with whatever limited scope, till 1967 and in this year came into effect the Maharashtra Public Libraries Act, 1967.

4.5 Other Libraries

From the earliest times, as shown above, there has been a trend of royal and court libraries. The modern period too had this category continued. Even the nobility or the elite did have the same trends and the following is a just an example of such libraries. Gradually a pattern emerged during the period for palace-based libraries to give way to state and public libraries, just as in European countries royal libraries became national libraries. A few examples will be illustrative.

4.5.1 *Saraswathi Mahal Library (or Tanjore Library)*

The annexation of Tanjore by Marathas and the rule of Raja Sarfoji (1798-1833) gave a great impetus to the development of a rare collection in this land. Being founded by Telugu Nayaks–of fifteenth and sixteenth centuries–the library had Sanskrit Mss. in Telugu characters, and manuscripts in Marathi came with the annexation of the library by the Marathas. The successive ruler brought Sanskrit manuscripts in large numbers, from Banaras during his visits in 1820s'.

In 1878-1880 appeared the first handlist of its collection, primarily by the efforts of Dr. A C Burnell. This subjectwise list had about 21,000 manuscripts. After completing this Burnell wrote to the Secretary, Government of Madras, "It may perhaps be asked if the library is worth the labour spent on it. I can answer unhesitatingly that it is. It is now a recognized fact that nearly all Sanskrit works of importance exist in different recessions. The Tanjore Library is unrivalled in this respect. It contains several good manuscripts of all the most important ones known as yet, including a few that are new... the Tanjore library, however contains additional manuscripts of most of the works of which I had discovered elsewhere and this is a matter of great importance. The preparation of this catalogue will therefore protect property of enormous value. Sanskrit manuscripts have long been very dear and the cost of making proper transcripts is now very heavy. As far as I can judge, it would not be possible to form a collection like that at Tanjore at a less cost than pounds 50,000, but many manuscripts are unquestionably unique" (as quoted in Kumar:1977:68).

This library became famous as Saraswathi Mahal Library. Personal collections were added to it from time to time. In 1921 it acquired one such collection of Jambunath Bhutt. In 1922 it received collections of local families named Kagalkar and Pàntanga Avadhuta. It is probably the oldest Oriental library in the country. The total collection presently is around 43,000 manuscripts and 15,000 books. Its language coverage is of eleven distinct scripts. This library is managed by the Tamil Nadu State Government.

4.5.2 *Tipu Sultan's Library*

While Hyder Ali in Mysore had a less time for cultural activities, his son and successor, Tipu Sultan (d. 1799) found some leisure for literary patronage. Reportedly this Tiger of Mysore, as is his historical name, had the rare gift of judging everyone's talent and gave suitable posts. Among scholars and men of learning some were entrusted with the task of education, some with writing of books and some with translation work. He founded a centre for liberal education, with a library housing books on various subjects. His collection included the books of the Maharaja Chikka Deva Raya of Mysore; books brought from Bijapur, Golconda, Chittur, Savanur, Kadapa, and among others his own writings.

The collection of Tipu was bound in leather. As stated elsewhere the art of binding had by this time developed to a very high level. On the bound book the practice in Tipu's library was to stamp Sultantat-e-Khudadad, or "Government Given by Allah". A few of the books were impressed with his private signet, 'Tipu Sultan'. The value of the collection can be seen from the details given by historians. The collection had in it a rare copy of the *Quran* written in the Calligraphic hand of Aurangzeb. Its price estimated at ninety thousand rupees. This copy found its place in the British Royal Library at Windsor Castle.

With the turn of tables, the English defeated Tipu in 1799, but could not immediately occupy all that the Tiger left. By the time they gathered courage to see the Tiger's possession, a lot of books were either stolen or were damaged due to carelessness. Only a fraction of the precious collection reached the conquered, about 2000 titles. It was about the same collection which the Court Directors wrote to the

Governor General that the Seringapatnam collections were preserved in the Company's Library. A major part of this collection must have gone to the India Office Library, and which set the pace for a special India Office Collection at London.

The catalogue of this remaining collection was compiled by Major Charles Stewart in 1808 and published at Cambridge. This catalogue shows the following number of books in each subject:

> *Holy Quran* (Scriptures) 44; *Tasawuf* (Mysticism) 56; Astronomy 20; Poetry 19; Commentary 41; Ethics 24; Mathematics 7; Hindi Poetry 23; *Wazaif* (Supplicatory prayers) 35; *Fiqh* (Islamic Law) 63; *Tibb* (Medicine) 62; Stories 18; *Hadith* (Traditions of the Holy Prophet) 42; Arts 19; Language 45; Turkish 2; *Ilahiyat* (Theism) 42; Philosophy 54; and Dictionary 29.

The compiler of this catalogue also states "The Library consists of nearly 2000 volumes of Arabic, Persian, and Hindi manuscripts in all the branches of Mohammedan literature" (Stewart:1809). Probably this set of books went to the Asiatic Society Library, Calcutta.

4.5.3 *Maharaja Sawai Ram Singh II's Public Library*

This Maharaja (1835-1895), established a library in 1865 meant for public use. He gave away hundreds of books and other reading materials from the age old *potikhana*, maintained by the Maharajas of this land. The public library was organized by an expert from U K Sir Frank Alexander Francis, who was available for advice and planning from 1866 to 1872. The library functioned systematically even after he left. With the efforts of T W Hendley the library was re-organised in 1881. Again in 1937 it was revitalized by Maharaj Sawai Man Singh II (1922-1970) (Sahai:1991:111). The library brought out printed catalogues. The present State Central Library of Rajasthan is housed in this building.

4.5.4 *Asafiya Library*

Mir Mahboob Ali Khan, Nizam VII (of Asaf Jahi dynasty) of Hyderabad, in India, opened a library for the public in 1891. It was then named Asafiya Library. Its collection had both Oriental and Occidental sections. Its purpose was to collect all prominent books on the orient. In 1896 it had 3876 titles (included Books and Mss.), in 1956 it had 62,332, and today it has 3,72,239 titles in its collection. It is today re-named as State Central Library of Andhra Pradesh. It works, as a State Library System, under the Andhra Pradesh Public Library Act, 1955. Its manuscripts were removed to the State Archives, and later shifted to another location, only to be forming a part of a system, named Andhra Pradesh Oriental Manuscripts Research Institute and Library.

4.5.5 *Salar Jung Museum and Library*

The Prime Minister's of the Nizam of Hyderabad, were called Salar Jung. Salar Jung III (1889-1949) inherited taste of art and learning from his family. He personally and singly developed a library of antiques and rare books. By the time of his death he had apart from thousands of other pieces of rare and valuable items, 51,000 books and manuscripts in oriental and occidental languages. This collection of library and museum was opened, by the order of the Government of India, to the public according to the benefactor's will in 1951.

4.5.6 *Khuda Bakhsh Oriental Library*

The elite classes also continued to gather literary works despite shortage of resources. One rare example of Mohammed Baksh (d. 1876), whose collecting efforts of a lifetime were dedicated to the nation as the Khuda Baksh library at Patna, in 1888. The son of this bibliophile, Maulavi Khuda Baksh (d. 1908), was entrusted the job, by his father, to continue to enmasse all literary masterpieces of oriental studies. As a result this library today is the leading Orientalia manuscript library in India. It was recognized as a library of national importance by the Government of India in 1969. It has today about 30,000 books and around 10,000 Mss. in its collection. It can be called a repository of rare and valuable oriental manuscripts. It has in fact, a proud possession of gold and illustrated rare manuscripts.

4.5.7 *Raza Library*

The Nawabs of Rampur, set up a library. While the actual founder is not known, it is likely that Nawab Faizullah Khan (d.1794) was responsible for the opening of the library. By the generosity of Nawab

Mohammed Said Khan (1840-1855) it was declared as a separate department in 1851, and named, "Kutub Khana-e-Riyasat-i-Rampur". As a building of its own was lacking, it is reported that Nawab Hamid Ali Khan (1889-1930) erected a separate building . He is also reported to have got compiled the handlist of Arabic and Persian books and Mss., in 1902 and 1928, respectively. To bring this library to the notice of the world at large, as a leading Oriental resources centre, the credit goes to Nawab Sir Raza Ali Khan (1930-1966). In 1974 it was declared by an Act of Parliament to be a Library of National importance.

Amir Minai, Hakeem Ajmal Khan, Ahmed Ali Shauq, and Imtiyaz Ali Khan Arshi, are reported to have been its Nazims. These were all men of letters. J A Chapman was probably designated as an advisor or Library-in-charge for some time. It had 9347 books in 1889; 1245 during the period of Ajmal Khan, and 24,115 in 1927. Presently it has over 55,000 books and manuscripts, of which 15,000 are rare manuscripts.

4.5.8 *Carey Library Serampore*

This library was found in 1800, to promote the missionary activities. The library formed the resource centre of the new college in 1818, named as Serampore College. The founding fathers of the college gave great importance to building the collection and in laying down clear guidelines for collection development. By 1822 it had 3000 titles and this went on increasing. Further, it collected books in over a hundred languages, like Sanskrit, Hindi, Urdu, Persian, Bengali, Oriya, etc. K S Diehl an American bibliographer, provided yomen service. She catalogued all the books, in the Carey Library - which were published before 1851. Today Carey Library is a proved and reputed centre for area studies research (Chatterjee:1991).

4.5.9.1 *Asiatic Society Libraries in Bombay and Calcutta*

Asiatic Society at Calcutta, formerly known as Calcutta Branch of Royal Asiatic Society, and Asiatic Society, Bombay formerly known as Bombay branch of Royal Asiatic Society, were founded by the approval of the East India Company. The planning of these was in line with the Royal Society in England. The Calcutta Branch was founded in 1784, and the Bombay Branch in 1805.

The Library at Calcutta, however, emerged only 1796. The library collection grew mainly from gifts, and Tipu Sultan's collection was the first major gift. In addition, it received in 1846 as gift all the Oriental collection from Fort William College. By 1820 it streamlined its functioning. It set rules and regulations for its users, and a base for collection development. By 1833 it published its first catalogue of all the thousands of books in its collection. Its collection grew from 30,000 in 1884 onwards, 1,27,000 in 1944 and 2,10,940 in 1987. Its coverage by subjects and languages makes it a unique collection in the area.

The library at Bombay was based on an existing collection, viz., Medical and Literary Society of Bombay (f. 1789). One distinction in the founding of this library, as against its Calcutta counterpart was, that this library at Bombay was aimed as a public library, and this was spelled since its inception. Though ironically it was named in 1804 as Literary Society of Bombay, its character, of public service was never undermined. It received gifts from private and government sources. It received all the collections of Agri-Horticultural Society in 1830, Geographical Society in 1831, Medical Physical Society in 1835, and so on. By 1970 its collection had grown to 4,46,000 volumes and in 198 it had 5,40,000 volumes. Its first catalogue was published in 1845. Interestingly, it was declared as public library only in 1947. Today it serves as national depository library as well as State Library for the Maharashtra State.

4.5.9.2 *Sanskrit College, Calcutta*

This was yet another institution established by the British East India Company in 1821. It was similar to the one already established in Benaras (f. 1791). Its vast collection must have definitely duplicated the titles at Asiatic Society Library, Calcutta. But nevertheless, it did serve as a valuable resource. Its first catalogue emerged in 1892 and consequently published its supplementaries up to 1909, in 12 volumes. Another catalogue of printed books was published in 1919. It has today reached a status and repute of a university library status, with thousands of documents useful for the scholars and researchers in Sanskrit and allied subjects.

In a period of nearly one hundred years, since middle of the nineteenth century, many literary societies emerged in the country. Some of these later became parent organizations of highly specialized and significant special libraries. Notable are Young Men's Christian

Association, Bombay (1844), Meteorological Institute, Poona (1875), Indian Association for the Cultivation of Science, Calcutta (1876), Bombay Natural History Society (1883), Deccan Education Society, Poona (1884), Anthropological Society of Bombay (1886), Servants of India Society, Poona (1905), Indian Institute of Science, Bangalore, (1911), Indian Research Fund Association, New Delhi (1911), Ismaili Association and Ismaili Dharmik Library, Bombay (1911), Bhandarkar Oriental Research Institute, Poona (1917), Benaras Mathematical Society or Bharath Ganitha Parishad, Lucknow (1918), Institution of Engineers, Calcutta (1920), Indian Chemical Society, Calcutta (1924), Indian Roads and Transport Development Association Limited, Bombay, (1926), PEN All-India Centre, Bombay (1933), Dawoodi Bohra Literary and Welfare Society, Bombay (1940), Bible Society of India, Bombay (1944), Taheri Scholarship Society, Bombay (1944), Indian Institute of Culture, Bangalore (1945), Indian Standards Institution, New Delhi (1946), etc.

4.6 **Professional Associations**

The first professional library association in the country was a regional body, viz., Andhra Desa Library Association (1914). A series of such professional groups started emerging from this point through out the country. All India Public Library Association (1918), Indian Library Association (1933), etc. were some prominent national groups. Indian Library Association, had in its first president Dr M O Thomas (Librarian of Annamalai University) and Secretary Khan Bahadur K M Asadullah (Librarian, Imperial Library). Its' objectives were to promote the library movement in the country; to promote training of professionals; to promote research in library science; to work for improvement of status and service conditions of professionals; and cooperate with international library organizations. Another leading national level organization is the Government of India Libraries Association (1933).

4.7 **Professional Leaders**

Indian as well as foreign professionals served in this period. Prominent leaders of this period include: Dr. M O Thomas, Dr. Wali Mohammed, Mr. John Sargent, Dr. S R Ranganathan, Khan Bahadur K M Asadullah, N N Gidwani, Asa Don Dickinson, W A Borden, Lala Babu Ram,

Dr. G T Kale, Abdul Majid, S Bashiruddin, I Venkata Ramanayya, S Mohammed Kaseem Ali Rasulpuri, K Selliah, Mohammed Safi, Lala Sant Ram Bhatia, Dr. Rahatullah Khan, A M R Montague, J A Chapman, John Macfarlane, Yusuffuddin Ahmed, Hari Sarvothama Rao (the Father of Library Movement in Andhra Pradesh), and N R Ray.

4.8 **Library Literature**

The literature in this field began to appear during this period for a variety of reasons. Certainly one of the causes was the influence of the Western Librarians who were present in the country, and who knew the importance of the literature for the country's professional development. The first journal, *Library Miscellany*, started in India in 1912, at Baroda. Between 1912 and 1987, according to a survey there emerged in India, 84 periodicals, 17 newsletters, and many annual reports. Of these periodicals only 40 are surviving. The publishing/sponsoring agencies of these periodicals are either professional bodies or individuals. There has been no commercial contribution or commercial involvement in this field.

Book publishers in India started bringing out reviewing journals and at times devoted a special number or few pages for library science. B H Mehta's Hints on Library Administration in India (1914), is considered to be the first Indian book on Librarianship. (Kumar, 1977. p. 89). The first foreign contribution to Indian librarianship came in the book Panjab Library Primer (1916) of Asa Don Dickinson, the University Librarian (1915-1916) at Punjab University. The first regional language library journal was in Telugu, entitled '*Grandhalaya Sarvasamu*', which began publishing in 1915.

4.9 **Education for Librarianship**

Education of library personnel started basically as inservice programme in Calcutta; in other places it resembled education for social work, for example in Vijayawada. The Imperial Library under John Macfarlane, organized between 1901-1906 an inservice training in library routine. The first formal course for training at Baroda, under Borden, commenced in 1911. It was aimed at creating a band of trained people. It had, in its first batch ten men and women. The course duration was one year. In 1913 a summer course of five months duration was started. Borden made some attempts at initiating a two-year postgraduate course in library science. But this did not come about, and it took nearly forty years to be initiated. Both the courses at Baroda ended in 1924 when all library services suffered a general setback. Andhra Desa Library Association started one month course at Vijayawada, in 1920. The intended participants of the course were social workers, however after 1934 its orientation towards library work grew stronger.

Dickinson started a regular course for inservice training in 1915 at Punjab University, Lahore. This was the beginning of training programme at University level. This continued till 1947. Between 1929 and 1931 Madras Library Association, offered a summer course every year that offered what is now called "bibliographic instruction" to general library users. This later evolved into an inservice programme to assist library personnel towards professionalism. The Madras University assumed responsibility for this course in 1931. From 1937 it was made a year long regular postgraduate programme and named diploma. A bachelors' degree course grew out of this in 1961. In these two historic achievements Madras stands as a pioneer.

The impact of Dickinson's efforts in Punjab bore fruits when Khan Bahadur Asadullah inaugurated a course in library field. This was in 1935, a programme that continued till 1947 as full-time Diploma in Librarianship and offered at the Imperial Library, Calcutta. R N Sharma rightly states "It was due to Asadullah and ILA (of which he was the first Secretary), that the Government of India started the fist diploma course in Librarianship in 1935, at the Imperial Library, Calcutta, which was taken over by Calcutta University in 1945" (Sharma, 1987. p.231). Concurrently, Bengal Library Association offered from 1937 onward a certificate course, which still continues. In 1938 Madras University was the first which offered a Diploma in Librarianship, this was later named as Bachelor's Degree. The first Master's degree and the doctoral programme in the country were started in 1948 at Delhi University.

In pre-independent India, Madras (1938), Banaras (1942), Bombay (1943), Calcutta (1945), and Delhi (1947) were the only five Universities offering degree course in Librarianship.

To get a glance at what was the course contents of the library training programmes, it is apt to list the papers that were taught in a Diploma course offered at Banaras Hindu University, in the year 1942. There were six theory papers and three practicals. The theory included:

Classification; Cataloguing; Bibliography, Book Selection and Reference Work; Organization; and General Knowledge. The practicals covered classification; cataloguing; and Bibliography and Book Selection. This programme was open for those having a plus two (or post-matriculate two year education, or intermediate or pre-degree, in the Indian terminology). The rules however were relaxable and a matriculate was also accepted if one had four years of service in 'recognized' libraries.

4.9.1 *Administration and Management*

Administration of library system continued with a little change into the modern period. The dawn of the twentieth century witnessed changes in administrative set up of libraries. Library administration started becoming scientific in outlook and humane in approach. Visits of foreign librarians and consultants, mechanized the age-old practices. So also Ranganathan's Five Laws brought changes in the theory of library profession. He clearly demonstrated the inter-dependence of staff, user and documents. Similarly, library personnel began to receive training, as seen above, in this period for the first time in the professional history of India.

Storage and preservation in the pre-independent period received little attention, except for the few directly funded British Government's scientific and technical libraries, etc. Library buildings were yet to be planned and built according to the library standards, developed in the West.

In the sphere of processing of books and storing the documents for retrieval Ranganathan's classification and cataloguing efforts were revolutionary. His Colon Classification scheme and Classified Catalogue Code revolutionized the processing methods. While its use in libraries was limited, its basics provided a base for much research and study in the world of librarianship, in India and abroad.

In the staffing pattern emerged much of the similar systematization. We find from the sources that in pre-war period the Librarians had received some professional recognition. For instance see the pay-scale given for trained and un-trained positions. In the case of a school librarian the trained personnel would get nearly double the salary of the untrained. A graduate with Diploma in Librarianship (with no past experience) was given the initial pay of one hundred rupees, which was only next to two hundred rupees received by Teachers with masters and three years experience. The un-trained would get fifty-five rupees as the initial salary (*India and Pakistan Year Book*:1949:48). What was the status and salary of other librarians in academic and public libraries needs searching the vast number of sources.

The history of the modern period and twentieth century will be incomplete without a glance at what Indians did and what factors were at work to promote library development in the country. The period saw a shift from private libraries to subscription libraries and later to free/open libraries. What forces and precursors were behind these and how did the people react to these are interesting questions. The answer to these questions lies in the fact that education and free thinking of nineteenth century was at the base. The western educated elite who started educational campaigns and founded academies kindled an urge for spreading the literacy and education for progress and for modernization. There came into the country western currents prompting every thinking soul to move towards better life and better living conditions. In the filed of librarianship these currents entered through foreign consultants or through Indians themselves who were returning home after training and exposure to the western librarianship.

Thus the seeds of the twentieth century library movement in India were sown in different soils of the country. Some soils were too fertile to immediately respond and react. Some others required additional manuring and greasing. In this period the first harbinger was Sir Frank Alexander Francis who was a consultant at Jaipur, in north India. He did his best to adopt the western notions of librarianship and he did succeed. Dr. A C Burnell at Tanjore was busy in a similar exercise on another soil of the south India. Burnell also did succeed in inculcating the western ideas of library and Tanjore still thanks him for this gesture. At a different level and from a different point of view worked the Christian missionaries in India, and these received a boost in the nineteenth century when American counterparts also appeared on the scene. Whatever sense of ideas these contributed, indirectly these people promoted education and literacy and in turn benefitted the development of a library movement.

Borden in Baroda and Dickinson in Lahore did introduce innovative methods, in public and university librarianship. More interesting and fascinating was the development of a movement which emerged on the professional scene in 1914, in Andhra Desa. The intriguing questions are who inspired the social leaders to work for libraries, for library associations, for professional training programmes, for professional literature, etc. Who must have prompted these souls to activate the masses. These leaders became forebearers of Ranganathan. Not only that these leaders worked for establishment of a library movement in the state, they also coordinated with the national personalities and established a national public library association, in 1918. The library movement in Bengal had direct influence of literary genius like Rabindranath Tagore. The library movement in Madras received direct influence of Ranganathan. Indian literature of library science has most on these developments in this century. In short the steps taken by the professionals did prepare a basic structure–unnoticed and unplanned.

There has been a change from time to time in the influencing and influenced relationship in India. UK was the first to bring in professionalism at a very large scale. The first library consultants in India, who started in nineteenth century were from UK. The first Indian trained professionals were from UK. Due to the British rule in India, it was easy for Indians to go to UK than to other lands. It could be hypothesized that Indians under estimated the advances in American librarianship. Another presumption is the US agencies that helped India in its independent period, neglected India earlier–neglected in both ways: in exposing American librarianship and in providing an exposure to visit American libraries.

How far Indian profession had developed in this period. There can be various measures and ways to judge the state-of-the-art. By the rate of progress made in the next following period, as will be seen in the following pages, this era did much of the ground work and on the whole no significant contribution is seen. There were undeniably contributors and there were stalwarts; what did they generate and produce. The fact is that the country was not stable politically, economically, and these hampered any strategy. Even the country as such was not progressing leaps and bounds.

In the editorial of Modern Librarian, Sant Ram Bhatia, had raised very pertinent issues. It was ending of the post war-era. "Where does the Indian Librarian stand to-day? What position will the Indian Librarian have in the post-war era? In the changing world will he have security of a free independent man, free from the worries and anxieties in the stress and strain of everyday life? Will he remain the ever- exploited instrument in the hands of a few who claim vested interests in the temples of knowledge? Or will he be allowed to serve the best interests of the society and the nation as a happy man?" (Bhatia:1945:47-51).

Before presenting a grand fatherly advice to the profession he realistically presented the prevalent trends: "To-day the Indian Librarian is working without the aid of the Government. That is the truth. Ill-paid, half-starved, unprotected, ill-equipped, groaning under the impact of the high prices and high expenses he is prey both to the whims of his masters and to his own staggering helplessness". He goes advising the professionals: "To the public librarian I would say: make your library a democratic institution, well-equipped, and well-administered. it is to be entirely a modern phenomenon... Do not depend upon the traditional methods of library circulation statistics. Know your readers: Know what they are reading, whether their reading is worthwhile; know who are the people or groups who do not use the library, and what are the reasons for their indifference, and whether they have legitimate reading needs which the library can satisfy. You are to see the political position of your library, its social relationship; you are to weigh technical and professional considerations... Provide a variety of techniques to assist the readers to find their books they need..." We may pause here. These were the thoughts of a senior professional. Did these help the profession in even attempting to think on these lines? There was hardly any!!! Ironically, India was not slow in reacting to the impulse of the library movement in the west, it did have a sense of public libraries in the nineteenth century itself. What made its progress slow (or rather stagnated the developmental process) was the level of literacy and financial support. There were even other factors, but these were also detrimental.

Bhatia, took pains to highlight the situation in each type of library and the required strategy to make the library a user-oriented centre. He very rightly commented on the position of the college librarian, stating that he "is still backward, still not fully trained to be a guide to the teacher and the taught". To the school librarians, he advised "You have in your hands a nation to build. Build it well", so that the citizens of tomorrow will be aware of the national interests and help the growth and development of the country. This he emphasized could be possible only if the student is provided with a wide background of unbiased information.

To build a better India of tomorrow Bhatia was equally conscious of the rural–the majority–population. He went to the extent of stressing the importance of this user and mixed no words in putting straight the idea that "Unless you start good library centres in every nook and corner of your rural area the country will remain steeped in poverty and ignorance". He included the special librarians in his review of the situation and even added the training aspect of the professionals. His last lines were addressing the library authorities, the planners of the future of India: "When there is nationalization of libraries in our country–which I hope will be soon if we are able to get a national Government at the centre–he is to be the leader of the community, the book producer and publisher: let the Institute of Library Studies train him for the future: Let educationists, in their plan, realize that without the aid of a good librarian and library their scheme will not make any strides. For the key of India's future progress lies in the hands of the Indian Librarian" (Bhatia:1945:47-51).

5

INDEPENDENT INDIA (Since 1947)

"Ranganathan is often accused in the West (usually by critics ignorant of his writings) of being over-theoretical, and of allowing a mystical pre-occupation with eternal truths to blind him to the practical problems of classifying documents. But like Plato, who also exhibits a certain pre-occupation with eternal truths, Ranganathan's main characteristic is a business-like determination not only to come to grips with difficulties, but also to propose feasible solutions. Nowhere is this demonstrated more clearly than in Part 7 of Prolegomena" (Foskett:1976:257).

This period saw many drastic changes, and in fact this period totally revolutionized the Indian scene of Library and Librarianship. It was an all round change in the environment. The country became independent and received a chance to develop its own resources. The developments in science and technology were faster than the other areas and this had an impact on the development of libraries in the country–Science and Technology library and documentation services are the most advanced in the country, and have developed links with international databases.

5.1 Academic Libraries

The academic environment received new definition with the establishment of a series of review committees and commissions, like: University Education Commission (1948), University Grants Commission (Called UGC, 1953), Kothari Commission (1964), to name a few. As a result of these, university and college libraries received support from the government and the other related agencies.

The Library Committee of UGC under Ranganathan prepared a set of standards and recommendations for library buildings, furniture, selection and ordering reading material, qualification, pay scale and status–all of which were accepted by the UGC and implemented.

One more factor worked for the progress of the libraries of higher education and that was the American aid (like PL 480 grant and Wheat Loan Programme). By these grants Indian institutions could purchase American books and scientific instruments. This enabled many academic and research libraries in India to develop rapidly. Under different programmes 145 American consultants came to India between 1910 and 1988, of this as many as 134 came between 1950 and 1988. (Kumar:1977:207, 217; Konnur:1990). Carl White, who offered his service as consultant in the Delhi University Library, presented his report on the library problems and its future. This Report "has a unique place in the history of university librarianship in India", and it "did attract the attention of librarians in India and abroad" (Konnur:1990:22).

The school libraries did start in pre-independence period. But they received some attention and acknowledgment in the post-independence period. One such activity involving the school librarians and libraries was a national Seminar on School Library held in 1962, at Bangalore under S R Ranganathan's chairmanship. Given the kind of majority of schools which are poorly funded by the government there are still many schools which don't have other minimum requirements of a school, and library is not at all in the priority list. Privately managed schools have libraries with a trained or untrained librarian to dole out books that are stored in the library. Service orientedness is neither expected nor offered in most of these libraries meant for the citizens of tomorrow.

Today the majority of academic libraries–especially, the institutions of higher education–despite some progress, share a bleak outlook.The national Policy of Education, 1986, has some hopes for progress in academic libraries. Although computer applications and cooperative ventures have made advances in many of these (with a proposition like INFLIBNET), problems of funds for modernization, more staff, proper and adequate resources are continuing to grow with the age of these libraries. So also there is no provision for library instruction. This sad neglect of the library user's needs has driven the libraries to be called and considered as storehouse rather than service-oriented and user-centred libraries. Even the schools of library and information science have not been able to take care of the growing needs related to the information needs of human beings and the impact of technology on human information behavior.

5.2 **Public Libraries**

The history of the public library of independent India has to its credit many professionals, but one in particular, can be singled out–Dr. S R Ranganathan. He began his career in the public library movement in 1930. The fruits of this emerged in Public Library Legislation, viz., Madras Public Libraries Act (1948); Hyderabad Public Libraries Act (1955), Mysore Public Libraries Act (1965), Maharashtra Public Libraries Act (1967), and West Bengal Public Libraries Act (1979, probably as posthumous award for Ranganathan's achievements). The process of legislation is still on and gradually one state after the other is reaping the benefit of this glorious Ranganathan heritage.

For illustrating the legislation, we may describe a few details of the first Act. It was an Act to provide for the establishment of public libraries in the state of Madras and the organization of a comprehensive rural and urban library service therein. The Act provides for the setting up of a directorate and state central library which receives five copies of each book printed in the state of Madras. It has also a provision for a library committee at state level which functions under the state government, and advises on library matters. For the collection of the library cess (or tax) a Local Library Authority was to be set up. This library cess was to be matched by the state in contributing an equal amount which would in turn go as fund for maintenance of the library. Each new Act henceforth considered the defects of the predecessor and rectified many defects and limitations. These defects became visible and even Ranganathan criticized the Government about some points in the Madras Act.

This legislative attempts apart, there have been other activities in the area of public librarianship. In 1951 the Delhi Public Library was set up. UNESCO collaborated with the Indian Government in its establishment. It is now the biggest public library in India. The total reading material is 8.65 lakhs. It has a network of branches and mobile libraries.

The Delhi Public Library, the Connemara Public Library, Madras, the Asiatic Society Library, Bombay, and the National Library, Calcutta, are the four depository libraries in the country, as established by Government decision in 1981.

The National Library, (the former Calcutta Public Library and the former Imperial Library), at Calcutta, has continued to expand, but it has not been able to act as an apex library in the country. There is a dire need for a national public library network to link, coordinate and cooperate the activities of the libraries at the national, state and the local libraries. In an ideal arrangement the State Central Libraries should alone be linking libraries to the national library in a hierarchical manner, but in practice there is lot of decentralization and chaos.

In the area of public library development the Raja Ram Mohan Roy Foundation (f. 1972) has emerged as a pivotal institution. Based on the name of the great social reformer of Bengal this Government funded body accelerated the library movement in the country. Its concentration areas are in literacy promotion programmes, supply of regional language books (to the extent of 80% of all its allocation for publications, leaving only 20% for the English language books), rural libraries, preservation of rare and out of print books and the establishment of Bal Kendras (Children's centres) in the country. The Foundation has of late started its official publication, Granthana (1990-).

For resource sharing and networking among the libraries there has been much said theoretically. It includes many suggestions and many resolutions. One such solution was offered by Keyes Metcalf, who had a repute in planning libraries. He felt that the local public library services in towns and colleges should be linked up with schools and other social agencies (Konnur:1990:38). There were many seminars on how India could effectively adapt the resource sharing methodology. A few states which have legislation, do form a network of libraries, like for instance the Andhra Pradesh Public Library system has evolved a state level centralization towards this end.

Leading libraries of each state have been designated as State Libraries (or theoretically called State Central Libraries). Ideally it has been suggested that there should be a hierarchy of public libraries: national, state, district, village, branch, mobile, etc. Whereas in practice only State libraries have emerged and others are still a dream. Almost all states and Union Territories, except Delhi, Sikkim Lakshadweep, Daman and Diu, have state libraries. Each state has one State library, but Jammu & Kashmir, Dadra and Nagar Haveli have two State Libraries each, and Gujarat has 3 state Libraries. The state library functions as apex library in some state, like Andhra Pradesh, Karnataka, etc. Divisional libraries exist in Andhra Pradesh, Bihar, Dadra and Nagar Haveli, Gujarat, etc. These divisional libraries perform same functions as state libraries, within the respective region.

5.2.1 *Five-Year Plans*

In the first five-year plan (1951-1956), a proposal was made to set up a National Central Library at New Delhi. This was to be based on nine state libraries - states which had some sort of networking. This plan period included a scheme for 'improvement of library service', wherein each state was to have a central or apex library, with district libraries and within each district there were to be circulating libraries. The Delhi Public Library, with Indo-Unesco collaboration emerged during this period.

The Second plan (1956-61) suggested forming a network (and a hierarchy) of all libraries in 320 districts of the country. The new copyright law (or the Delivery of Books Act, 1954), and amended in 1956 to include Newspapers, prescribed now that every Indian publisher will gift one copy of a publication to each of the three libraries in Calcutta, Bombay and Madras. Yet another scheme was added in the plan: to amalgamate public library service in rural areas with adult education programmes. An Advisory Committee for Libraries was set up under K P Sinha, in 1957, to enquire and recommend matters relating to reading needs of users and public library structure in India.

During the Third plan (1961-1966) the government agreed on having four national libraries in New Delhi, Calcutta, Madras and Bombay. Accordingly, Delhi became the forth depository in 1982.

In the Fourth Plan (1969-1974) a working group was st up under Dr. V K R V Rao to prepare a programme for library development. It was in this period emerged the Raja Ram Mohan Roy Library Foundation in 1972, for the development and upliftment of public libraries in India. From this plan period working groups were called upon to present proposals for each five years.

Fifth plan (1974-1978), Sixth (1980-1985), Seventh (1985-1990) and Eight (1990-1995) are on the way making progress. During the Fifth plan the National Science Library was developed, as a part of INSDOC. In 1976 was enacted the National Library of India Act, based on the recommendations of V S Jha, who chaired the Reviewing Committee for the National Library. The Committee defined the basic features of a National Library and included in its recommendations, measures to improve working of this apex library. In 1985 was appointed a Committee to draft a National Policy on Library and Information Systems under D P Chattopadhayaya. Under the Eight plan there is a proposal to set up a National Commission on Library and Information Services. It is also proposed to establish an Institute of Information Science, and to link this Institute with NISSAT, NICNET, INDONET, and INFLIBNET.

5.3 Special Libraries

This refers to the libraries that are attached to scientific, technical, and cultural institutions or attached to various government department. In India these special libraries have received comparatively high support from their parent organizations, compared to academic and public libraries which have frequently been neglected.

As the stature of library and information science as a profession increased, networks for specialized information were established. In the broad field of social sciences the government of India set up the Indian Council of Social Science Research (ICSSR) in 1969. This body in turn established the National Social Science Documentation Centre (NASSDOC) in 1970. The latter's activities/service, include photocopy, compiling union catalogues and bibliographies, reference and referral, indexing, abstracting, consultancy, resource sharing, data activities, international collaboration, compilation of directory and conducting of surveys. Six regional centres of ICSSR are spread throughout the country, which are engaged in documentation activities in the respective regions.

In the field of pure sciences, the Government established Council of Scientific and Industrial Research (CSIR). Under the CSIR the important body that functions is Indian National Scientific Documentation Centre (INSDOC) founded in 1952. The latter's activities are acquiring and preserving all scientific serials, reports etc., based on Indian needs, publishing current awareness tools, reference service, photocopy and translation service, manpower training, compiling union catalogues, etc. Among other significant national level developments are the National Medical Library, and Indian Institute of Agricultural Research Library.

Under the Department of Science and Technology, called DST, emerged in 1977 the National Information System for Science and Technology (NISSAT). This network was a brain child of Dr. Peter Lazar. NISSAT was based on the existing infrastructure. It aims on integrating and coordinating the available resources, service and activities. Its main components are:

English but suffered from their small size and prestige and with their fascination for cataloguing. Library associations seemed to be numerous, small, contentious, and professionally ineffective. The poorly paid librarians themselves seemed wary and nervous, in some way sensitive, in other ways insensitive, the quality of life affecting their behavior, the quality of bureaucratic red tape affecting their success" (Harvey:1973-1974).

What the professional leadership felt of India's achievements in this era, can be guessed from the following observations and comments of Prof Kaula: There were only six students in library school at Madras, and seven at B H U, in 1945. "Today we have large number of applicants of admission with high academic degrees" (Kaula:1984: 103). "In the 1940's the teaching was conducted in the University Library as a wing of the library. There was no independent department of library science and today there is hardly any teaching being done as a wing of the library. The teaching in 1940s was done by the library staff and there were no full time teachers and today there are full time teachers with very few working librarians associated with the teaching. The teaching is 1940s was oriented towards the work in the library, the student having greater opportunity to work in the library against what we witness today. The teaching today is more theoretical with less dependence on library work. In fact several universities students do not have opportunity to visit the university library nor nay one to guide them in the working of the library... In 1940s there was only the post-graduate Diploma course, against several courses available today leading to B Lib Sc., M Lib Sc and specialized degrees. No one could think of working for Ph D those days against several universities having provision for research work. The content of the course in 1940's was small with few books and few journals available for study. In 1980's there are quite a large number of books and also journals. So the student of today has to undergo more hard work and study more comprehensively than the student of 1940's... Further "'Library Science' was not a recognized discipline and the society was not convinced that it had scientific content. But today it is a recognized discipline and had several adherents too. The dimension of library science in 1940's was limited and there were alien courses attached to it. But today library science itself has become quite vast and its dimensions extended into areas of information science, communication science, computer technology, and so on".

6

LIBRARY DEVELOPMENT IN THE STATES

The history of the librarianship and library science in each of the States and Union territories is also interesting and gives a clearer picture of the country's library history. These divisions were a result of redrawing the map of India on the basis of linguistic groups.

6.1 Andhra Pradesh

In the southern part of the country, it is situated in-between the states of Karnataka on the west, Tamil Nadu on the south, Orissa in the north east, Maharashtra in the north west and Bay of Bengal in the east. Hyderabad is the state capital. The state was called Hyderabad state after independence, and received its present name in 1956. Andhra Pradesh includes the Nizams' (ruled territory) state of Hyderabad, a part of the Vijayanagara dynasty's territory, and a part of the Bahmani ruled lands. Of the libraries which lived long one is most notable, the Sayidia Library, Hyderabad (10th century). It survived for ten centuries and in 1970s started its decline and in 1980s was closed to the public. It reached its heights of glory by storing some rare documents of British rule in south India, along with correspondence of Clive, Hastings, Wellesly, and Tipu Sultan. The library culture of Vijayanagar empire, Qutub Shahi's and Asifjahi's did pave the way for patronage of learning and libraries. Libraries were either patronized by the state or were maintained by the elite. In the beginning of the present century many libraries came into being. Financial support was given even to libraries that were established during the people's movement. The Asaf Jahi style of architecture is visible in the buildings erected by the Nizam, viz., State Central Library, Osmania University Library, etc.

The language of the majority of the people in the State, and hence the first language of the state is Telugu. The use of the language and its literature must have been earlier than 2nd century AD. Evident from the Pali and Sanskrit inscriptions of this region, is the fact that there was a usage of Telugu, and which indicated the common usage of the Telugu words by all. It was by fifth century the first existence of Telugu inscriptions is traced in history. The first piece of Telugu literature is a translation of *Mahabharata* dated to be of 10th century AD. Its educational history is evident from the census reports: 3.3% in 1951; 12% in 1961; 21% in 1971; 29.5% in 1981, and 45% in 1991 indicating that there is a vast field yet untouched for the future librarians–to work in collaboration with literacy workers.

Among the elites who built personal collections during the rule of Nizam VII Sir Krishan Prasad, Raja Rai Rayan Sharma, Raja Shiv Raj Daharmavant, Venkata Ranga Rao, Venkata Rama Reddy, Ameen Jung, Sir Nizamat Jung, Salar Jung III, and many others.

Libraries were attached to government departments too. The present High Court Library was originally attached to department of Judiciary. The Department of Umur-i-Mazhabi (Religious Affairs), was responsible for libraries at Mutts, Mosques, and other religious institutions.

Among prominent libraries, still in existence are Jamia Nizamiya Library, Hyderabad { (f.1875 according to P S G Kumar, (see Kumar, 1977; and f.1892 according to Taher, *et al*, (see Taher,1989)}; Nizam Club Library (1883), Asafiya Library (1885)–now called State Central Library whose manuscript collection has been separately developing since a few decades and is named as Andhra Pradesh Oriental Manuscript Library–Dairatul Maarif (1900), Sri Krishna Devaraya Andhra Bhasha Nilayam { (f.1901 according to A A N Raju, (see Raju, 1989); and f.1914 according to P S G Kumar, (see Kumar,1977)}, Osmania University Library (1917), Sri Vemana Andhra Bhasha Nilayam (1923), etc.

The growth of free public libraries, as anywhere in India except for Baroda, is a post-independent feature. The enactment of the Andhra Pradesh Public Libraries Act, 1960 (originally called Hyderabad Public Libraries Act), has been a boon for the growth of the library system in the State. There is state Central Library and there is a network of District level city level and village level library system. However the State Central Library, which should have been acting as an apex library for the system, has not played a strong role. In reality, the State Central Library is a local/regional landing library, and shares this activity with a few other regional libraries in the state.

Among the University Libraries Osmania, Andhra and Sri Venkateswara were forerunners, and today there are ten universities, and the city of Hyderabad itself has six universities, viz., Osmania University, Andhra Pradesh Open University, Telugu University, Andhra Pradesh Agricultural University, Jawaharlal Nehru Technological University, Hyderabad University, and Central Institute of English and Foreign Languages (a deemed to be university).

The Andhra Pradesh Library Association (APLA), founded in 1914, was the first professional body in the country. Its official organ, *Grandhalaya Sarvasamu*, was the first professional periodical in the country. Literature in Telugu, Urdu and English has been written in the field of library science. The other active professional bodies include Academy of Library Science and Documentation (ALSD), and Andhra Pradesh Public Library Association.

The education for librarians has been offered at Andhra and Osmania since a long time, at Bachelor's level. Master's and doctoral level were added later on. The other Universities offering professional courses are Kakatiya University, Sri Venkateswara University, Sri Krishnadevaraya University and the Andhra Pradesh Open University. This was the first Open University in the country to start the professional course for training of working librarians. There is, presently, a six level educational system for Library and Information Science: certificate, diploma, bachelor, master, M.Phil (pre-doctoral), and doctoral. This education is offered by the University at the higher levels, and by professional bodies and government recognized institutes at lower level. We can name one or two institutes that run the training programme, Central Institute of Library Science, Hyderabad, Institute of Library Science, Hyderabad, and State Institute of Library Education and Training (SILERT), Hyderabad. The state has developed a network of public libraries, and its State Central Library, supplemented with regional libraries, district libraries, etc. forms a model for other states. And this model is suggested here, despite the fact that there is much that is required to be done, to call it functional (Inamdar:1984; Raju:1988).

6.2 Assam

This is situated in the northeastern part of the country. It is situated in between the boundaries of Nepal in the west, Bhutan in north and even touches Bangladesh on its south.

Its palace library in Kamrupa has been reported to have existed. Hieun Tsang informs about the King Bhaskaravarman's gift to Harsha Vardhana of Kanauj. In the 15th century we find Ahom Kings (who gave their name to this territory) were strong rulers. The other houses were used in this period for storing of books and archival material.

The literacy growth rate in this state has been 3% (in 1951); 27.4% (in 1961); 28.1% (in 1971); and 43.42% (in 1991). This growth rate also speaks of the development of adult education activities in the state. The first language of the state is Assamese. The earliest extract book in this language is *Prahlad Charita* by Hema Saraswathi.

This state has been underdeveloped in libraries despite its literary fame for Buranji's in prose of 13th century, and neo-Vaishnavaite literature of the 15th century. Its centres (called *Namgharas*) are still a place of attraction, not for reading purpose, but to hear neo-Vaishnavaite verses.

The year 1903 saw the first public library in this state. It was named Assam Government Public Library and was housed at Shillong. Later in 1956 it was named State Central Library of Assam, and shifted to Gauhati. There were attempts to build more and more libraries, beginning this development. District Libraries and subdivisional libraries were linked to the State Library.

The founding of the first library group, Assam Library Association in 1938 under Kumudeswar Barthakur paved the way for founding hundreds of rural libraries. The Association collaborated with Dr. Ranganathan in preparing a Draft Public Library bill, in 1964. However, the state is yet to get its bill passed in the state legislature.

The state has been offering professional education since long for entire North-east India. It has Bachelors (1966-), Masters (1979-), and doctoral (1988-) programmes at Gauhati University. Degree course in Library Science started in 1966. The library journal in Assamese *Granthalok* started in 1971 has ceased now. There is hardly any textbook of library science in this language (Buragohain: 1988).

6.3 Bihar

This state is in the north-east of India. It is surrounded by Uttar Pradesh in west, Bangladesh in east, Madhya Pradesh in west, Orissa in south, West Bengal in south east and Nepal in north. The name Bihar (Vihar) is the gift of Muslims as they saw many Buddhist monasteries (=Viharas) in this land. Bihar has its importance in being the land of Buddha (for Buddhists) and Mahavira (for Jains). Bihar like Uttar Pradesh has significantly contributed to Hindi and Urdu literature in the past. It has a lead in the country with its oldest Nalanda, Odantipura and Vikramshila University libraries. Details of few of these have already been described.

The library patronage of the Mughal Governors of Bihar was very well continued, to some extent, by their descendants and Abu Zafar Nadvi stands testimony to this (Nadvi, 1945, 1946). While there were libraries in each period in this land, these were not an instrument of mass education. Hence these libraries would not form a part of the present sense of public library structure. A true pattern of such a structure emerged only since a hundred years (Mishra:1964).

The literacy rates in this state are: 10% in 1951; 18% in 1961; 20% in 1971; 26.21% in 1981; and 38.54% in 1991. It is one of the least literate states, and is the crux of the problem for the public libraries in particular and librarianship in general.

The Bhagalpur Institute Library (f. 1834) is the oldest known library. The special feature of this library is it was open to public every evening–to say it was the beginning of public libraries and a humble attempt was made by making it part-time service. The Gaya Public Library (f. 1855) was founded on the basis of subscriptions and donations. The Khuda Bhaksh Oriental Public Library (f.1888) has a lead in the city of Patna. Rampur Raza Library at Rampur (f. 1889), received royal patronage and was kept open for public. Its manuscript collection is far more than the Khuda Bakhsh Library. By an Act of Parliament both of these libraries have been made libraries of national importance. The Patna University was established in 1919. The Sinha Library (f. 1924), was converted into the State Library in the year 1956. This State Library is managed by a private trust. It has a collection of 1,50,000 volumes. The public library movement received impetus from the new ministry set up in 1935, under the Minister of Education, Dr. Syed Mahmood. This minister was responsible for setting up thousands of literacy centres in the state. It requires a details study to see how these effected the growth of reading tastes and reading needs (Pandey Sharma:1992; Mishra:1964; R S P Singh:1991).

Bihar Raja Pustakalaya Sangh, earlier called Bihar Library Association, was founded in 1936. It is a leading professional body and its organ is Pustakalaya.

6.4 Delhi

New Delhi is the capital-city of India today. Old Delhi and other adjacent places are brought together to be called the Union Territory of Delhi, since 1956. As against the State which is a decentralized division, a Union territory is directly administered by Parliament through the Home Ministry. Tradition has it that Delhi has lived seven lives, so as to say there are seven (some others report 15) locations where people lived at different times in the vicinity of the present place. The popular Hindi or Hindustani (also called Urdu) originated both as a tongue and a script in Delhi and Agra (Agra is now in Uttar Pradesh). The language was born here but grew in the Deccan Plateau is a part of history, and receives a national importance today through the world of film and television. Delhi is situated in between Haryana in north, Rajasthan in west, and Uttar Pradesh in south. It has had a history of plunder and splendor.

Its public library tradition has had private sponsors/supporters (the example of Saint Nizamuddin's library, (and government support (for instance, during Delhi Sultanate and Mughal period). Of the existing public libraries Hardyal Municipal Public Library (1862), Marwari Public Library (1915), Raghumal Vedic Library (1915), Fatehpuri Muslim Public Library (1928), Rama Krishna Mission Free Library (1934), are a few of the significant ones. The present leading public library is Delhi Public Library (1951). This public library holds the prestigious position as fourth national depository library–in the entire country. It has a public library network which has no parallel in the south Asia. These two features place Delhi in forefront among the library-cities of India.

This city-state has a history of its educational patronage as is West Bengal and other British presidencies. Its literacy rate has been 37% (in 1951); 52.7% (in 1961); 56.6% (in 1971); 61.06% (in 1981); and 76.09% (in 1991).

Among the oldest known libraries the Zakir Husain College (formerly Delhi College, f.1824), forms an example of college libraries. Similarly among the Government libraries, are Department of Legal Affairs Library (f.1869-70), Central Secretariat Library (formerly Imperial Secretariat Library, f. 1891), etc are prominent.

A library course of one year was started in 1955 by Delhi Public Library Association. A diploma of two years commenced in 1962.

Delhi University started the first degree course in 1947 under the able guidance of DR S R Ranganathan and Prof S Das Gupta. Carl White, of University of California–served as a consultant at the University of Delhi Library. This consultancy resulted in initiating yet another phase of library development of Universities. Carl White Report has a unique place in the history of university librarianship in India.

The Delhi Library Association was formed in 1953. This body and the Department of Library and Information Science each have their official organ,viz., *Library Herald* and *Journal of Library and Information Science*, respectively. The Indian Library Association was founded in Calcutta in 1933 (shifted to Delhi in 1946, but was back to Calcutta in 1953, to return for permanent seat at Delhi in 1964). Its official organ *The Indian Library Association Bulletin* continued to serve despite the transfers of its parent body (Vashishth:1988).

6.5 Goa

Goa also comprises of Diu and Daman, is located in the west coast of India. It is surrounded by Maharashtra in the north and the remaining border by Karnataka. The name Goa appears in *Puranas* as Gove, Govapur and Gomant. The Muslims knew the land as Sindebur and the Portuguese as Goa Velha. Its rulers are many in history, notable ones are, Kadamba, Bahmani, Vijayanagar, and Portuguese. It was the Muslims who introduced the mobile transport system (horse) through Goa. And it was the Portuguese who introduced the printing press and printed the first book in the country in Goa. Portuguese whose presence made. It was a Portuguese seat from 1510 to 1961, being a holder of sea port the conquered were always strong and did not allow British or other forces to get in from this part of the country. Its literacy rates are: 30.7% in 1961; 44.7% in 1971; 55.86% in 1981; and 76.96% in 1991.

Its present State Central Library (f.1832), is older than the Calcutta's Public Library. In 1836 it was named "Bibliotheca Publica". In 1897 it was given the status of a national library, being named "Bibliotheca National de Nova Goa". Its collection consisted of books, journals mainly in Portuguese, French, Latin and a few in Konkani and Marathi. Today its collection is around 1,30,000.

Among the academic centres which existed noteworthy is the College of Rachol which has an outstanding library. This college was later called Seminary of Rachol. Its collection was listed and published in a catalogue of 1900. The oldest private libraries, as traced by historians is the Saraswat Vidyapeeth (f. 1899), followed by Shri Mahalaxmi Pradadik Vachan Mandir (f. 1907), Gomti Vidya Niketan Library (f. 1912), Saraswati Mandir (f. 1913), etc.

In 1983 was formed Gomantak Granthalya Sangh, a professional body, under the leadership of B D Satoskar. This association offers a certificate course of two months duration. There is no such course at the university level (Rodrigues:1988).

6.6 Gujarat

One of the states attached to the border of Pakistan, it lies on the Western part of India. Among its other neighbours are Maharashtra in the south and east, Madhya Pradesh in northeast and Rajasthan in north. Gujarat has its name from *Gujara* (a subtribe of Huns). It came into existence as a state in 1960, when Bombay State was divided linguistically: Marathi speakers (getting Maharashtra) and Gujarati speakers (given Gujarat). Literature in Gujarati is likely to have emerged in 12th century A C.

Its library history is traced from 5th century, with the Maitraka's building a monastery. We have the name of the monastery to ascertain the history of the library. Being a renowned monastery its library collection must have been very valuable. The existence of an earliest palace library in this land is evident in the period of King Siddharaja Jayasimha (1094-1143). This was brought into Anhilvad in 1140 A C, as a booty of war from Paramara Dynasty of Malwa. This collection originally belonged to King Bhoja of this Dynasty. Another palace library was maintained by Kumarapala Deva (1143-1174), whose successors were reported to have destroyed the collection (Dar:1960; Nadvi:1945, 1946). Muslim rule in Gujarat both in its provincial period and as an independent period built many libraries. Furthermore, Sultan Mahmud Bagda (1458-1511) is said to have had a palace library. The academic libraries in this historic context include, the hundreds of Madrasa which came into existence in the medieval period and continued to exist later, at Ahmedabad, Surat, Cambay, Pattan, etc, and these have all been mentioned in the earlier pages. Gujarat leads the country in having the first known private printing press–owned by Bhimjee Parak in 1674. It had the first Church libraries at Surat, established in English factories. Gujarat of 19th century had the highly educated community of Parsi's who founded libraries (some of which exist even today as public libraries and reading rooms).

Its literacy rates are: 30.0% in 1961; 35.8% in 1971; 43.75% in 1981; and 60.91% in 1991. Despite all efforts in the first quarter of this century the literacy rates in this state are comparatively very low. There are evidences that as early as 1906 and 1907 a few individuals joined to start Mitra Mandal Libraries. The scheme was to share resources and books by jointly subscribing on a village basis. The scheme started with 150 such villages coming together. We do not know as to what happened to it later (Kumar, 1977. p. 83).

This is a state whose history of library development though short is marvelous, and probably, unparalleled in the annals of the Indian history. The ruling monarch, Maharaja Sayaji Rao Gaikwad, initiated the development programme, whose history is unique in the country. W A Borden, an American consultant Librarian, provided all planning and implementing skill and brain. Baroda therefore, was first in many library activities in the country. For instance, it initiated "Open Access" in 1910; started a library journal in 1912; and began library training programme in 1912. But this golden period was short lived. By 1924 with the death of the monarch all progress came to a halt. Probably library was not required by the masses but it was imposed from above (Ramakrishna Rao:1961:142).

Presently three State Central Libraries exists in Gandhinagar, Baroda and Ahmedabad. The first public library in the state emerged in 1849 in Ahmedabad. This was a native library, and now it is called Himabhai Institute. This state has a long tradition of academic centres of Muslim learning, and still some exists. One instance of this is the Pir Muhammad Shah Dargah Library, Ahmedabad (Taher:1986).

The leaders of the library development in this state include T D Wakins, Motibhai Amin, Kudalkar, Newton Mohan Dutt, and others.

Seven universities offer library science degree course in the state. Twelve bodies, including private and government offer certificate courses of six month duration. Of all these universities M S University, Baroda offers teaching in English medium, and the others offer in Gujarati (Shah:1988; Upadhayaya:1991; Qureshi:1972).

6.7 **Haryana**

Haryana is located in the north India with Punjab in north west, Himachal Pradesh in north east, Uttar Pradesh and Delhi in east, and Rajasthan in south west, and emerged in 1966. It was born as a result of separation of Punjabi speaking Punjab and Hindi speaking Haryana. The name of the state probably originates from *Hari* (=green) and *ayana* (=home), denoting the fertility of the country side.

Its literacy figures are: 19.9% in 1961; 26.9% in 1971; 35.84% (in 1981); and 55.33% in 1991. Its library history is also not very old. The district library of Ambala (f.1957), became the State Central Library of Haryana.

Haryana Library Association was founded in 1967. A newsletter is published by this professional body. It offers a six month course which was changed to one year duration in 1981. Another diploma course of two years is offered for women, since 1968. The University of Kurukshetra started the degree course in 1969 for the professional training. For the regional languages professional education there is no literature and they have to forcibly rely on English and material in languages of the other neighboring states.

This state became the eight in the country to enact library legislation, in 1989. Its State Library is in Ambala Cantt (Raj:1988).

6.8 **Jammu and Kashmir**

This state is on the tip of northern India. Situated between China and Pakistan this state lies in a strategic position. Its one-third is adjoined with Pakistan as Azad Kashmir. It has been in a dispute between Pakistan and India since post-independent era and a part of the problem lies in the plebiscite and the Simla Pact. The literacy rate of this state has been 11% in 1961; 18.6% in 1971; 27% in 1981; and 32.68% in 1991. The language most common in the State is Kashmiri. It probably evolved out of the *Apabrahmsa* prevalent in the area around 10th century A C. The earliest known literary piece is belongs to 13th century A C.

In terms of library tradition it has a long history. Taxila which flourished for a thousand years was near its border, and must have been quite a traffic zone for this reason.The location of Taxila is said to be on West of Rawalpindi (in present Pakistan).The Chinese scholars must have crossed the Kashmir valley each time they went to Taxila or nearby other institutions. Hieun Tsang, a Buddhist-Chinese traveller in his seventh century Indian travelogue has recorded the existence of a palace library in Gandhara, during the rule of Kanishka the Kusana King. Hieun Tsang was assigned the task of reading and giving a commentary on Buddhist scriptures. Sultan Zainul Abideen who ruled in

15th century, set up technical schools to train people in paper manufacture, binding and other related techniques. In supply of ink it was once famous (Kumar:1977).

Probably the year 1919 heralds the era of public libraries in the state, which saw the establishment of Sri Pratap Singh Library at Srinagar. This state has two State Libraries, one each at Jammu and Srinagar.

The first professional body in this state emerged in 1964. The State has presently two universities, University of Jammu and Kashmir (f. 1948) and the University of Jammu (f. 1969). The first professional course offered was in the year 1971. It was at Srinagar in Kashmir University, as Bachelors degree (Shafi:1988).

6.9 **Karnataka**

The state of Mysore emerged as a result of reorganization of the country, in 1956. Mysore meant buffalo town. It was renamed Karnataka in 1973. It is situated in south India, and surrounded in south west by Kerala, south east and east by Tamil Nadu, Andhra Pradesh in the north east, Goa in the west and Maharashtra in the north. This state is one of those which has along library tradition. Prof. K S Deshpande rightly observes "Epigraphic evidences are available to show that a great many libraries were attached to universities and religious maths" (Despande:1962). Therefore there is a vast amount of material available for research in the Hindu and Muslim periods of history of this lands. Its tradition of libraries encompasses a number of dynasties, like Hoysalas, Chalukyas, Kadambas, Rasthrakuthas, Vijayanagara, Wodeyars, etc. Kannada is the first language of the state. Much of the Kannada literature was of religious nature, and Jains contributed largely to this by the first and the second centuries A.D. The library of Singeri has already been mentioned in this book.

The existence of a library tradition in palace libraries, academies and religious centres has been already elaborated. In passing we can mention here some significant ones: the Jain collections at Moodibidre (the Kashi Jains of) South Kanara; the palace library of the Wodeyars, Mysore; the Sringeri Mutt Library, Sringeri; Tipu Sultan's Library, Mysore; Mahmud Gawan's College Library, Bidar; Asari Mahal Library of the Adil Shahi's, Bijapur; etc. The Asari Mahal Library was a prestigious and reputed as it had in its staff scholars like Waman bin Pandit, Hussain Khan, and Manjan Khan. The Sringeri Mutt Library received grants from far and near, and the Vijayangar rulers grant-in-aid was one such instance.

Its literacy rate has been progressing slowly: 3.0% in 1951; 25.4% in 1961; 31.5% in 1971; 38.41% in 1981; and 55.98% in 1991. Its literary history in Kannada language dates to 9th century, when Kavirajamarga was composed by the King Nirpatunga.

Public libraries have been established in this state by both the government and the public bodies in the recent history. The Tipu Sultan's Library, described above, was one specimen of the library tradition, and indicates the tastes of the rulers. So precious was the collection that many significant manuscripts from this Library went to different libraries of the world. The British Government in order to curb anti-British movement established a series of native (public) libraries. The first, so far traced, has been at Dharwad. Probably the first subscription based public libraries set up by the government, was at Bangalore and Mysore, in 1914. The former is today the City Central Library and the latter is the State Central Library. Private agencies like Karnatak Vidya Vardhaka Sangha (f. 1890) established its own public libraries at Dharwad. Karnataka became third state in the country with Public Library Act, 1965.

Library science education at certificate level was first initiated by the Government in 1962. A diploma for women was introduced as under graduate study programme, at Women's Polytechnic in 1963. Karnataka University was the fore runner to start a degree course in 1963, and today five universities offer the degree course. Documentation Research and Training Centre (DRTC), offers a specialized course (since 1964), leading to Associateship in Library and Information Science. The leading university in terms of training professionals, apart from Karnataka University, is Mysore University.

Mysore Library Association was formed in 1929 and later named Karnataka Library Association. Based at Dharwad it is a leading professional body. The professionals in Karnataka University wisely decided to keep up with times and they started Timeless Fellowship, in 1964, which was regular till recent years, and is likely to be revived soon. "Library Science with a Slant to Documentation" (f. 1962), is an official publication of DRTC, and is the oldest periodical in the state. In the regional languages there have been few books for professionals. Karnataka Granthalaya is a serial in this regional language (Ijari:1988).

6.10 **Kerala**

This southern most state was formed in 1956 and included Malabar (from the Madras state) and Travancore and Cochin. It is situated between Karnataka in north Indian Ocean in the west and Tamil Nadu in the east. Its first language is Malayalam. Its culture is distinct for other neighbouring states. Asoka's inscription is the first source to know the existence of this state. It is mentioned as Kerlaputra. The language evolved with its own identity in 825 A C, which coincides with the commencement of the Kollam Era. Its own literature probably dates back to 1373 A C. A Tiruvitamkot stone inscription in Malayalam script proves this point (Kumar, 1977. p. 21). Its library tradition is yet untapped from historical sources. The oldest library traced is Trivandrum Library Society's Trivandrum Public Library (1847), followed by Kottayam, Cochin Public Library (1869), Public Library and Reading Room (1870), and so on. The Trivandrum Public Library was declared as State Central Library in 1959.

A state which has a strong tendency towards literacy, Kerala, has had literacy growth rates from 6.0% in 1951; 46.8% {in 1961, with an addition of a part (Malabar) from its neighboring state}; 60% in 1971; 69.17% in 1981; and 90.59% in 1991. By 1992 the state reached hundred per cent literacy. Its library development has two distinct features:

1. Part of the state (Malabar) came under the jurisdiction of the then Madras State, and by this it has been a beneficiary of the Madras Public Libraries Act, 1948. This benefit was extended to Malabar till 1989 - when Kerala government passed the Public Libraries Act.
2. The existence of about 5000 subscription libraries which are affiliated to a leading professional body (Kerala Grandhasala Sangam) - these libraries function as cultural and information centres. There is a very good response from the public in using these libraries (Taher, 1990).

The first professional body that emerged in the State was All Kerala Library Association at Trichur in 1931. The main person behind this was Kunhirama Menon. All Travencore Library Association emerged in 1933. This survived for three years and was formed again in 1956 as Kerala Granthasala Sangham (or Kerala Library Association). Another group emerged in 1937, Malabar Vayanasala

Sanghom (or Malabar Library Association), and its President was E Raman Menon. The state has a longer tradition of experiments in adult education. The Government of Cochin started libraries in villages to promote adult education, in 1926. This was on an experimental basis.

Library science education is offered by the public library and the library association. Kerala University offers degree course, beginning from 1961. Calicut University too offers a degree programme. The Trivandrum Public Library (f. 1847, now called State Central Library), offers certificate course. The Kerala Grandhasala Sangam also offers a similar course.

Grandhalokam, and *Vijnana Kairali* are two serials covering professional literature in the regional language. There are many books on professional subjects in this language. Incidentally, these library trends and movements have been existing since decades, as seem from above, and this state has the highest literacy in the country. Thereby implying that the leadership and literacy can move the public library development, and the support of the government is not always necessary. It is the people who have strived for the progress of the library and library profession (Augustine:1990; Pandey Sharma:1992).

6.11 **Madhya Pradesh**

The centrally located state (Madhya meaning centrally) is Madhya Pradesh, and it emerged as a result of linguistic organization in 1956. It is surrounded by atleast seven states, and prominent are Rajasthan on its west, Uttar Pradesh in the north, Maharashtra in the south and Orissa and Other in the east.The state has a mixture of cultures - Rajput, Muslim, Maratha, British, Hindu etc. - as an impact of their respective rule. The literacy rates in this multi-cultural state is: 6% in 1951; 17% in 1961; 22% in 1971; 27.82% in 1981; and 43.45% in 1991. Its state language is Hindi.

Its library history is still unearthed and needs a few more generations to do this gigantic task. Malwa, the ancient capital of attraction in this region, had educational centres and libraries. Notable is the Palace library of Paramara Kings. The state has five regional public libraries, viz. Bhopal, Gwalior, Rewa, Indore, and Jabalpur. Each of these cities, has a historical importance. The princely states of Bhopal and Gwalior had their respective royal libraries, like Hamidia Public Library of Bhopal (now called Maulana Azad Central Library), Madhya Pustakalaya at Gwalior (1899), and Yuvaraj Sarwajanik Pustakalaya of

Ujjain (1914). The oldest public library in the state probably is the General Library at Indore (1954). The first government library was established by British government as Central Library at Gwalior in 1927. Like Kerala this state too has subscription libraries. There are 137 such libraries run by registered bodies.

Of the eleven universities in the state, the oldest is the Sagar University (f. 1946), but however it was Vikram University which was first to start degree course in 1957. Certificate courses are offered by the public library in Bhopal and Gwalior (f. 1958).

Madhya Pradesh Library Association (f. 1956), at Bhopal, is a leading body. Keeping in line with the need of regional language professional material, the Indore Library Association started a quarterly "Pustakalaya Sandesh" (f, 1967) (Mishra:1964; Wadikar:1988).

6.12 **Maharashtra**

The state lies in between Gujarat in the north west, Madhya Pradesh in the northeast, Andhra Pradesh and Karnataka on east, and Goa on the south west. It brought together the Greater Bombay/Bombay State/Bombay presidency and few other surrounding areas, called Maharashtra, (or big state) this state emerged in 1960. Historical records as back as those of Hieun Tsang refer to this name. The land of Marathi language, this state occupies a substantial portion of the Deccan Peninsula. The literary history of this language probably commences from 10th century, with an inscription in Marathi, at the Gomateshwara statue, Shravana Balegola (presently in Karnataka). Its literacy growth has been from 13% in 1951; 29.8% in 1961; 39.2% in 1971; 47.37% in 1981, to 63.05% in 1991, is comparatively better than other states, but requires much more effort.

The first library set up by the East India Company was in Bombay in 1715 (Kumar:1977:33). Of the present leading public libraries that were opened by the British prominent are: Literary Society of Bombay (f. 1805; also called Bombay Branch of the Asiatic Society), and Bombay General Library (f. 1830, now Peoples free Reading Room and Library). In the same period emerged the Victoria Technical Institute Library, Nagpur (1806). The Britishers also established a series of native (public) libraries. The first so far traced are at Bombay (1823) and Ahmednagar (1838). Among other prominent libraries are: Poona Sanskrit College (1821, later called Deccan College), Albert Edward Institute Cowasjee Dinshah Hall and Library, Poona (1875), Bai

Dinabai Nusserwanji Petit Trust Library, Bombay (1895), Mumbai Marathi Grantha Sangrahalaya (or Public Library), Bombay (1898), Servants of India Society Library, Poona (1910), and Sadar Muslim Library, Nagpur (1925).

The Library Development Committee, of the Government of Bombay, under A.A.A. Fyzee's Chairmanship, recommended a comprehensive library system. These formed a base for later developments in the state. The Government gave grants to public libraries, as a follow up. There is no separate State library. The Asiatic Society Library functions both as State Library and as a regional depository Library. Due to the recommendations of the Fyzee Report, the Government established three regional libraries at Poona, Dharwar and Ahmedabad in 1954-55. (Mahajan:1988).

The education for library profession started with certificate course offered by the library associations. The first such a course was offered in Poona in 1947. Bombay took the lead in introducing degree course as early as 1943. Today there are 19 centres offering certificate courses and seven universities offering degree in library science.

There have emerged many professional bodies in the state. Probably, the first professional body in the state was the Maharashtra Library Association (1921). To uplift the public library services strives a professional body Maharashtra Rajya Granthalaya Sangha (f. 1962). There is another association which strives for the up lifting of Health science libraries. Yet another works for College Libraries. Only due to consistent attempts the Maharashtra Public Library Act, 1967 was passed. However, there is no cess levied under the Act. The State Library Council consisting of the representatives of the library associations take policy decisions. Maharashtra is the fourth state to have library legislation. Literature in the regional language has been increasing to meet the professional demands (Mishra:1964; Mahajan:1988; Chahande:1991).

6.13 **Manipur**

This is one of the northeastern states which was established in 1972. While this state has its history since 10th century, the historical records really begin from 1762 when its ruler Raja Jai Singh, signed a Treaty with the East India Company. It was independent from British control till 1890. It is situated in between Assam in the west, Nagaland in the north, and Myanmar in the east. It is largely isolated from the country.

The state language is Manipuri. It has had however, serious problems in retaining its literary heritage. For instance its vast literature was put to ashes (between 1707 and 1748) - during Vaishanvite influences - forcing it to undergo devastation for seven years, between 1819 and 1826. Its history of Library and literary traditions, then, must be both exciting and interesting. While formal education entered in the state around 1870s its history of royal libraries is as old 475 A C. We are told that its Royal Library was supervised by a council of learned (Pandit, *Loisang*). Its literacy growth rate has been 30 % in 1961; 32.9% in 1971; 41.9% in 1981; and 60.96% in 1991.

Its first public library, viz., Imperial Public Library started as a subscription based in 1938. It ceased functioning in 1960s. In 1950 started the Manipur Public Library, which was made State Central Library in 1958.

For a long time the professional training requirements of this state were met by neighbouring states. Its first university library emerged in 1980, and a degree course in library science in 1986. A certificate course was started by State Central Library in 1982. It has very little library literature in its regional language.

The Manipur Library Association was founded in 1987. The State has its library legislation, and this is called Manipur Public Library Act, 1988 (Singh:1988).

6.14 **Meghalaya**

This state, is in the northeastern corner of the state and was formed in 1972. North of it is Assam and on its south is Bangladesh. Meghalaya has a meaningful name in its historic background, (Megha= clouds, alaya= home). This natural position of the country was such that it never gave a home to a foreign ruler and largely managed their own government. They mostly remained secluded. The literacy growth patterns are 18.5% in 1961; 29.5% in 1971; 33.22% in 1981; and 48.62% in 1991. Its library history is far more recent, than other states. The year 1903 became significant in its history as in this year was opened a library by the then government of Assam in shillong. Its audience was supposed to be the government officials. This limitation by the user group resembles to some extent the Secretariat Library in New Delhi, and the Library of Congress in Washington D C.

After the formation of states, Meghalaya was separated from Assam in 1956. The Government library also came under the state of

Meghalaya in 1974. But part of the collection was taken away by the Assam Government. The State Central Library of Meghalaya emerged in 1956. Historically, a major public library based on subscriptions was founded in 1962, and it was called "Rabindra Smrita Granthalaya". The state has still to develop its own programme for education and training of Librarians. (Chandel:1988)

6.15 **Orissa**

This state is inbetween West Bengal on its east, Madhya Pradesh on its west, Bihar in north and on its south is Andhra Pradesh. The first language of the state is Oriya. The beginning of the literary history of this state is probably from the 11th century. Cultural history of this state goes back to hundreds of years. Prof Mahapatra says "Archaeological evidences reveal that there were libraries in the ancient Orissa (then called Utkal Kalinga) with Buddhists shrines and sculptures". Despite its long history it has had a slow progress in its literacy rate: 3% in 1951; 21.7% in 1961; 26% in 1971; 34.1% in 1981; and 58.55% in 1991.

The structure of Oriyan Caste System is of interest for library history. Next to the Brahmins is the class of Karanas (=the writer), who claim the Kshatriya status; with pen as their weapon rather than the sword). There is a need to search contribution of this class to literature and to the development of private libraries, if these writers maintained any personal collections. The oldest library recorded in history is Raghunandan Library at Puri (1821), among the colleges is the Ravenshaw College, Cuttack (1816). Among the loose-knit public libraries is a State Central Library named 'Hare Krishan Mahtab State Library' at Bhubanewsar. The state public library bill is long pending in the State Legislative Assembly.

Of all the professional associations, Utkal Library Association (f. 1944), is the oldest and the most popular. Teaching of library science at university level has commenced only recently. Of late literature for professionals in the regional language has also taken its shape. (Panda:1992; Mahapatra:1988).

6.16 **Punjab**

Punjab lies in the Northern part of the country. Jammu and Kashmir on north, Himachal pradesh in the east, Pakistan in the west, and it has many more states around. The word Punjab is derived from its geographical location. In Persian *Punj* means five and *ab* means water. Ibn Batuta is the first historic source referring to this land as a separate unit. The first language of the state is Punjabi. Punjabi literature appears to have originated in 12th century. The Punjabi writings of Baba Farid laid the ground for the Bhakti movement in this state and was appealing for both Hindus and Rajputs. Like Baroda and Gujarat, Punjab also received an American Librarian - Asa Don Dickinson - who organized and laid the ground for its library growth and development. He created the base for the development of university librarianship in India. He was the one who brought Dewey Decimal scheme and introduced open access system in the country.

Punjab that exists today was undivided before 1947 and was quite large and probably one of the most active states. Pre-partition activities include establishment of Punjab University library at Lahore (f. 1882); Punjab Library Association (f 1916); commencement of its official organ 'Modern Librarian' (1930-); and starting of another professional library journal '*Indian Librarian*' (1946-), by S R Bhatia, etc.

Dayal Singh Library was founded in 1908, in Lahore, later shifted to Delhi. Lala Lajpat Rai's Servants Of People Society and Tilak School of Politics Library was set up in 1921. After independence this library was shifted to Shimla, and thence to Chandigarh. It was Lala Lajpat Rai who named it Dwarka Das Library. Its educational and literacy rates are: 3% (in 1951); 24% {(in 1961) which then included Haryana}; 33.7% in 1971; 40.7% (in 1981); and 57.41% (in 1991).

Punjab Library Association founded in 1948 moved from Shimla to Chandigarh in 1952 and later to other place, with the formation of states–first Himachal Pradesh, which took over Shimla; and later Chandigarh, which itself became an independent Union territory.

Library literature in English started as early as 1915 when the American Library consultant published Punjab Library Primer. Later few books have appeared in Hindi and Punjabi to meet the growing regional demands for the professional literature (Mishra:1964; Singh:1991; Trehan:1988).

6.17 **Rajasthan**

In-between Haryana in its north, Madhya Pradesh on south, Uttar Pradesh in the northeast, and Gujarat in the south, this state lies on the western border of India. Despite it being in a desert it has had period of literary and library growth since a few centuries. This state which emerged from former state of Rajputana, has a long standing library history. Jaipur, incidentally was and is presently also its capital city.

There was always some literary contribution made by the ruling class. Maintaining libraries was probably the minimum they did, and in this they never failed. Palace libraries of Anup Sinhji at Bikaner, Raja Sawai Jai Singh II at Jaipur, and a few more in places like Jodhpur, Jhalwar, and Bharatpur, were famous and well maintained. It was in this state that the great sufi-saint Chishti lived last, in Ajmer. Here is his tomb, and it was due to this presence that Muhammed Ghori built the first Madrasa in the country in Ajmer. It was in 1191. The Madrasa without a library was unimaginable, and hence must have had a valuable and precious collection.

This former state of Rajputana must have had many educational and religious libraries, and whose history needs unearthing from all flowery anthologies of this land. The Rajputs took pride in education and learning and even their *harems*, imitating the Mughals, were no where less. It was the queen Jodha Bai who was the first to enter the Mughal family and promoted the feeling of brotherhood among the Muslims and Rajputs. Rana Khamba (d.1469) of Mewar, a famous ruler of India, was a poet and an man of letters. He had a good collection of manuscripts. In this period Jain monks took shelter in desert, along with their *granth bhandars*.

Maharaj Sawai Jai Singh II had a library, consisting of not only manuscripts, but also printed books. He added to his collection hundreds of printed books, between 1704 and 1716. The Maharaja Sawai Ram Singh (1835-1895) took a British Librarian, as consultant and advisor, Sir Frank Alexander Francis, to improve the library system. He worked as an advisor from 1866 to 1872. The Maharaja Public Library was established at Jaipur in 1866. Again, Sir Mirza Ismail as Prime Minister brought a new life for the library movement, in 1940s. He implemented the plans of Pratab Rai Mehta. Introduced by him was a scheme of village libraries and urban libraries. Children's section was started in 1944 in the Palace Library. It has published its catalogue of books, the first edition had appeared in 1883. Today this palace library building houses the State Central Library, at Jaipur.

Its educational status is in a low profile and this is evident from the literacy figures: 3% in 1951; 15% in 1961; 19% in 1971; 25% in 1981; and 38.81% in 1991.

Rajasthan Library Association (f. 1962) under Prof. Basheeruddin's presidentship made history. The same association made bigger strides under Presidents like N N Gidwani, Satish Chandra, and others. (Sharma:1988).

The first library science course was offered in 1956 by the state government. In 1961 was started the first degree course at the University of Rajasthan (f. 1947).

6.18 **Tamil Nadu**

This state was originally called Madras state, which emerged from the then existing Madras province and Madras presidency. It is located in the western coast of India. Madras as a city though important in the British annals was neglected at the cost of exploring Bombay and Calcutta (Shield:1977. p. iii). The language of the state is Tamil, and hence its name is land (=nadu) of Tamil. Being surrounded by Kerala in west, Andhra Pradesh in its north; Karnataka in the north west, it has also a newly born state, that of Pondicherry, on its northeast. Pondicherry, or Puduchcheri, in its original name, was a part of Tamil Nadu, but it requires time to write its own history. Library history of Tamil Nadu has had many ups and downs. While little is known of its age old history (civilization with a long and complex urban tradition), and of golden period of Tamil culture, the recent history has been very interesting.

Palace funded special collection is identified in the Tamil inscription, dated 1251, which belonged to Raja Raja Chola (985-1013). The library had in it collection Devaram Hyms of a seventh century saint. More so because it formed the base from where Ranganathan had his start.

Among its oldest existing libraries are the Saraswathi Mahal Library, Tanjore (flourished in 17th century); Madras Literary Society (f. 1818), Connemara Public Library (f.1896), Madras (the present State Central Library, and the fourth national copyright depository library); Fort St. George Library, Government Oriental Manuscript Library, Madras (1837), Adyar Library, Madras (1886), etc. Its educational history has developed quite rapidly in a century of British and French supported institutions. The literacy in this state has however not been compatible with this growth of academies. The literacy rate has been 18% {(in 1951) which included then Malabar, now in Kerala)}; 31% in 1961; 39.5% in 1971; 45.78% in 1981; and 63.72% in 1991.

The first university library in the state was opened in 1904, and that was Madras University Library, which had the first professional librarian in the person of Ranganathan himself in 1924. The education for librarians was first started in 1929 by the Madras Library Association, with the intention of initiating the lay towards the use of library. Madras University took over this course in 1931, and from 1937 it was made a regular post-graduate diploma. In 1961 it was re-named as Bachelor's degree.

Interestingly, Madras was the first state in the country to have the public library legislation in 1948. And the geographical boundaries of this covered Malabar, (i.e.,a portion of the present Kerala state), and remained so until the enactment of the Kerala Library Legislation in 1989. (Sarma:1991). The libraries and the profession in the state developed all through due to the sole efforts of the Madras Library Association (f.1928).

6.19 **Tripura**

Tripura emerged in 1956 as a Union Territory; and in 1972 it was declared as a state. It is surrounded by Manipur, Mizoram and Bangladesh.

The royal libraries of the state have long history. Only one known is the Palace Library established by Maharaja Bir Chandra Manikya Bahadur in the later half of 19th century. This was later named as Birchandra Public Library, and was taken over by state government in 1953. It became the State Central Library in 1973, and housed at State capital, Agartala. The library movement in whatever shape it existed, was all by the initiative of the government.

Its literacy was 2.3% in 1901, 42.1% in 1981 and 60.39% in 1991. Agartala is one of the leading cities with highest rate of literacy in India. The state has three library Associations, viz., Nikhil Tripura Granthagar Parishad; Library Employee's Local Committee; and Tripura Library Association (Chakravarty:1988; Sharma:1988).

6.20 **Uttar Pradesh**

This is the biggest state in India, in terms of population and size. It is situated as a heartland of the country in between Haryana, Himachal Pradesh in north, Rajasthan in west, Bihar in east and Madhya Pradesh in the south. Its libraries too have Hindu, Muslim and British impact. Its library system though entirely knew has had base from the eight hundred year rule of Muslims.

Of all the places in the state, Oudh and Lucknow, being capitals of the respective rulers, had a very strong library tradition. Kavindracharya, a scholar of repute, lived in Benaras, in sixteenth century, had a collection which dazzled the eyes of his guest Bernier, the European traveller. Another European traveller in 19th century was amazed by the royal library at Lucknow, and was very disturbed by the deteriorating state of affairs. He was a witness to the disposal of very valuable documents as thrash by the descendants of aristocrats and by those who were suppose to be care takers. He saw the royal collections of different families in Oudh and Lucknow.

It educational history has been more of traditional than modern. Its literacy growth has been evidently slow : 12% in 1951; 17.6% in 1961; 21.8% in 1971; 27.38% in 1981; and 41.71% in 1991. One of its oldest public libraries the Government Public Library (f. 1863), at Allahabad. A voluntary library run by British Indian Association is the Ammirud-Daula Library, at Lucknow (f.1882). This library had a drastic improvement when Wali Muhammed assumed his office as Honorary Secretary in 1937. He modernized the library. The State Government set up a Government Central Provincial Library in 1949 at Allahabad. Since its inception it was designated as a depository and recipient of books under Copyright Act, 1889. It was declared in 1958 as the State Central Library. Another public library (f.1863) was Allahabad. Since 1975 it is one of the Government libraries. The oldest Sanskrit College Library, Benaras was started in the country by British patronage in 1792. The leading Madrasa libraries in the country emerged in this state known as Nadwat-ul-Ulema, Lucknow (1893, library in 1901), Darul Uloom Deoband, Deoband (1866).

Of the 16 universities, only seven are offering degree courses in library science. The Uttar Pradesh Library Association offers four-month course. Another two-year course is also offered lately.

The leading and most active professional body is Uttar Pradesh Library Association (f.1935, active since 1965). *Lucknow Librarian* is its official organ which started appearing from 1962. *Pustakalaya Samvad Patrika*, is another Hindi news quarterly published by the Association (Shrivastava:1988; Sharma:1988).

6.21 **West Bengal**

West Bengal is surrounded by many states, including Other on its north and Orissa in south. Bengal originally one monolith land, was divided according to its populace, as Muslim majority land (East Bengal; the present Bangladesh) and Hindu majority land (West Bengal). Bengali is its official language. The word Bengal or Bangla is derived from the ancient Kingdom of Vangaor Ranga. The Sanskrit literature of 3rd century mentions this name.

There was a conscious behavior in King Devapala providing funds for duplication of literary works. He is said to have funded the project of making copies of a Mss. available in the Nalanda University, may be to store in his own palace library. The rulers of Bengal were also patrons of literature and art, and libraries did not fail either in receiving their rightful. The office of the Librarian was called Tahwildar, see for instance, the Nawab of Murshidabad, Muinuddawla had in his library Hafiz Asadullah, as Tahwildar.

The English landed first in this Eastern part of the country and the state has therefore a strong-British-tradition of libraries. But its mass education and adult literacy programmes have had a low profile. It literacy has risen from 9% in 1951; 29.3% in 1961; 33% in 1971; 40.88% in 1981; and 57.72% in 1991.

The missionaries, traders, and learned, each had reasons in establishing and maintaining libraries. The libraries which have made history and still flourish are Calcutta Branch of Asiatic Society Library (f. 1784; also called Asiatic Society of West Bengal), Calcutta Madrasa (f.1781), Calcutta Public Library (f. 1835; now the National Library of India); Serampore Public Library (1871); and Calcutta University Library (f. 1880). Dr. Nihar Ranjan Ray was appointed in 1937 the first Librarian of this University.

Bengal Library Association was founded in 1925 at Calcutta. Within a year of its establishment this body made considerable efforts to generate interest and awareness about libraries. It made use of public forums to create this momentum through over 25 radio lectures on libraries and library movement.

The first diploma course was started by Khan Bahadur Asadullah at the Imperial Library in 1935. The Bengal Library Association started its certificate course in 1937. Calcutta University started its diploma (later named as degree) in 1945. Literature in Bengali, the regional language, has been enormous, in books, journals, etc.

Bengal has been professionally, probably, most active as it was here that the Indian Library association and, the Indian Association of Special Libraries and Information centres,were formed; and a host of other professional activities, that were initiated.

West Bengal Public Libraries Act, 1979, simply gave a boost to the already motivated and spirited professionalism. In December 1988 it was this state which hosted a joint conference, probably for the first time in the professional history of India, of Bengal Library Association, Indian Library Association, and Indian Association of Special Libraries and Information Centres (Fazle Kabir:1989; Saha:1988).

7

CONCLUSION

When one surveys the rich and longstanding history of libraries in India over the past two or more millennia, one cannot but be struck with the great diversity of collecting activities and the proliferation of libraries, especially in the 20th century. Building on the foundation of scholarly and princely collections, academic libraries, specialized libraries, and popular libraries have joined the array in more recent decades. In some respects all the types of libraries have come into existence in India that one finds in the most advanced countries on earth. However, despite how adequate they appear in descriptive tables and in organization charts, there is ample room for reasonable progress and a great distance to go to catch up with the best library systems, support, and practices experienced elsewhere.

One of the most striking holes in the library fabric of India are the public libraries. Their condition–in reality, as contrasted with public relations statements–is generally poor from the central state libraries to the city and village libraries and so on to the provision of library materials for the rural population. Public libraries in India are, in fact, still to be born, to be called "public" and to be called a "library", at least in the modern sense of user-centred, service-oriented, balanced-collections, centres of graphic records meant primarily for use. May God bless the state and central governments and inspire them to establish Junta libraries which should be proper expression for public libraries (Watkins, 1969).

While the modern period gave a free hand to British, there rule was of little significance to the masses since the native education and libraries did not receive much encouragement. An exception were the few learning centres and libraries which were sponsored by colonial interests. Why they were 'sponsored' is not an issue here. There were many reasons, most importantly to use imperial powers in a right fashion, in a right manner, and in a right time, while at the same time exploiting and draining much of the valuable literary resources to the

Mother country.

The modern library movement, and the increased tempo of library development, is clearly a phenomenon of the 20th century. While other nations experience similar exceptional development in this century, one seems to have expected more from India, because of its learned history. However, for India modernization of mind and spirit was postponed form the 16th century to 20th century. Despite a longstanding ten-century history of paper and over a four-century history of printing technology in India, the majority of Indian libraries even today exist in a middle-age scenario, in terms of acquisition and storage, with even poorer concentration on processing (packing and re-packing/content analysis), and least of all on dissemination.

A glance at the library situation reveals that the library orientedness is still lacking among the users, professionals, and the sponsors, alike. The participation of the government is only of a marginal level. Atleast sixty percent of population is still illiterate. In the states where library legislation has been brought in, literacy figures have no links with the period of library legislation. To quote from Professor Marshall "In surveying the national scene in India today, in the field of libraries, one cannot but feel depressed at the very discouraging panorama that presents itself, in most aspects, save a very few. For instance, in public libraries, the present situation is dismal and despairing. Years roll by, but the figures of public libraries continue to be stagnant. Of the different states of the Union, only four so far have initiated some efforts for the establishment of public libraries through library legislation. A recent study, however, has disclosed the fact that implementation of this legislation has failed to make an effective impact (Marshall:1973:230).

A common notion is that the longer the period of library legislation in a state, the higher the rate of literacy and library awareness must be. In fact, there is a need to study comparatively, why legislation has been brought in, and what is its impact in those states which have this Act. One more notion held by many is that library legislation brings support from the government–moral, financial and material. Another supportive factor, a notion that probably came from Ranganathan's thought, that library legislation would lead to networking and cooperative systems would appear in course of time. Have these results emerged in the way the promoters of library legislation envisioned? The answer is a simple negative. Legislation has not translated itself into support. The population clearly has not mandated public library service–or other types of library service–for that matter. The reasons for this situation, in comparison with the attitudes in some other rapidly developing countries, is difficult to explain and remains to be studied seriously.

Another issue is the role of the profession. If the issue involved is creating an information culture and a library culture how has the profession itself functioned to fulfil this role. Also are the questions of the ethics of profession, sociology of profession and the politics of profession. The profession has grown considerably and has on the whole performed well. There are, however many, issues and problems which our successors will have to tackle.

Further, the Indian Library profession has not yet decided as to what level it should go in extension activities. In some cases the Librarians have ventured to become specialists and in some other cases the possessive-mind of the traditional librarian is not willing to give up even clerical jobs, although giving up these clerical jobs, would allow the Librarian to devote for User-centred services.

Rajgopalan has rightly remarked, "It is generally, acknowledged that our libraries are under utilized in relation to investments being made on them. Non-use and low-use of libraries amount to wastage of facilities being made available. May be low literacy rate, lack of reading habits, etc. are the causes for low use from the side of patrons... User education programmes must be organized by libraries in a way that libraries are fully utilized" (Rajgopalan: 1987).

This hints at another matter that needs to be addressed through in-depth planning. That is, only twenty per cent of Indians are urban dwellers, and the remaining eighty per cent are rural dwellers. If library service is to be extended on a universal basis what is required is:

1) the society must be made conscious about the 'need of information';
2) the people should make the government feel that the emerging information society needs–apart from food, clothing and shelter, - information for survival, information for development, and information for progress; and
3) library professionals should assert their role positively in the society, create user-friendly situations, and be more user-based than collection-and-classification-based librarians.

Ranganathan's words about the reasons for the paucity of Indian library history, quoted in the opening lines of this book, should offer challenge for any historian or library professional. His words are not sacrosanct. Even if little interest in library history is evinced by historians at large, the profession can take up this search for the history of library and librarianship in India. What is required is inspiration and momentum to undertake this task. Compared to resources of yesterday, the profession today is mature enough and capable to achieve this activity by itself, rather than wait till Doomsday for some one else to cut the harvest. If Indian librarians cannot appreciate their history enough to rediscover, analyze, and recreate it, they need not wait expectantly for others to do so.

7.1 **Agenda for Research**

The basic agenda is writing of an exhaustive and comprehensive history of library and librarianship in India. While the present work has followed the broad time periods, any future history can be differently written: (a) it can be a history of dynasties and libraries in those times, (b) it can be by the advances in technology–the pre-inscriptional age, the post-inscriptional age, manuscript (before the use of paper) age, post-manuscript age, paper age and post-paper age, (c) by pre- printing and post-printing times, (d) history as seen from the eyes of travellers and their works, (e) history before and after the advent of Westerners (primarily Europeans) in India–the common notion is that the West 'caused' every advancement in science and technology in India. (f) Urban patterns versus the rural patterns of library growth, (g) impact of western educated elites on the growth of libraries *vis-a-vis* the effect of the anti-west campaigns who were against the use of English language and adoption of English culture and, (h) in the periods as Ranganathan suggests: Vedic, Buddhist, Muslim and Medieval, and we may add the later periods.

In short, whatsoever may be the classification in writing the past, history should be accurate, authentic, verifiable, reliable and unbiased. It should try to avoid the nineteenth century techniques of wilfully being carried away by western philosophies of writing history–which ultimately necessitated Independent India rewrite its own history. The issues involved in this context are: (1) identification of impact of factors/forces/precursors involved in the process of development; (2) establish a regular discussion group in the annual meetings of the national level library associations in the areas of public, academic and special librarianship; (3) publication of a serial to keep abreast of the progress in historiography and historic researches; (4) introducing in some library schools a course on library history; (5) search the role India has played in South Asia and in Asian context of Oriental, International and Comparative librarianship.

There are other agenda for the research and study. These are broad-based and require an area study approach in dealing with the following, for the purpose of highlighting the comprehensive nature of the field: Perform team research with historians in the subject area of (1) economics (to know the economic library history of the country, to identify the sources of funds for the different types of libraries, to study the patterns of growth and development in different economic periods–periods of high inflation, periods of recession, periods of normal conditions, periods of political crisis, etc., to know what types of subscription libraries originated in the British period and what is the present fate of such libraries– if they have survived how did they, and if they have modified their position as 'free' libraries what factors prompted them in changing their behaviour, and patterns of subscription and membership in these libraries); (2) art (to know what role has art played in the library history, or to know the place of art history in the context of library and its location, structure, design,etc.); (3) sociology (to link up aspects like literacy, reading, literary patronage, educational patterns, class and tribal differences and the result on the use or non-use of libraries [where entry of one community or communities has serious restrictions], and the role of the book in the Indian social scenario of the past : with special reference to the family life and its behaviour – did educated parents encourage book habits? did reading form a part of the daily routine? did reading get restricted to light material ?); and (4) Politics (How far is 'book burning' linked with religion? Was there any impact of political forces in book burning or it was always spiritual? and did it exist in the periods of 'benevolent' rules–periods when India had art and literature 'patronizing' kings ? or is it a fact that political historians never thought about such factors ?).

At a micro level there is a need to study, for instance: (1) what was the function and role of the library–when their was a mix up of roles with museums, archives, and records department, (2) functional levels in each period and in each dynasty in the Indian history, (3) growth and development of each professional organization and its role in the country's overall professional outlook, (4) level and degree of professionalization in the education and in library schools–as it has evolved,

(5) legal aspects of library and librarianship: copyright rules, censorship, freedom of expression, library legislation, role of governments, role of individuals, and role of associations, (6) professional vs. non-professional's–level and degree of–involvement in generation of professional literature, (7) patterns of collection development in libraries: traditional vs. modern, historic collection vs. non-historic, oriental vs. occidental libraries in India, academic vs. public libraries, etc. (8) state-of-the-art of manuscript collections: acquisitions, processing, storage and dissemination patterns: do any of these differ from city to city, from state to state, from language to language, and so on, (9) What traces exist of the bibliographic tradition of the past, and if it exists what were the developments in ancient, medieval and modern periods, (10) nature of book trade, publishing, marketing and links with the profession– how strong and how week, where do the twain meet, (11) physical bibliography as it evolved in the country, (12) Classification and cataloguing patterns in different traditional and modern libraries, and how far did these libraries accept the Ranganathan's model and how far is non-Indian, (13) did the libraries in the past adopt any sort of marketing strategy to sell their goods, if yes what patterns and trends prevailed, if no, what were the reasons for the management to be so passive in catering to needs of those for whom the library exists–for whom is all the show and with out the user how the existence is justified, (14) to what level and degree is the historic aspect covered in the library schools–bearing in mind that no school offers the history of library as a separate course.

It is befitting to end the book with a quote from Prof. Marshall, to whom this book is dedicated:

"If I may be pardoned a concluding personal note, I am one of those very fortunates, who, long years ago, found his work. The long working life that the benign providence ordained for me in this profession has been to me a very rewarding experience. Let me wish all my fellow professionals the same good luck and the same happiness that has been my reward in the profession. Experience tells me, however, that to attain that happiness, a changed approach and a changed outlook are necessary. And as a parting gift, let me indicate the secret of that changed outlook and the key to that happiness, in the words of an Urdu poet, rather freely translated:

Mita de apni hasti ko
Agar martaba chahe to,
Ke dana khak se mil kar
Gul-o-gulzar hota hay.

(Fold up your ego, if you wish for respect and reverence. For, the seed, only when it mixes with dust, sprouts into a tree or blooms into a flower)".

Presidential address delivered by Professor Marshall at the Eight Conference of Indian Association of Special Libraries and Information Centres, Bombay, 1969.

APPENDICES

APPENDIX I

SELECTED CHRONOLOGY OF NOTEWORTHY EVENTS

(Material has been selected from P S G Kumar's *Indian Library Chronology, Herald of Library Science, Indian Librarian, Modern Librarian* and few other sources)

I. **Ancient India** (3000 B C -1206 A D)

3000 B C Script–Mohenjodaro
The script in use was picto-phonographic, i.e., non-alphabetical, the writing runs normally from left to right, exceptionally from right to left in the case of first lines, resembling the semitic/Arabic languages

2000 Script–Boghaz Koi Inscription
This was discovered in 1907 by Dr. Wincklev, which speaks about the existence of writing (or literature), and the presence of Aryans in India by 14th century B C.

1000 Southern India
Sage Agastaya introduced both Sanskrit language and Aryan culture; his disciple composed the first Tamil grammar, the *Tolkappiyam.*

1000 Vedas–Documented
Vedas were written by Vasukra, a Kashmiri Brahmin, ending the oral transmission practice.

850-700 Script–Brahmi
The parent of all the modern Indian Alphabets, Brahmi, was imported in Western India through the sea route.

8th Century Education–Contents
The educational process was known to be by Sruti-Smriti, with no reference to teaching of alphabets.

8th Century Education–Centres
Taxila, Kuru, Panchala, Videha, Matsya, Usinara, Naimisranya and Kasi.

6th Century Script–Kharoshti
A form of Aramaic imported in North-West India, during Persian rule; script used on stone, coins, and metal plates; written in irregular, elongated and cursive script, this was also written from right to left.

5th Century Script–Word Game
Viniya Pitika and *Nikyas* mention a list of games of which one is called *Aksharika* (lettering). It is the guessing at letters traced in the air in a play-fellow's back.

4th Century Writers
Panini refers to the existence of *Lipikara* (scribes or authors); implying the existence of a literary genre, and presence of different kinds of authors (viz., *Mantrakara, Padakara, Gathokara, Slokakara*, and *Sabadkara*). Panini also makes a mention of the principles of 'book' making as *Krita Grantha* and *Adhikritya Krite Grantha*, and planning of treatises as *Tantra Yukti*. His grammatical *Sutras* use the words *akshara* (or alphabet) and even *lekhaka* (or writer).

4th Century Nearchus
'Paper' was made out of cotton, reports Nearchus, a Greek traveller, and admiral of Alexander the Great. Ink was used to write on wood or cloth.

327 Writing Material–Stone
Greek presence in India was recorded by the erection of twelve altars of square stone in Indian scripts as a monument of Alexander's expedition.

325-321 First Indian Empire
Chandragupta Maurya inaugurated the first Indian empire, which included a major portion of the Indian subcontinent. In the end of his

reign he converted to Jainism, which didn't evince any influence on Jainism, as he became an ascetic. Kautiliya, was his prime minister, who is ascribed to as an author of a treatise on political economy, viz., *Arthashastra.*

320 Jain Literature
The First Jain Council which met at Patliputra framed the Jain Canons.

2nd Century Multiplicity of Scripts
Lalitha Vistara, mentions along with ink, and pen the existence of 64 scripts "Which is the writing Sir, which you wish to teach me? Is it the Brahmi, Kharosthi... (of the) 64 kinds", (a question put by Buddha to his guru Viswamitra).

2nd Century Manuscripts–Palm Leaf
Palm leaves came in use in South India for writing.

2nd Century Writing Material
Writing with ink on a relic vase is traced at a stupa of Andheri; ink-pots with ink stains were found at Harinarayanpur (West Bengal).

268-231 Inscriptions–Rock
Asoka the Great (268-231) had his edicts engraved on rocks, in Prakrit (in the Indian boundaries, and in Greek and Aramaic in the areas where his empire extended); his sole ambition was the expansion of Buddhism and hence he was a major source for the growth and spread of that religion and its sacred literature; one of his rock inscriptions became the official emblem of India since 1947.

1st Century B C Writing Material–Golden Ink
Use of golden ink in a Kharosthi manuscript, is evident from a stupa near Taxila.

1st Century A C Script–Kharosthi
Kharosthi lipi was found on the Bhurja Bark of the Dharmapada from Khotan.

1st Century Language–Prakrit
Hala, a ruler of Satavahana (dynasty of Andhra), wrote *Gadha Sapta Sati* in Prakrit.

1st Century Writing Material
Brahminical use of birch bark, palm and *bhuja patra* was common in North-West India; Buddhists used wood.

1st Century Writing Material–Pen
Copper pen with point divided by a cut (as in nib), found at Taxila.

2nd Century Language–Telugu
Inscriptions, in Prakrit and Sanskrit, included Telugu words.

2nd Century Literature–Tamil
Sangam literature of Tamil started appearing.

2nd Century Writing Material–Copper Plates
Sacred writings in the period of Kanishka were on copper plates.

2nd Century Sanskrit Literature
The greatest Sanskrit poet and play writer Kalidasa is said to have composed his works in this period.

2nd Century Archives
Satraps of the Upper Deccan registered all documents and preserved in the *Phalka-Vara* (or state record office).

200-300 Writing Material–Clay Tablets
These were used in the Gupta period.

280 Education–Centre
End of Taxila University and its Library.

3rd Century Writing Material–Bricks
Inscription on brick of 11-1/2 × 9-1/2 inch have been traced, one such was at Gopalpur village (Gorakhpur District, Uttar Pradesh).

3rd Century Writing Material–Leather
Use of leather as a writing material commenced.

300-400 Painting
Vishnu Dharma-Mahapurana elaborately discusses the rules for making chitras (or painting).

300-750 Classical Age of India
The migration of Buddhist influences and reduction of Jain political support saw the emergence of the Gupta's, whose patronage of art, architecture and literature was hitherto unparalleled.

4th century Centres of Learning Library
The Nalanda University had its library in three buildings: Ratnasagar, Ratnadadhi and Ratnaranjaka. Probably, Ratnadadhi, was nine storeyed.

414 Fahien
Fahien, the Buddhist Chinese traveller, left the country after collecting large number of manuscripts on Buddhism. He went to many places, including Patliputra and Tamluk monasteries.

454 Jains–Canon
Famine and massacre of Jain monks led to a threat of extinguishing to literature. Hence the Council, called Vira-Samvat met at Vallabhipur, (in Kathiawar, Rajasthan), to arrange the sacred literature. This event is called *Pusthakarohana of the Jain Agamas* (or the reduction of the Jain canons). Tirujnana Sambandar a Tamil Saivaite destroyed many jain scriptures in South India and killed many monks to revive Hinduism.

484-528 Library in Literature
A major contribution to Sanskrit literature appeared in this century. Kautiliya's *Arthashastra* (a work of major importance in Sanskrit; the kernel of the book was originally written in 320's B C, but interpolations continued till 528 A C) mentions the designation of the officer (or adhyaksh) responsible for the for the collection of manuscripts: *Nibhanda Pustaka-Sthana*. This work mentions about the state-of-the-art of the legal and royal documents of the Malwa kings, who were exposed to attacks by the Huna(s). It also speaks of wooden shelves used for storage of manuscripts.

6th Century Writing Material–Aguru Bark
In *Bana*'s Harsha Charitra (which is first of the major historical biographies in Sanskrit), we find that King Bhaskaravarman sent presents to Harsha Vardhana, which included anthologies written on the bark of *Aguru* trees.

6th Century Huna(s) Invasion
Huna invasions lasted for over a hundred years. King Mihirakula, a Huna and a patron of Saivism, is recorded in the Buddhist tradition as uncouth and extremely cruel for his destruction of their monasteries and libraries.

559 Library–Funds
Maitraka Monastery at Vallabhi (now Wala, Maharashtra) received a grant from King Guhasena I.

7th century Writing Material–Brass
Brass inscriptions, particularly in Jain *Upasarayas* (or Temples), found place on pedestals.

629-642 Hieun Tsang
This Buddhist Chinese traveller informs us of the preservation technique: Kanishka got transcribed the *Tripitaka* Texts on copper plates, placed these in stone boxes, and got a *stupa* erected on it. He informs about the then existing script which had 47 words. He also informs about spacious reading rooms in monastery libraries, observes that the kings appointed a person specifically for keeping of records. While he visited many academies, he spent probably longer time in the palace library of the Kushana King, Kanishka in Kashmir.

672-685 Itsing
Itsing, the Buddhist Chinese traveller (the last of the trio-resource-persons, with Fahien and Itsing on the history of ancient India), informs about the fine and costly paper used for religious purpose, mentions the existence of text books both for basic and specialized education, describes minutely about the pooling at one place of scriptures and commentaries for the sue of the monks. He maximized the use of the libraries, carried copies of four hundred manuscripts from Nalanda, and many more from others.

708-715 Entry of Muslims
The warriors entered into India from Sind, Sufis too entered the country from North, the traders however were used to the sea route and all of them came from the western and southern coasts.

9th century Script
Emerged the Sanskrit alphabet, a distinct form other than the Brahmi script (Davids, 1903, p.155)

825 Malayalam
With the Kollam era appeared a distinct language 'Malayalam', along with a distinct geographical unit 'Kerala'.

The earliest inscription in this language is the Tiruvitamkot stone inscription of 1373.

10th Century Bengali
It evolved through Sanskrit and Prakrit. Proto-Bengali character was a peculiar cursive script and developed a little later out of Nagari script, in next century. By 16th century Bengali was enriched with Persian words. The first prose work *Pratapaditya Charitra* appeared in 1801.

10th Century Muslim Public Library
Sayidia Library of Deccan was founded. It flourished till recently, being a world famous centre of Oriental collection.

983 Marathi
First inscription is traced in Shravana Belgola (Karnataka). First book '*Dayaneshwari*' a treatise on *Bhagvad Gita* appeared in 13th century. The first printed book appeared in 1805, entitled *Balabodha Muktavali*, a translation of *Aesop's Fables.*

1000-1100 Kashmiri
It evolved out of the *Apabrahmsa* prevalent in the valley. Later it adopted the *Sarda* script in 13th century; then also appeared the easiest known work '*Mahayana Prakasa*' in pure Kashmiri.

1089 Writing Material–Indian Paper
Paper manuscripts appeared (Marshall, 1983)

II. **Medieval India** (1206-1757)

12th Century Script–Nagari
Prevailing in north India, it moved to south Indians Nandi Nagari.

12th Century Oriya
The language of Odisa or Oriya/Oria saw the emergence of its literature. Its retilineal script, developed into curvilinear form by 14th century.

12th Century Printing–Stone Block
Stone inscription at Kamala Maula Mosque of Dhara (Rajasthan).

12th Century Librarian–Status
At Nagai, the library staff were given the status and pay equal to that of the faculty, as the librarian was also supposed to be a guide for the students.

12th Century 'Burning of Libraries'
The Somapuri monastery was destroyed by a fire, it was renovated by Monk Vipulasrimitra.

12th Century Writing Material–Metal Plates
This became a popular source for written communication.

12th Century Persian
Emergence of this Language and Literature in India.

12th Century Duplication of Manuscripts
Sri Siddharaja Jayasimhadeva appointed three hundred scribes. He ordered 1,25,000 copies to be made of a text book useful for the students.

1191 Madrasa Library
Muhammed Ghori set up the first Madrasa Library, under the royal patronage at Ajmer (Rajasthan).

13th Century Assamese
The earliest extract work in this language '*Prahlada Charita*' appeared. Beeranji or Prose Chronicle took its birth with the initiation of Ahoma Kings.

1290 Muslim Librarian
Jalaluddin Khalji appointed Amir Khusro (d.1325) as the first Palace Librarian in the Delhi Sultanate period. This poet laureate of Hindustani (later Urdu), who carried the title of Prince of Poets continued to serve even the two consecutive successors.

14th Century Endowment Library

The sufi-saint Nizamuddin Auliya (1325) lived in Delhi, and as a philanthropic practice his library became after him a property of the *Wakf* (i.e., endowment or Trust). It was open for all. Muslim Librarianship has many samples of the Endowment libraries.

14th Century Mosque Libraries

This library attached to a Mosque or situated near the mosque was the only and the first kind of public library medieval India experienced (Marshall, 1983).

14th Century Mushaf-Bardar

The Librarian of the Delhi Sultanate reportedly was at times designated as *Mushaf-Bardar.*

1351-1388 Firoz Shah's Sanskrit connexion

The 1300 titles found in Nagarkot Temple library, were by his order translated into Persian. He didn't Burn Libraries, rather developed many.

15th Century Education–Physical Bibliography

Sultan Zainul Abideen, of Kashmir, established technical schools where people were taught paper making, book binding and other allied arts.

1526-1530 Mughal Imperial Library

Babur founded this library. It formed the main collection of the Mughals, and each of the subsequent rulers did possess personal collections too, in the *Harem.* The *Shuhrat-i-Am* (or public works department built Madrasas and Madrasa Libraries

1526-1530 Khat-e-Baburi

Babur a literary genius, evolved his own style of writing called *Khat-e-Baburi*, or *Babur-i-Hand* (writing).

1556-1605 Akbar's Contribution

Akbar established the Imperial Library on a sound footing: he classified, catalogued, appointed people of merit to different tasks in the library, acquired books from all possible means, established a department of libraries, the Head of the library was called *Nazim* or *Mutamad* and the deputy was called *Darogha* or *Mohtamim.*

1556 Printed Book–European Language
The first known book is St. Xavier's *Doctrina Christa* printed in Portuguese language at Goa.

1577-1578 Printed book– Indian Language
The first printing in Indian characters was said to be done at Ambalakkadu in Cochin.

1578 Printed book–Translation
A Tamil Translation of *Doctrina Christa* by Harique Henriques was published. Fr. Souza writes "This is the first printed book which India saw born in its own land".

17th Century Urdu
Emerged the language called Hindustani, with a mixture of Hindi, Arabic, Persian and Turkish words. In the beginning it was called *Zaban-e-Urdu-e-Mualla* (or the language of the exalted camp), with a later simpler forms from *Zaban-e-Urdu* and simply Urdu. Probably the first Urdu printed book appeared in 1804, as a translation of Persian version of *Hitopadesa* or Indian Ethics, printed at Hindustani Press.

1604 or 1605 Book Exhibition
Jesuits arranged an exhibition of their books to the Governor of Lahore.

1715 Library Catalogue
Ziegenbalg prepared an inventory of manuscripts in his library (situated at Tranquebar); it contained 119 books by Hindu authors; 21 by Roman Catholic authors and 14 by himself.

1739 Nadir Shah
His invasion and loot of valuable materials, including the peacock Throne, and illustrated manuscripts, was only one of the last nails in the process of decline of the Mughal empire.

III. **Modern (British) India** (1757-1947)

1767 News Paper
It appeared in Calcutta by the efforts of William Bolt.

1770 Public Library

A public library was run by Mr. John Andrews, at the Old Fort, Calcutta; this library circulated books; and circulated its catalogue, also sold the books like a book store.

1780 Weekly

A weekly Newspaper *The Bengal Gazette* was published by an Irish person, James Augustus Hicky, with a self-quote: "A Weekly paper open to all parties, but influenced by none".

1780 Calendar

Rustom Caresajee of Bazar Gate Street in Bombay printed the first calendar.

1781 Oriental Studies Centre

Calcutta Madrasa was the first British inaugurated institution, founded by Warren Hastings the Governor General of India. Consequently emerged in Banaras a Sanskrit College in 1792, a was founded by Jonathan Duncan.

1784 Oriental Public Library

Royal Asiatic Society of Calcutta was opened by the British, which later became Asiatic Society of Bengal. Its purpose was to provide an access to library, with limitations of the types of users and limitations of subscriptions. In 1788 it started its official journal *Asiatic Researches*, which stooped at last in 1939.

1792 Multilingual Periodical

Bombay Courier was printed in English, Marathi and Gujarathi.

1800 Paper Industry

First paper mill emerged in Calcutta, with the personal involvement of Mr. Carey. He was a source for the existence of the Carey Mission School at Serampore, providing education in modern subjects.

1805 India Office Library

The Court Directors wrote to the Governor General that the Seringapatnam Collection (of Tipu Sultan) was preserved in the Company's Library at Calcutta. This formed the basic stock round which the Company's library later known as India Office Library developed.

1806 Science Library

A science library was established by the Victoria Technical Institute Library, Nagpur.

1808 Registration of Libraries

The British Government in Bombay Presidency started a scheme for registering libraries to which copies of books to be published from the "Funds for the Encouragement of Literature" were to be given.

1811 Extension activities

Lord Minto ordered public librarians to serve the college community in the respective areas.

1813 Funds–British

While renewing the Charter of the East India Company, The British Parliament declared that "it is the duty of the country to promote the interest and happiness in India", and by legislation empowered the Company to spend not less than a lakh of rupees on the revival and encouragement of learning.

1817 College

Raja Ram Mohan Roy was one of those who opposed the opening of the Oriental Centres by the British. He himself pioneered the cause of eradicating literacy in the country and resolved to open the first collegiate institution on western lines in the country. It was Hindu College, at Calcutta.

1818 Literary Society Library

Madras city had this first literary society library, it is today the oldest public library in the country.

1818-1831 Calcutta Library Society

This society tried to its best to market itself and soon grew into prominence. It received media coverage too. It was a public library limiting its access to subscribers. But it closed in 1931.

1818 School Book Society

To publish school books and meet the continuing demand for school books this School Book Society was opened as an Indo-European enterprise.

1819 Old Hindi

The first printed book of Old Hindi (Braj Bhasha), *Sudamacharita* was printed in Calcutta at Sanskrit Press.

1820 Publishing Society

Mehtaji Durga Ram, a leading social reformer, started the "Pustaka Prasaraka Mandali", a tract publishing society with its litho press in Bombay.

1832 Scientific Periodical

Journal of Asiatic Society, Bengal was the earliest scientific periodical.

1832 Kannada

A mix type of Telugu and Kannada type faces provided the basis for the first book, *Desantriya Prayanammu*, a translation of *Pilgrim's Progress*, at Mission Press, Bellary.

1835 Access to All

The Hindu College (when it was also called Presidency College), was thrown open to the non-Hindus. The increasing number of the users required appointment of a Librarian. His salary was rupees thirty per month. This was the first appointment of a Librarian, in a modern Indian institution.

1835 Medical College

The Calcutta Medical College Library was established, as first professional college.

1835 National Library of India

The seeds of the future national library were sown in this year by opening the Calcutta Public Library, which was amalgamated with other collections in 1903 to become Imperial Library and finally in 1948 it became the National Library of India.

1835 Indian Press Enactment

This allowed freedom of expression in the country and a freedom to own a press by an Indian, which brought a drastic difference in the number of presses owned by Indians henceforth.

1837 'Library Habit Prize'

Lord Auckland declared this prize for the students who received the greatest benefit from the use of the library. In 1849 the condition for award was modified with the introduction of an examination of the subject in which the student had read.

1851 Prisoners' Prize

Dr. Walker introduced this in Agra Jail in 1851. Various concessions were granted to induce the inmates towards education. Books were offered as prizes as an incentive to future applications. It was a system of mutual instruction.

1853 Presses and Publications

The Bengal Government asked the District Magistrates to make available requisite information to Government about native presses established in their respective jurisdictions and the publications brought out by them.

1854 British Policy

The British Government in its resolution of Jan 11, 1854 expressed its desire to establish libraries and extend reading facilities to larger district areas.

1856 Request for Copyright Provision

The Court of Directors requested the Government to direct to have the India Office library supplied with one copy of each work of every description in original Bengali, published by the native presses of Calcutta.

1857 Sepoy Mutiny

The British army pundered Bareili and Oudh libraries after the revolt (Dalvi:1989:251).

1867 Press and Registration Act

Press and Registration of Books Act was passed; the Act provided that every publication must have the printer's name and address, and also that of the publisher, printed on it. One copy of the book be sent to England, and two copies to the Government for information.

1885 Theosophical Society Library

Col. Olcott sowed the seeds of this library. It became later famous as Adyar Library and Research Centre. It is an important resource centre of Indological studies (Kaula:1989:119)

1885 Librarian Honoured

Sri Nanda Kishore Singh, Librarian of the Maharaja Public Library, Jaipur, was made a member of the State Council, the Supreme Executive Body in the state.

1885 Calcutta Municipal Library

Minister Mackenzee submitted a plan to convert the Calcutta Public Library into a purely municipal library free to the public. The Government approved his plan.

1886 Punjab Public Library

A Commission was appointed on the Punjab Public Library, Lahore. The report was favourable on its usefulness, the Government sanctioned a special grant and also commended it to local bodies throughout the province.

1890 Amendment of Press and Registration Act

The Act of 1867 was amended giving a provision to three copies to be delivered to the Government of British India free of cost. There were more Acts passed in 1911, 1914 and 1922, modifying the details. But it was in 1954 was the passing of Delivery of Books (Public Libraries)Act which made four depositories at the national level

1901 Union List of Serials

List of Scientific Periodicals in the Bombay presidency was brought out.

1901 Training Programme

The first in service training programme started at Calcutta Public Library.

1902 Deputy Librarian

The Syndicate of the Calcutta University appointed an additional graduate assistant to look after tits library on a scale of Rs 50-6-80, the person to be appointed being required to give a security deposit of Rs. 1000.

1903 Imperial Library
Imperil Library Act was passed, and the founder subscribers were paid Rs. 500 each as compensation for the transfer of the ownerships; the basic aim was to transfer it to a library of reference and to make a repository of every work written about India. John Macfarlane was the first Librarian of the Imperial Library.

1904 Indian Universities Act
This Act was passed. It contained statutory provision for the universities to erect, equip, and maintain university libraries.

1906-1907 Mitra Mandal Libraries
A society of friends (*mitr*) worked on this project successfully by sharing monetary resources to run libraries in 150 parts of the Gujarat State.

1908 Library Directory
A List of Most Important Libraries in India was published.

1910 Borden's Achievements (US)
W A Borden is the first American and the initiator of Indo-American Library exchange, and the first importer of Dewey's professionalism (being a student of the first batch of Albany School started by Dewey in 1887). Borden invented a classification system known as Borden Classification Scheme and Alphabetical Author's Surnames. He was the state library advisor on the public libraries; he introduced the first library school in the country in 1911, the first school which had ten men and women participants, and which by chance initiated the women's education era in the profession too; he started the first network of libraries at the state level; he initiated the practice of public carrying books by travelling libraries for free services in villages; he contributed for the emergence of the first professional serial *Library Miscellany* (1912, it stopped in 1919); and he started the first local library group, i.e., Library Association, Baroda

1914 Library Conference
The first library conference was organized by the first 'State' level Association: viz., Andhra Desa Librarians Association.

1914 Library Literature

The emergence of Indian books started with B H Mehta's, *Hints on Library Administration in India.* This was published in Surat. This is the first Indian contribution to the field.

1915 Foreign Hand

Asa Don Dickinson was the first foreigner who wrote his book and got it published in India, i.e., the Library Primer. He was an American advisor and later the Librarian of Panjab University.

1915 Training Abroad

H H Das was the first to go for training in Librarianship. He went to University of London.

1915 Library Directory

Andhra Desa Library Association brought out its Directory of Andhra Libraries. This was the first reference book in area studies.

1915 Telugu Library Literature

The first publication in this language was the serial *Granthalaya Sarvasamu*. It was the official organ of the Andhra Desa Library Association.

1916 Honorary Librarian

The first Honorary Librarian appointed was Prof. Jadunath Sarkar, at Banaras Hindu University, Banaras (Varanasi, U P).

1918 Saraswathi Mahal Library

This library at Tanjore was opened to the public and a Managing Committee was appointed.

1918 Library Pilgrimage

The Andhra Desa Library Association started the first Library Pilgrimage in Bhimavaram Taluk (West Godavari Distt., Andhra Pradesh).

1918 National Library Conference

The first All India Library Conference met at Lahore, under the leadership of Asa Don Dickinson.

1918 National Public Library Conference

The first All India Public Library Conference met at Madras which was convened by Andhra Desa Library Association. Khudalkar of Baroda presided the meet, and it was resolved to form the All India Public Library Association (f. 1920). It had its headquarters at Vijayawada. Its official organ *Indian Library Journal* appeared between 1924 and 1927.

1919 Regional Language Books

The first book in the regional language was published in Telugu in 1919 *Pracheena Granthalaya Charitra* (history of ancient libraries) by Kolachalam Srinivasa Rao.

1924 Ranganathan's Librarianship

He was appointed as Madras University Librarian and sent for training to London. On his return he assumed his job.

1927 Documentation List

Ranganathan initiated the first Documentation List. It was on New Radiation, and distributed to the audience at a lecture of Sir C V Raman.

1926 Extension activities–University Library

Madras University Library, started delivery of books at the residence of the graduate members of its library in the city on payment of a rupee. The next year saw the extension further to under graduates in the city and to all faculty even out side the city.

1927 Five Laws of Library Science

He expounded these to the audience of Annual Conference of South Indian Teachers Union.

1929 University Library–Open Access

Madras University Library followed the open access system.

1929 College Librarians Association

Ratanchand Manchand, Librarian Hailey College, Lahore with the assistance of other college librarians formed The Fifteen Libraries Club.

1930 Independent Library
Connemara Public Library (f. 1890) was separated from the Museum and released from the control of the Superintendent of Government Museum.

1930 All Asia Educational Conference
This had a section on Library Service. The Conference met at Banaras, the library session was presided by N M Dutt. The conference in its resolutions included the suggestion to the Inter-University Board for operating a scheme of inter-university loan of books and bound volumes of periodicals, a union catalogue and standardization of pay scale for university libraries.

1931 Malayalam Library Literature
Grantha Viharam, is the first title published in this language, as a serial. Intended to be a quarterly,its second issue never appeared. This serial was the organ of Samastha Kerala Pustakalay Samithi, and under the guidance of C C Kunji Rama Menon in Trichur.

1931 Model Public Library Bill
Madras Library Bill and Bengal Library Bill were introduced in the respective Legislative bodies. Madras Library Bill got the support and appreciation from the Governor of Madras Sir George Stanley and even the members of the body, like Swami Venkatachalam Chettiar, Basheer Ahmed Saeed, and Hameed Khan.

1931 Reading Habits–School
Madras Library Association started a scheme of awarding a prize to the best essay by a school student, with a pre-condition that the prizes were to be given for three consecutive years and later this programme to be taken up by participating schools.

1931 Mobile Library Service
A free travelling library service was started, by Madras Library Association to serve the villages in a radius of 82 miles from the town.

1931 Prison Library
Madras Library Association started the first prison library.

1931 Mailing Discount
The Madras Library Association got an agreement with the Local Railway Companies at Madras to charge half-rate for book parcels, for books loaned by libraries to libraries and individuals.

1931 School Curriculum–Library Hour
The Director of Public Instruction in Madras required all schools to provide one hour for library, in every week.

1933 Rural Library Service Conference
The All India Public Library Association arranged the first All India Rural Library Service Conference in Madras which was presided by Dr M O Thomas. Here was formed an association, All India Rural Library Service Association whose President was Dr. Thomas and Secretary Hilda Wood.

1933 Government of India Libraries Association
This was formed at Delhi.

1933 Colon Classification
This was the first comprehensive Indian scheme, and was the master child of Ranganathan.

1933 Indian Library Association
It was formed at Calcutta during the All India Library Conference. Its President was Dr M O Thomas and Secretary Dr. K M Asadullah.

1933 Mahatma Gandhi and Seth Maneklal Library
Mahatma Gandhi laid the foundation stone of this library at Ahmedabad.

1933 D P I's Order for Library Period
The order issued stated: At least one period of library work every weak in all schools of Madras.

1933 Title 'Granthalaya Udayama Pitamaha' Conferred
This was conferred for the services rendered by M N Amin to develop and improve rural and travelling libraries in Baroda.

1934 Marathi Books

Literature in regional language of Maharashtra was initiated by R S Parkhi's book *Granthalaya Sastracha O, nam*; or ABC of Library Science.

1934 Freedom of Expression–1st Amendment

The Indian Wireless Telegraph Act, passed. It prohibits the unauthorized recording and public communication of broadcast emissions and re-broadcasts.

1934 RAJARATNA–Award

Newton M Dutt was given this award by the Maharaja of Baroda.

1934 Catalogue Code

The world's first catalogue code was brought out by Ranganathan.

1934 Commercial Indexing Service

The Guide to Indian Periodical Literature appeared as a first key to the literature in humanities and social sciences, from Gurgaon in Haryana.

1935 Floating Library Service

Central Library of Pedapalam (Andhra Pradesh) started serving in boats to passengers between 30 villages.

1935 Indian Librarianship Abroad

Kumar Munindra Deb Roy Mahasai, MLC (Bengal), spoke of Indian Library movement at Second International Conference of Libraries and Bibliography, Barcelona, Spain.

1935 Khan Bahadur

K M Asadullah BA., FLA, Imperial Librarian, was honoured by the title of Khan Bahadur on the King-Emperors' Birthday. He is the first Indian Librarian to receive this title. He is also the first to hold the Fellowship of Library Association (FLA), London.

1935 Abstracting

The first service was offered by National Institute of Science with its *Indian Science Abstract*. It stopped in 1940.

1936 Proposal for Post Graduate Course
Ranganathan's proposal to Madras University was not accepted because "the subject was not a discipline of sufficient calibre for which the university can give a degree".

1936 Colon in Chinese
Translation of the scheme took place.

1937 Dewey Expansion Committee
Indian Library Association appointed this body to invite librarians using Dewey to send in, their suggestions on expansion of Dewey's scheme.

1938 Diploma in Librarianship
Madras University started the first diploma course at University level.

1939 All India Library Directory
This was the first edition, and the first national listing.

1939 Fyzee Committee Report
The Government of Bombay Presidency appointed a Library Development Committee with A A A Fyzee as its President. It recommended a graduated scheme for library development in Bombay in six stages.

1940 Congress Library
The Dr Rajendra Prasad, President of the premier political party of the country, appealed to publishers and authors to contribute to the Research Library of the All India Congress Committee Office. The library was established for the study and investigation of the country's problems, national and international.

1940 Urdu Library Literature
Intezam-e-Kutub Khana, or management of the library was the first book in this Language, the second commonly used tongue in the country.

1941 Manuscript Libraries Association
At the All India Oriental Conference, Hyderabad, was formed All India Manuscripts Libraries Association. P P Subramaniya Sastri as President and Kunhan Raja as Secretary were elected.

1942 Foreign Student

B I Palmer, FLA, was permitted to audit the post-graduate course in Madras University.

1942 "Deccan Libraries" Prize

The State Asafiya Library, Hyderabad, established by the Nizam, announced three prizes for best article on Deccan Libraries, as apart of its Golden Jubilee celebrations and exhibition. The occasion was also of the meeting of All India Oriental Conference and Indian Historical Congress.

1943 American Centre

First American Library, called United States Information Service (USIS) was set up at Calcutta.

1943 Education–Admission Requirement

Inter-University Board resolved to admit only graduates to the Diploma course. This was for standardization in the country.

1943 Library in India Series

Punjab Library Association started this series.

1945 India Book League

It was an association of men and women of goodwill, who recognize the place of books in their daily lives and seek to spread knowledge amongst the people of the country. It was a membership based group. It did emerge as a great body of the leading intellectuals of the country (Bhatia, 1945. p. 63).

1946 Department of Library Science

Delhi University was the first to start a Department of Library Science. This was also the first University to introduce masters and doctoral Programmes, in 1948.

IV. **Independent India** (Since 1947)

1948 National Library Librarian

By an Act of Parliament the Government of India changed the name of the Imperial Library to National Library. B S Kesavan became the first Librarian of the National Library of Independent India.

1948 Doctor of Letters (D.Litt)
Ranganathan was conferred this honorary degree by the Governor General of India, Lord Mountbatten, in admiration of his services to library profession. He was awarded the title Rao Sahib in 1939; and received another D Litt from Pittsburgh University in 1964. In 1957 he was awarded Padmasri by Dr. Rajendra Prasad, President of India.

1948 Pre-natal Processing (C.I.P)
Ranganathan gave the idea to the world and offered advice on this in an address at the Library of Congress.

1948 Librametry
Ranganathan is the first person who initiated the idea of quantification in Library Science. Its presentation as *Bibliometrics* by Alan Pritchard, in 1969 followed later (Ravichandra Rao, 1983.p. 179).

1948 Madras Public Libraries Act
The Governor General gave his assent and this Act came into force. The Connemara Public Library was made the State Central Library, under the control of Director of Public Instruction. This is the first enactment in the country, and the first in series of library legislations in the states and union territories.

1948 Library Research Circle, Delhi
This body started meeting at Ranganathan's residence periodically to discuss issues and problems facing the profession.

1949 Masters Course
The first master's degree course was offered in Delhi University, as two-year programme, and it replaced the Bachelor's Course.

1951 Doctoral Study
Delhi University was the first to start the doctoral programme, with the registration of D B Krishna Rao, who with this facility became the first Ph D holder in the country.

1951 Documentation–Government Documents
P N Kaula systematized the documentation service for the first time in the country in the area of Government documents, in the Library of the Ministry of Labour and Employment.

1951 Continental Federation of Associations

The Ninth All India Conference was the meeting place of foreign delegates who had agreed to form Asian Federation of Library Associations.

1951 Ranganathan Endowment

Ranganathan Endowment for Library Science was formed with S Das Gupta as Chairman and P N Kaul; as Secretary.

1952 Book Trade–Incentives

The State Government exempted books of all kinds from the Sales Tax.

1952 Book Trade–Federation of Associations

A Federation of Book Sellers and Publishers in India (FBPI) was formed in Delhi, during a conference of representatives from different associations from various states.

1953 British Council

The first library was opened in Bombay to serve central and north India, through two types of membership: postal for scholars living outside Bombay and corporate membership for institutions.

1953 Ohio's Children's Gift

Children who use a village library in Ohio State, U S A donated $2,500 to India for Children's books.

1953 Literacy House

Welthy Fisher started a new kind of literacy programme in this house at Lucknow. It was a first experiment to reach villages with library kits for literacy classes, bell-bicycle-libraries, workers" mobile libraries and other types of services. The UNESCO's Iraq International Literacy Award was given to this institution in 1988.

1954-1962 Wheat Loan Programme

The major foreign grant for the development of libraries and information activity was a US project. Twenty American Consultants visited under this programme. US lent support through the Wheat Loan programme for Libraries and Librarians in India, and within eight years it released an amount of $1,700,000. About twenty libraries received more than 24,000 publications in 1956 through the United States Book Exchange Programmes.

1954 Institutional Status
Banaras Hindu University was the first in the country to rank the University Librarian as an Officer, who would be an ex-Officio permanent member of the Academic Council and University Court, as well as Convener of the Board of Studies and Examiners of the Department of library Science.

1954 University Grants Commission
For the standardization of the education in the country the Government set up the University Grants Commission (U G C) at Delhi.

1954 Syed Bashiruddin
He was the first Librarian in the country to receive the status and Scale of University Professor. He was the Librarian of the Aligarh Muslim University.

1955 Soviet Books
The Soviet Academy of Science presented books on various subjects to Maulana Abul Kalam Azad, first Union Education Minister.

1955 Special Libraries Association
The Indian Association of Special Libraries and Information Centres (IASLIC) was founded in Calcutta. Dr. S L Hora was its first President.

1956 Library Literature Exhibition
As a part of the All India Educational Exhibition the Delhi Library Association organized a exhibition of Indian Library Literature. P N Kaula brought out his bibliography on the same theme.

1956 Publishing–Awards
To reward for excellence in printing and designing of publications the Government of India started the annual prize programme.

1956 Full Time Lecturer–Aligarh
First full time Library Science Lecturer in the country was appointed at Aligarh Muslim University.

1956 Chair of Professorship
Ranganathan gifted one hundred thousand rupees to the University of Madras for this Chair in Library Science. The occasion was the centenary celebrations of the University. The University announced the establishment of Sharda Ranganathan Chair in Library Science during its Centenary Celebrations in 1957.

1958 Film Library
This was founded at Delhi, by the Federation of Film Journalists, as an appreciation of the services of Dada Saheb Phalke, the Father of the Indian films.

1958 Chinese Books
China donated 12,000 books to the Viswa Bharathi University.

1958 Japan's Gift
Japanese Government sent a generous gift of 1802 books and 200 periodicals. Of these books 1450 were in Japanese, and, 452 in European.

1958 National Bibliography
The Central Reference Library released the first issue of the Indian National Bibliography.

1958 Foreign Language Education
IASLIC offered a part time course in Russian.

1958 Mailing Rates
The Government of India reduced the book parcel rates to half of the actual's.

1959 Media library
The Local Library Authority, Madras introduced audio-visual aids.

1959 International Catalogue Code
Ranganathan laid down the standards for formulation of this code.

1959 Gold Medal–Awards
One individual K Mahalingam, of the Delhi University Library donated four thousand rupees to the University for instituting this award to be given to the first in first candidate. Similarly the Delhi

Library Association instituted the award for distinct contribution to the profession by an individual.

1959 Qualifications

UGC announced the decision that the essential qualification for Senior posts was a higher professional degree. This meant to show the increase in the value of the professional advancements.

1960 Indian Donation

India donated one million yen to the new Library of the Ohtani University at Kyoto.

1961 Rockefeller Foundation Grant

Rs 1,90,000 was given to the Department of Library Science of the University of Delhi, for professional development.

1961 Sharda Ranganathan Library Science Lectures

Another Endowment was created by the generosity of Ranganathan's students, to further the cause of Library Science, and the lectures to be delivered under the auspices of any university or any library association.

1961 Indo-American Joint Programmes

There have been many such programmes. One of them is the low-priced text book scheme; the others include sponsorship of professional to USA, sending or inviting library consultants to India as experts and advisors.

1961 Documentation Training

The Documentation Research and Training Centre (DRTC) was founded by the Indian Statistical Institute at Bangalore with Ranganathan as Honorary Professor (Kaula, 1977).

1962 Academic Libraries Association

This Indian Academic Libraries Association came into existence at the Fifth Wheat Loan Workshop at New Delhi.

1962 Indian Collections

The commencement of Library of Congress's PL 480 Acquisition Programme led to purchase of Indian books for 31 US participating libraries. This has resulted in collection development of Indian books on a foreign soil. These books are now accessible on computerized databases through the efforts of these American libraries. This also initiated the publication of Accession List, which is up to date as a tool for Indian publications.

1963 Women's Training

Government Polytechnic for Women were started with Diploma in Library Science courses at Ambala, Bangalore, Chandigarh, Delhi, and Jalandhar.

1964 American Studies Research Centre

The Centre, set up as a registered autonomous body under the Government of India's Registration of Societies Act, is at Hyderabad. It is the first and the largest in its size outside USA and caters to the researchers and scholars in the area of humanities and social sciences. Its trans-national environment has been a model for many libraries.

1964 Council for Library Development

Indian Council for Library Development was established at Sharda Society, Ahmedabad. It included many specific aims and objectives for the promotion of library science.

1967 Audio Visual Librarianship

First comprehensive indigenous source on this theme appeared, viz., M S Hussain. Audio-Visual Librarianship: A Select Bibliography of Articles, Books, Documents and Pamphlets published during 1961-1966.

1965 National Research Professor

The Ministry of Education appointed the first of its kind, a professor with a salary to devote entirely his services. This offer by the government indicated the changing attitude of the bureaucracy towards the status of the profession as on par with the other traditional disciplines.

1966 National Advisory Board

The Government of India set up a Board with the Union (federal) Education Minister as its chairperson, to advise the Federal and State Governments on all matters pertaining to libraries specially regarding establishment, improvement, reorganization, popularization and coordinated development of libraries.

1966 'Great Book Club'–Aligarh
General Education Centre of the Muslim University Aligarh started this to foster reading habit, as a part of co-curricular programme.

1966 National Federation of Associations
Federation of Indian Library Associations (FILA) was formed at Chandigarh. Its aim was to federate the activities of library associations and to coordinate the work of librarians.

1966 UNESCO Book Coupon
UNESCO provided $ 60,000 worth of coupons to the Indian National Commission, 1966-1967, as a programme to reduce government's foreign exchange cost and bring savings for the buyer.

1966 National Book Fair
The first National Book Fair was held in Bombay, sponsored by the National Book Trust.

1966 Education–Publishing Industry
First refresher course for book sellers was offered in New Delhi by the Hindi Publishers Association. Of the topics selected one was 'storage of books'.

1967 Reading Week
A Reading Week was organized by Rajasthan Library Association, Jaipur. A souvenir was released on this eve with essays on library and reading of books.

1967 Round Table–Copyright
To consider the various problems of literary and artistic work copyright the Federation of Publishers and Booksellers Association of India organized the Round Table Conference, at Delhi. The occasion was the second National Book Fair.

1968 Terminology
A seminar at Pune discussed the problem of terminology of library science. It had taken note of what all was resolved in a previous similar meeting (1965). It concluded with a list of 2,000 terms. Its concern was in the regional languages and in 1969. Another seminar in the year 1968 was organized at Delhi, by the Standing Commission for Scien-

tific and Technical Terminology in the field. The seminar took note of the previous meetings and resolved with a list of 5,000 terms. Similar meeting was again held in 1969 and organized by the Commission on Technical Terminology of the Union Ministry of Education. It finalized 1,500 terms.

1968 Library Day and Library Week

To promote reading habits and market their services and facilities the Indian Library Association resolved to have a National Library Week from 14 to 20 November each year, and 14th to be as National Library Day.

1968 Oriental Studies

Nizam's Charitable Trust, Hyderabad, sanctioned a grant-in-aid to translate to Telugu the available masterpieces in Urdu, Arabic and Persian.

1969 Institute of National Importance–Act

Khuda Bakhsh Oriental Public Library, Patna, was declared by an Act of Parliament to be an institution of national importance. By this Act it ceases its private position and it receives support by the Government of India.

1969 Association of Teachers

For the development of rapport between library schools and promotion of education for librarianship there emerged Indian Association of the Teachers of Library Science, at Bangalore. D B Krishna Rao was elected the Chairman and P N Kaula the Secretary.

1969 Preferential Professionalism

In its policy to revise periodically the qualifications required the UGC has to take note of what the Government has to say. While UGC had made higher qualification as essential, the Government in its notification in 1969 de-professionalised the status and made it 'preferential'.

1970 Central Reference Library

Due to the policy made, the Central Reference Library was separated from the National Library. Central Reference Library has been the base for the publication of the Indian National Bibliography.

1970 American Blessing Bliss Remembered
DRTC celebrated the centenary of H E Bliss, and the participants in this meet including Ranganathan and A Neelemaghan paid tribute to his contribution.

1970 UNESCO Māndram Award
A fine Teacher received this award, and he was V Thillainyagam, Librarian Coromondal Library, Madras. The event was the celebration of the International Education Year.

1970 Books Instead of Garlands
The feelings of the State Minister of Education were conveyed to schools by a circular of Director of School Education, Madras, "That it would be better and more appropriate if distinguished visitors and guests were invited to participate in school functions are presented with books instead of garlands and desire that this practice may be followed in schools".

1970 Wall Newspaper
The first wall newspaper was brought out by the Press Information Bureau, of the Government of India. It was in two languages, Hindi and English.

1971 'Book Chain' Programme
To share the meager resources and permit maximum use of school books, the Lok Milap Trust, Bhavanagar (Gujarat State) offered free loan of sets of 50 books to secondary schools. The period of loan for each school was one week.

1971 Minister of Public Libraries
The first minister of State for the Libraries was A Madan Mohan and the portfolio was first of its kind in the country.

1971 Lady Librarian
The first lady Librarian at a senior post was Mrs Rajendra Chopra, who became State Librarian, State Central Library, Chandigarh.

1971 Rail-Staff Libraries
Transport authorities had long neglect the information needs of rail staff. The first relief was in providing mobile libraries for staff work-

ing at road-side stations, on the North Eastern Railways. One on Samastipur-Narkaityaganj (Darbhanga section in Bihar) and the other on Gorakhpur-Gonda loop (in Uttar Pradesh).

1972 National Library Bill

Lok Sabha received the National Library Bill for legislation. It was introduced by Prof S Noorul Hasan, Union Education Minister. The bill then was referred for detailed study to a Joint Select Committee of both the Houses (Upper and Lower).

1972 Late Dr Ranganathan

The Father of Library movement in India, whose contribution to the library world stays in ideal, verbal and oral plane, passed away.

1972 International Book Year

While the world celebrated this Book Year, India went ahead a step in the zeal to promote reading and hence the Government appointed a national Committee to do the needful. Abul Hasan, Book Promotion Officer, Ministry of Education and Social Welfare was made the Secretary.

1972 American Aid–Book Trade

USAID provided monetary support of one hundred thousand rupees to the Federation of Publishers and Book Sellers Association, to bring out a directory of Indian Book Industry.

1972 Raja Ram Mohan Roy Library Foundation

One of the most important establishments which emerged for the promotion and acceleration of library movement was this Foundation. It has been working at a massive scale. It has selected old and well known libraries and supports for their maintenance and preservation of books. It has extended its activities to literacy promotion campaigns and to rural book deposit centres.

1972 Documentary Film on Libraries

A step ahead towards VCR era, as early as 1972, when India hardly had TV sets, a film on Indian Libraries presented a vision for the future. The producer of the Film 'Yuraj Singh', deserves ranking among Indian Media Librarians. The title of the film is 'Badte Kadam', in Hindi.

1973 Transit Library
A long distance train, Jayanti Express on an experimental basis opened a library in railway carriage. It lent books on monetary deposit.

1973 Braille on Wheels
While there have been some attempts in the public libraries in the country to have Braille section, Delhi Public Library initiated the process of mobile Braille Service.

1974 Educational Standards
By the standard of Library Science examination in India it was resolved that MLS in the USA is equivalent to the Bachelors in India (and not equal to the Master's Degree in India). This is the evaluation of the Standing Committee of the Association of Indian Universities, New Delhi.

1974 Institute of Librarians
At Calcutta emerged this body to promote library, information and documentation activities. It was registered as a national voluntary organization.

1974 North India Association
As the country has been larger than the time of Muhammed bin Tughluq, the North Indian Library Association was established by Librarians from the northern states. The President of this was Nasib Chand and Mrs S A Bhagi General Secretary.

1974 National Council of Assocation
P N Kaula on his own initiative, on consultation with professional leaders set up a National Council of Indian Library Associations. There was a good acceptance and 35 organization came forward to join this body.

1975 Telecommunication Network (Education thro' media)
With the advancement in the networking of the box the Government of India started the education through this media to cover 5,000 villages.

1975 International Conference
The third meeting of the International Conference on Classification Research, was in Bombay.

1975 Inter-Library Resource Centre

The Indian Council of Social Science Research Centre (ICSSR) and the Jawaharlal Nehru University, jointly established this at the documentation Centre of ICSSR, in New Delhi. It houses withdrawn and less used books in social sciences, and in this respect it is the first cooperative venture of academic and research libraries in the country towards cooperative storage and resource sharing (Kaula:1976:71)

1981 Cooperative Library

A national cooperative library was set up by the National Cooperative Union of India, in New Delhi. This is the first attempt in this sector to build a nationwide library system. Its objectives include maintaining liaison with academic and research libraries (Kaula, 1981.p. 113).

1984 Open University

Andhra Pradesh became the first state in India to start a professional course as a part of its distance education program. This is a first informal programme in the world. It was introduced at the Andhra Pradesh Open University. Being the first experiment in the non-class room professional training it brought a great revolution in the patterns of education and training of librarians.

1986 Survey of School Libraries

The National Council of Educational Research and Training (NCERT), conducted a sample study of library facilities and their utilization in secondary and high schools. This sample was limited to four states. This is the first sample study by a government body of the school libraries. The NCERT worked on this project under the Deptt. of Measurement and Evaluation, Survey and Data processing (Kaula:1986:108).

1986 Asiatic Society Library

The Governing Council of the Asiatic Society, Calcutta decided to close the library and its Museum, after a life span of 202 years. It was, however, reopened after renovation of the old library (Kaula:1986:180)

1986 Integrated Master's Degree

The North East Hill University started first course in the country of this type. The course has two phases, the first phase of two semester leads to a bachelor's degree, and on the continuing for another two semesters leads to Masters' degree. The same year saw the integration of the library school with the university. This in fact was a reversion to the pattern of the past. These changes were in line with the UGC's guidelines. And based on the suggestions of the UGC's Library and Information Panel (Kaula:1986:119).

1987 Centenary of Library Education

University of Nagpur hosted the annual conference of IATLIS, on the theme of One Hundred years of Library Education.

1988 E Mail

The Government of India introduced the computerized Electronic mail system. It started its operation with the collaboration of the National Informatics Centre using the INTELSAT network. As an experiment this system is limited to the Department of the Posts (Kaula:1988:281).

1988 Joint meeting of ILA and IASLIC, Calcutta

This was an historic event when Bengal Library Association hosted the joint meeting of both the national professional associations. Such a 'mela' was probably for the first time in the Indian annals. It was to hold 34th All India Library Conference of the ILA and 13th National Seminar of the IASLIC.

1988 DISNIC

The National Informatics Centre Network (NIC - f. 1973 and set up in 1977 by Government of India) initiated a District Information System (DISNIC) to effectively work at district level all over the country.

1992 IFLA Conference at Delhi

India was proud host for the first time of this International conference at Delhi; IFLA being the association of associations and hence the importance of this international meet.

APPENDIX II

SELECTED LIST OF FOREIGN LIBRARY CONSULTANTS

(Selections from P S G Kumar's *Indian Library Chronology, Herald of Library Science, Indian Librarian* and *Modern Librarian*)

{Note: The terms consultants, advisers, visitors are not used in exact literal sense. These are Librarians or Faculty basically, who came to India as foreigners, either on prior appointment or there services were availed as advisors and consultants. Some came as invitees for a specific programme and on their travel stayed and exchanged their ideas and even advised. This note is to clarify the difference in the usage of the term 'consultants'}.

1866-1872 Sir Frank Alexander Francis, (UK)
This person was one of the earliest advisors in the country. He was a British Librarian. He served the Maharaja Sawai Ram Singh (1835-1895), Jaipur.

1878-1880 Dr A C Burnell (UK)
He was at Saraswathi Mahal Library, Tanjore (Tamil Nadu). He came from U K. He was the responsible for continuation of the work for the compilation of a manuscript catalogue of this library.

1910-19 W A Borden (USA)
Maharaja Sayaji Rao Gaikwad of Baroda, made W A Borden an American Librarian, Director of the State Libraries. Borden revolutionized the library system, initiated educational programme, and publication of literature. He is the first foreign Library Director at a State level and also the first American in this position.

1915-1916 Asa Don Dickinson (US)
The first foreign Librarian at the university level, Asa Don Dickinson was made the Librarian of the Punjab University, Lahore (now in Pakistan). He was the one who initiated the first course of three month duration at University level.

1924, 1939, 1947 Welthy H Fisher (US) & 1953

She has been a source of high value for her experience in literacy campaigns and outreaching programmes. She set up a Literacy House in 1953, at Lucknow, which was mean to promote literacy and reading habits among the rural masses living around this city. Its experiments succeeded and it set up six types of libraries, like halting mobile libraries, workers mobile libraries, and district deposit libraries.

1942 and 1965 Bernard Ira Palmer (UK)

B I Palmer, FLA, was the first foreign course auditor at Madras University, and he visited many libraries including the Imperial (National) Library, Calcutta. Back at home he was Deputy Chief Librarian, Public Library, Action. Probably in 1942 he was wished many happy returns (to India), and so he was again in the country in 1965. He made a complete tour of the country visiting all major cities and major library Schools. In 1965 he was Education Officer, Library Association, London.

1944-1946, 1953-1955, Maureen Patterson (US) and 1982

As a specialist in South Asian Languages and Literatures Maureen has been serving Indian culture in number of ways. She made three visits and each time left her impressions on the soil. Being the Bibliographer and Head of South Asia Collection at Chicago University, then, she must have been influencing her colleagues in US too. She was an advisor even to the Library of Congress on collection development in this area.

1951, 1954 and 1956 Luther Evans (US)

Evans, came to India in different capacities, as Librarian Columbia University, as Librarian of Congress (or The Librarian, as he is called in the Congress Library), and as Director General of UNESCO. He was in India for three times and he addressed many meetings. He even had an opportunity to advise the professionals. He gave theme based lectures on Role of UNESCO, Importance of archives, etc.

1951 E J Carter (France)

Carter, Head of Library Division, UNESCO, visited India on a two week visit. He had elaborate discussions with the members of Indian Library Association, and was very positive about his plan on how Indian library movement could further its cause.This much of his interest in Indian librarianship indicated the level of empathy he had as a foreign librarian and an outsider.

1951 Frank M Gardner

This former Librarian of Luton Public Library, came to India on a consultant. It was UNESCO's project on Delhi Public Library. Gardner was also involved in the group discussion which kept Carter occupied.

1951 Edward Sydney

The Government of India liberally invited foreign advisors from time to time and so Edward Sydney was on such. He was appointed for the first six months of the starting of the Delhi Public Library as its Foreign Advisory Director.

1952 J B Reid

This Foreign Documentation Specialist was one of the first staff in Indian National Scientific Documentation Centre (INSDOC). INSDOC came into existence in the same year, and was well starting with a band of foreign advisers like Reid. The basic function of INSDOC being Documentation, its choice of best of foreign hands was most appropriate. Reid was to assist in the planning and programming of the Documentation projects.

1952 A L Gardner

For the huge task of Documentation in Indian and Foreign languages the INSDOC authorities had to consider development of special areas. Scientific Translation was therefore assigned to Gardner.

1952 E K Osloni

For the Mechanical Processing activities at INSDOC, Osloni was appointed.

1952-1955 Avila A Pelletier (US)

He was appointed at INSDOC to work as an advisor for Printing and Reprographic Services. He was originally head of Publications Sections of the Technical Information Division in LC.

1957-1979 Dorothy L Clark (US)

Probably the longest term an American could spend as an active Librarian in India, Miss Clark has that distinctive position. She served two institutions, the first half of the period in USIS Bombay, and the second half in American Studies Research Centre, Hyderabad. Her contributions to the latter have become the pillars of the library.

1957 Ralph Shaw (US)
The American Library Association and Library Association, London, have been one of the main source for consultants and advisors. Dr. Ralph Shaw, president of American Library Association visited India and was keen in knowing more about the Indian library practices. He addressed a meet of the Government of India Libraries Association, on the topic Mechanization of Bibliographies. His primary task in India was to provide expert consultancy on the development of agricultural information network. He worked in close association with Dr D B Krishna Rao, the Librarian of Indian Council of Agricultural Research (According to Konnur, Prof Shaw visited India in 1956–see Kumar,1977. p.227 ; Konnur, 1990. p.31).

1957-1958 Archie McNeal (US)
He was a specialist on education and being a working Librarian (at University of Miami Library, Florida) he provided ample of advice on academic and research libraries.

1958 John Alden (US)
He was a walking encyclopaedia on book preservation. His services were utilized by the National Library, Calcutta. His three months tour of various manuscript libraries culminated in a report he wrote. Back at home he worked at Boston Public Library.

1958 Agard B Evans
The Government of India, was well advised by people around to avail the services of foreign librarians. This was a policy. It included the opportunity given to Agard Evans, Chef Librarian, Minister of Works, London. He was on an appointment to give his expert opinion on planning and implementing of Documentation service in the National Buildings Organization.

1958-1959 Jennings Wood (US)
Some Librarians and consultants came as specialists in acquisition of Indian material. This was possible under the PL 480 programme. They surveyed the market place as well as libraries to identify the appropriate materials. Wood was one such specialist.

1957-1964 Jack Dalton (US)
Dalton had been to India seven times. He was on a variety of programmes. He went to different Indian libraries, and addressed many including the Delhi Library Association's meetings. He was back at home, the Director, Public relations Division, ALA, and Director of Library School, Columbia University (Kumar records his visit to have been in 1959, whereas Konnur places him in 1957; see Kumar, 1977.p.245, and Konnur, 1990, p.41).

1959 B Holt (US)
She was the Consultant, India Wheat Loan Office, Delhi. And during her period of consultancy she was very useful for the Indian library community. She even addressed meetings, for instance the meeting of the Delhi Library Association.

1959 A Letts (Canada)
She came as a Consultant under the Colombo Plan. She was former President of Canadian Library Association. During her visits to Indian libraries she could very easily transfer the Canadian Librarianship. She addressed the members of the Delhi Library Association and spoke about the Canadian Library Development, which gave some similarities to Indian scenario, and a food for thought on how India could further her library development.

1959 M Lorch
A UNESCO Technical Expert on Scientific Documentation, Philippines, Dr. M Lorch visited India. He gave his lecture on Libraries in Philippines and other places.

1959 Keyes Metcalf (US)
As a consultant-librarian the visit of Dr. Metcalf must have been very useful to the Indians. Metcalf, was Library Consultant with the Rockefeller Foundation (and formerly Librarian, at Harvard University). This visit must have given a boost to the era of Rockefeller funded libraries in India, which were spread across the country. He spent his time in India at different libraries in Delhi, Calcutta, and Bombay. His expertise in planning libraries must have been very valuable and at opportune time Kesavan and Ranganathan took his suggestions for various programmes.

1961 Carl Hintz (US)
Rajasthan University is one more which received visiting faculty. Prof. Hintz made an extensive study of the training programme at fifteen library schools in the country. He limited his study to university level, and didn't include the education given by other institutions. He made many suggestions for the improvement of the existing system. He spent four months in this project and resumed his position back at home as University Librarian, University of Oregon, Eugene.

1961 Laurence Kipps and Ceilia Kipps (US)
This couple was one of the joint consultants, like Russells and Chapmans. They did much constructive work in their brief period of stay of eight months. Apart from providing consultations, they evaluated the US aid and actively involved in zonal workshops, organized by the Ministry of Education, India. They were officiating as specialists on behalf of the Wheat Loan Programme, and came from Harvard School of Business.

1961-1962 and Katherine S Diehl (US) 1967-1969
She worked earlier as Librarian at Serampore College, near Calcutta, and later as a researcher. She systematized the College Library. As a researcher she has contributed substantially in the area of Indian Studies. She has extensively contributed the history of printing in South Asia.

1962 Engracio Basio (Philippines)
The Principal Librarian, College of Agriculture, University of Philippines, visited India to hold discussions on the Indian library situation as against his own. He was on a deputation from his Government to visit agricultural libraries in eight South East-Asian countries.

1963 R E Mc Burney
McBurney visited India and lectured at various places, including the National Physical Laboratory, New Delhi. He was Chief Technical Information Service, NRCC and also Chairman of the FID's Technical Information to Industry.

1963 Dr. John Charles Finzi (US)
Director, Library of Congress Book Procurement Centre, Delhi also visited different libraries and spoke at various institutions. He also

spoke, on the invitation of P N Kaula, at the Library of Banaras Hindu University (Kumar states that him as Librarian of Congress, see Kumar, 1977.p.292).

1963 Quincy Mumford (US)
He was the Librarian of Congress. He visited India and addressed many library groups in different cities.

1963 Anis Khurshid (Pakistan)
The professional links of India and Pakistan remained intact despite the physical and political boundaries. Anis Khurshid's visits to India, (without ignoring other Librarians in Pakistan some of whom are products of the Indian Library Schools, See Husain, 1974), demonstrates this fact. Anis Khurshid visited many libraries and library schools, like those in Nagpur, Bangalore, Madras and Varanasi. He was then the Head of the Department of Library Science, Karachi University, and also Assistant Secretary, Pakistan Library Association.

1963 David T Ray (US)
An expert in Indian languages, David was then Cataloger, Morris Library, University of Illinois. He visited 22 libraries in different cities and and well received. He addressed also at Uttar Pradesh Library Association's Varanasi Branch.

1963 A J Wells (UK)
Tours of libraries was sometimes also associated with a participation in one single project or seminar, or programme. Wells, FLA, and the Editor of the *British National Bibliography* lectured extensively on the themes of Bibliography and Documentation.

1964 and 1964 Lester Asheim (US)
To advice on the developments in theory and practice internationally, and India being one in the schedule, Asheim made two trips to India. He was also to identify the areas in which ALA could send consultants to foreign countries. In this programme he visited library schools and libraries in many places in the country.

1964 Sarah K Vann (US)
Consultants have been on their trips to study and advise on many areas. Vann was on an exclusive project of finding out the Indian contribu-

tions to Dewey Decimal Classification Scheme, and provide consultancy on how best it can be adapted. She officiated on behalf of ALA, as Director of this Field Study.

1964-1985 Henry Scholberg (US)
Consultants who frequented India for various reasons included Scholberg. He visited at least eight times this country, for projects like book acquisition, speech giving, and research.

1965-67, 1974, Dr. Kenneth R Logan (US) 1981, 1984 and 1986
He is the South Asia Librarian, University of California, Berkeley. He is a specialist in Hindi and has an interest in modern history and politics of India. His first visit was to work as US Peace Corps Volunteer, to work with the Government of India Small Scale Industries Institute Library, Kanpur. In 1974, 1981 and 1986 he visited on a collection building project as well consultation with Library of Congress Office, New Delhi. In 1984 he was invited for a lecture. In this trip was also arranged a Smithosnian Museum tour of India.

1965 Carl White (US)
The author of the renown *White Report*, White was a special consultant to plan the development of Delhi University Library. He opened a new era of University Librarianship in India by writing this 184-page report. He laid a foundation for study of libraries in India.

1966 Morris A Gelfand (US)
To advise on the education of librarians, specialists like Prof. Gelfand were sponsored. He undertook teaching work for three months and also did a tremendous job of analyzing the activities of the Library School at University of Delhi. He submitted his findings of the state-of-the-art to this University. Prof Gelfand headed the Library School at Queens College, N.Y. His report was the first of its kind in suggesting that the master's programme be taken as (an intermediate) step to award doctorate. May be it has support in the present M.Phil research degree which Delhi was first to initiate–which is a pre-Ph.D research programme.

1966-1967 John Russell and Margaret Russell (US)
Consultants like Russells contributed substantially to collection development in the annals of Indian library history. John advised the

American Studies Research Centre, Hyderabad on various aspects. His report on developing a balanced collection stands on its own. Margaret collaborated in this programme and provided advanced ideas on cataloguing the material in the Centre's library. They also visited many other libraries. Russells hailed from University of Rochester (Taher and Kumar, 1990).

1966-1967 H Tyler Gemmell (US)

Among those consultants who concentrated on a single library and brought exhaustive changes in the system, is the name of Gemmell. She came under the US-India's Women's College Exchange Programme. She served her period of stay, of one term, at Isabella Thoburn College, Lucknow. The library received much awaited expertise and special attention during her presence.

1968 Don W Jett

The spurt of agricultural and medical institutions in the country required special consultants from abroad. Jett came in to speed up the library development of one such libraries, viz., University of Agricultural Sciences, Bangalore. His report on the present and future plans made a history in case studies.

1968 George S Bonn (US)

Another consultant on training programme came Prof Bonn, from Library School at University of Hawaii. His stay of a few months led him to evaluate the Indian libraries at Delhi and the type of education required in this context. He served as a visiting Professor in Library School at the University of Delhi.

1969, 1974, 1983 Eugene Garfield (US)

The world famous information scientist and the promoter of citationalia, Garfield visited India thrice. He was simply amazed by Ranganathan. Apart from his Sharda Ranganathan Lecture on Citation analysis in relation to third world, he humbly related his work to Ranganathan in another lecture he gave at Madras University.

1969, 1984 and 1989 Merry L Burlingham (US)

She is a South Asia Librarian, University of Texas, Austin. She has been to India as a student, as collection building specialists and as a field officer in the area. She has a speciality in Hindi and has had much professional interaction with the South Asia libraries association.

1969 Ahmed al-Qaisi (Iraq)
He visited India to hold discussions with Indian librarians on library and information issues. He was a UNESCO Fellow and Librarian, Supreme Council of Scientific Research, Government of Iraq.

1969 Derek Langridge (UK)
Langridge came to India on the invitation to deliver the Sharda Ranganathan Lecture at Bangalore. He visited libraries at Madras, Calcutta, Delhi, Bombay and Poona. He was Principal Lecturer at the North Western Polytechnic School of Librarianship, London. This expertise in teaching was fruitfully utilized in India by his lectures he gave at the above-mentioned places, and this experience was made long lasting in India when he presided in the same year in the meeting of teachers of Library Science to form the Indian Association of Teachers of Library Science (IATLIS). Luckily, IATLIS was also born in this fruitful year.

1970 John F Harvey (US)
This former Dean of Library Service, University of New Mexico, has made a remarkable contribution and continues to be a consultant for different libraries in the world. In India he visited innumerable libraries and his observations find a special place in the annals of Indian library history. He visited libraries in Hyderabad, Bombay, Delhi, and others.

1970 Pauline A Atherton (US)
Another American professional in India was Prof. Atherton. She was President-elect, American Society for Information Science (ASIS) and Associate Professor School of Library Science, Syracuse University. He was on an invitation to deliver the Sarada Ranganathan Endowment Lectures. He associated while in India with the founders of the first teachers organization, viz., Indian Association of Teachers of Library and Information Science. He also spoke at other library schools in Bangalore and Madras.

1972 V Yu Afemov (USSR)
He visited many libraries in Delhi. He addressed a special ILA audience on Nation Wide Information System–its Organization and Activities in the USSR. Afemov was from the Library of Academy of Sciences, USSR.

1972 Jack Wells (US)

A South Asian Bibliographer at Wisconsin University, Jack has a speciality in Indian history. He was in India for months and he advised many libraries, including Tamil Nadu State Archives, Bombay University Library, Asif Jah (State Central) Library, Hyderabad, and Delhi University Library.

1975 Ravindra Nath Sharma (US)

Sharma stands today as one of the leaders of Indian Library historians. He visited his former abode many a times, but this was an American funded trip (funded by Colgate University, Hamilton, N Y and American Institute of Indian Studies, Chicago, IL) to work on the archives of the History of Rajputs in Bikaner, Rajasthan, and to develop an Indian collection for the Colgate University Library. This sort of work while is not directly involved in consultancy projects, but it is an eye opener for the concerned authorities that the collection which they care–not is very highly valuable in the Modern Western World. By this trip Sharma was able to advise the concerned authorities on the issues of organizing a modern library and what were the most essential and required priorities.

1975 Jean M Perreault (US)

Prof Perreault visited India as a distinguished speaker at the invitation of Sharda Ranganathan Endowment. He also addressed many other professional groups and students at library schools in Delhi, Hyderabad, and Madras. His Sharda Ranganathan Lecture was on 'The idea of order in bibliography'.

1976 Dr. Peter Lazar (Hungary)

Dr. Lazar visited a number of libraries in Calcutta, Madras, Hyderabad, Chandigarh, Varanasi, Mysore, etc. He addressed many professional gatherings, hosted by ILA, IASLIC, etc. He is Director General, Hungarian Central Technical Library and Documentation Centre, Budapest (Kaula, 1976.p.75).

1976 Dr. D J Urquhart (UK)

He was on an invitation by the Government of India to build a cooperative programme between India and UK in the field of Information Science. Dr. Urquhart is the former Director of British Library Lending Division, Boston Spa, Yorkshire. He addressed the Delhi Library Association meeting and other professional audiences.

1976 Dr. A M Abdul Huq (US)
He visited India, his former home, and gave extension lectures on the library development in US. Dr. Huq is Asstt. Prof. at St John's University, School of Library Science, New York.

1976 Mrs. Mozelle Isaac (Australia)
She was on a short visit to observe library practices in Calcutta. She spoke at many professional meetings. Mrs. Isaac is affiliated to the Sydney University Library, New Wales.

1976 Dr. William J Cameron (Canada)
On the invitation of Sharda Ranganathan Endowment Dr. Cameron visited India. He gave the Sharda Ranganathan Lecture at DRTC, Bangalore. At home he is the Dean, at Library School, University of Western Ontario.

1976 and 1985 Patrick R Penland (US)
Prof. Penland, an author and scholar on Indian library scenario, has a distinction of living in US and working on India, with contacts and personal visits. He has been a Visiting Professor, a doctoral advisor, editorial consultant, and has much more to pen. He delivered a series of lectures at DRTC, and was a distinguished speaker at other library schools, including Bangalore, Mysore, Trivandrum, Bombay, INSDOC (Delhi), and others. Back at US he works at University of Pittsburgh.

1978 Charles P Bourne (US)
Prof Bourne advised many libraries and library schools. He was on invitation of the Sharda Ranganathan Endowment, to deliver the keynote address on Technology in support of library science and information service. He went round the country meeting professional groups and spoke at various library schools, like Bangalore, Madras, and Delhi.

1979 Jo Manning (US)
The American Centre Libraries, Library of Congress's Delhi Office, and American Studies Research Centre, Hyderabad have been primary centres for the consultants and advisors. Jo visited the latter and in his short visit he left behind many suggestions for the growth and development. He witnessed a period of major change and development in the history of this library.

1980 and 1982 James Agenbroad (US)
In the area of automation and computer applications there have been of late a few consultants, and Agenbroad probably felt necessary to up date the Indian technology. His visits to different libraries at Bombay, Kanpur, and Delhi were with this felt need. He extended his helping hand in the area Indian adaptation of computers, in the context of regional languages and the multiplicity of scripts.

1980, 1985 F W Lancaster (US) and 1991
He visited India twice and in both these trips he has been a distinguished speaker at a number of meetings. Prof Lancaster, hails from Library School of University of Illinois. He actively participated in the seminar, at INSDOC's Asian Regional Seminar on Construction of Thesaurus, he was the resource person. He also visited libraries in Pune, Bombay, Madras and Delhi. His ideas of paperless society took the Indian Librarians in to disney's world.

1981 and 1990 Dr. James H Nye (US)
Bibliographer for Southern Asia, Jim has a specialization in Sanskrit. He has been to India on different programmes and for different purposes, including acquisitions, research, and as a leading collaborator of the National Bibliography Project. This project is aimed at compiling a bibliography of 60,000 books in the sixteen official languages of India.

1981 Peter R Lewis (UK)
Mr. Lewis, Director General, Bibliographic Service Division, British Library, U.K., visited different libraries in Calcutta (Kaula, 1981. p. 113).

1981 and 1987 Paul Wasserman (US)
Indian librarians had opportunity to hear from this great expert, and UNESCO consultant, during a seminar in 1981. The seminar had an international audience. He travelled extensively in 1987, and covered a large part of the country, from Punjab to Delhi and to Pune. In this trip he was a resource person at the seminar held in Punjab.

1983, 1984, Dr. David Magier (US) 1986 and 1989
Dr. David, a specialist in Rajasthani, heads the Asian Collection, Columbia University Library. He visited the country for various reasons, which includes research, collection building in his library and as a field specialist.

1983 Hilary Burton and Trudy Brekelbaurn (US)

With the growing specialization in information technology in the science and technology, India kept pace and progressed. The International Crops Research Institute for Semi Arid Topics (ICRISAT), Hyderabad, availed the services of this Team. It concerned the evaluation of the Sorghum and Millet Information Centre. A user survey formed the basis of their project and they elicited much relevant information. They came as Technical Information Specialists from USDA Agricultural Research Service and Texas A & M University, College Station, respectively.

1983 Miles M Jackson (US)

This Hawaiian Librarian, championed the cause of transnational connections in the world of libraries. Being an resource person of encyclopedic nature on International Librarianship, his trip of a month was fruitful in creating an idea of comrade in the profession. He was a keynote speaker at many conferences at Calcutta, Bombay, Madras, Delhi,and Hyderabad. Prof Jackson is the Dean of Library Science, University of Hawaii, Honolulu

1984 Daniel J Boorstin (US)

This was another Librarian of Congress, who visited India on the invitation of the Indian Council of Cultural Relations. He visited many prominent libraries at Varanasi, Calcutta, Madras, Bombay and Delhi. He gave his expert advise at many places. He reviewed the working of the LC's field office at Delhi. He had discussions on the programmes with Prime Minister Indira Gandhi, and with his own colleague E Gene Smith, Field Director at the Delhi Office.

1984-1985 Ronald Chapman and Ellen Chapman (US)

Another consultant-couple, ıich came to India was Chapmans. They were on a special project to catalogue the hundreds of the US Government Documents available in the American Studies Research Centre, Hyderabad. Ronald worked on the projects like evaluation and competence of staff. Ellen worked on evaluating the library collection. This classification of jobs apart they joined their heads to solve many issues, and together visited many other libraries in the country. They conducted a user survey and submitted its results to the authorities (Taher and Kumar, 1990).

1986-87 and 1988 Theodore A Mahr

He visited in 1986-87 on Indo-American Fellowship and in 1988 he visited India under the sponsorship of American Institute of Indian Studies sponsorship. His specialisation is law libraries and he made extensive survey of Indian law libraries.

1987 William Bates (US)

This USIA Book Officer visited India to advise American Studies Research Centre on collection development (Taher and Kumar, 1990).

1987 Bob Usherwood (UK)

He visited India as a consulting faculty in SNDT University, School of Library and Information Science, Bombay. He was a resource person in many workshops and seminars, in Calcutta, Pune, Lucknow and Madras. Mr. Usherwood is a Senior Lecturer in the School of Information Studies, University of Sheffield.

1987 William Webb (US)

Webb, the famous author of Information Sources in Social Sciences, very humbly offered his expertise to the Indian libraries. Webb Report on the development of American Studies and American Library Programmes in India will go in a long way, in achieving two purposes: in informing the library authorities of the trends and needs and in informing his sponsors, the US Government about the state of the art of collections and use patterns (Taher and Kumar, 1990).

1988 Ms. Noreen McMorrow (UK)

She came as a visiting faculty and addressed in many Library Schools, including Jadavpur University, Calcutta. Back at home she is a faculty at University of Strathclyde, Glasgow, UK.

1988 Ms. Frances Wood (UK)

The British Council Specialist Tourist Programme, enabled Ms. Wood to visit the country. She visited many library schools and actively participated in many seminars and assignments. She is a Senior Lecturer, School of Information Studies, University of Sheffield.

1988 Ms. Kyllikki Ruokonen (Finland)

Ms. Kyllikki visited the libraries in the city of Hyderabad. She is the Librarian, Helsinki School of Economics and Business Administration.

1988 Richard Greenfield (US)
In the most neglected areas of study and research did venture Richard and came out with his findings, about the status of Law collections in the American Studies Research Library, Hyderabad. He offered his expertise as Information Specialist. A Library and Book Fellow of the ALA, his visit also included participation in a series of lectures and workshops. He visited many libraries in the country.

1988 Dr. Leo Egghe (Belgium)
Dr. Egghe is the Librarian and Professor at Limburgs Universitair Centrum, Belgium. He extended the Indian thinking on Bibliometrics by his expert advise and lectures. As a visiting faculty he lectured at many library schools and was of immense help to the community of professionals.

1988 Donald G Davis Jr. (US)
His visit was the first of its kind to study the stature of library history and librarianship. His project led to much discussion and debates and impressed on Indian minds the need to write on this neglected subject. He toured in different cities to feel the glory that was India and grandeur that was Indian subcontinent.

1989 and 1990 Donald Johnson (US)
Don has been to India on collection building project. He has his area of interest in Jain Temple collections scattered in Rajasthan, Bhandarkar Oriental Research Institute, Pune, and other manuscript libraries.

1989 Hill Shaw (UK)
Ms. Shaw visited the libraries in Bombay and addressed the professional groups. She is the Customer Support Manager, British Library Document Supply Centre, U.K.

1988 Dr. Jashu Patel (US)
Among the Fulbright Scholars and specialists Dr. Patel, offered his expertise to the SNDT University, Bombay. He extensively toured the library schools in the country. Prof. Patel, is in the Deptt. of Library Science and Communication Media, State University of Chicago.

1989 Faye Powell (US)
A Fellow of American Library Association, she came as a Social

Science Bibliographer to the American Studies Research Centre, for over seven months. She is Asstt. Professor and Social Science Librarian, Portland State University, Portland, Oregon. She enabled planning extended service to the users, and conducted survey to analyse the book and journal collections in Social Sciences.

1989 and 1993 Prof. Rosalind Miller (US)
She visited in both the periods as Fulbright Scholar. In 1989 she was at Madras and in 1993 she was affiliated to American Studies Research Centre. At Hyderabad she was the chief facilitator for a two-day workshop for schools, on information use skills for teachers, students, administrators, and librarians. Prof. Miller is at Georgia Tech. Atlanta, Georgia.

1990 John Sims (UK)
Mr. Sims is the Curator, India Office Library. He was on a special visit to Indian libraries and of great help to communicate the value of manuscript collections.

1990 Graham Shaw (UK)
Mr. Shaw is the Deputy Director of Oriental Collections, British Library. He visited many libraries in India.

BIBLIOGRAPHY

Abul Fazal. *Ain-e-Akbari*. Tr. F Galdwin. London, Unwin, 1918.

——. *Akbarnama*. Tr. H Beveridge. Calcutta, Biblio India, 1897-1921.

Adhikari, P. *History of Library Movement in India, 1901-1947*. Ph D Dissertation. Allahabad University, 1986.

Agarwal, J N. "Libraries in Ancient India", *Indian Librarian*, 8 (March 1954), 141-44.

Ahmed, Rafique S, "Imperial Library of the Mughal Kings", *Proceedings of All Pakistan Historical Conference*, 1 (1951), 392- 393.

Aligarh Library Journal. Aligarh Muslim University, Aligarh, Department of Library Science, vol. 1, 1972.

Ali, Muzaffar, "Oriental Librarianship and Development of Libraries in New India", in *Development of Libraries in New India*. Ed. N B Sen. New Delhi, New Book Society of India, 1965.

All India Conference of Librarians. *A Chapter in Library History of Indo-Pakistan*. Ed. Mumtaz Anwar. Lahore, American Publications, 1980.

Allaudin, Shaikh and R K Rout, "Personal Library of Abdal Rahim-i-Khanan", *Granthana* 2:2 (1991), 179-182.

Altekar, A S. *Education in Ancient India*. Benaras, Kamla, 1948.

Amin, Motibhai M, "The Library Movement in Charotar Mitra Mandal Libraries–The First Library Movement", *Modern Librarian*, 7 (1936-1937), 30-38.

Anand, Virendra K. "Library and librarianship in the city beautiful: An overview", in Souvenir. Calcutta, Bengal Library Assn. 1988. pp.44-48.

Andhra Pradesh (India). Committee on Private Libraries. *Report of the Committee on Private Libraries, November*. Hyderabad, Deptt. of Public Libraries, Government of Andhra Pradesh, 1979.

Annual Report of the South Indian Epigraphy. Department of Epigraphy, G.O.I.

Ansari, Shahabuddin. *Kutab Khana Dari Ek Taaruf*. (Urdu trans. of J

K Gates's Introduction to librarianship). New Delhi, Taraqqi Urdu Bureau, 1984.

Anuar, Hedig, "Asian Librarianship: Its Background, Emergence and Development", in *World Librarianship: A Comparative Study*, Ed. Richard Krzys and Geston Litton. New York, Dekker, 1983.

——. "Patterns of Library Service in Asia and the Pacific Islands", *Library Trends*, 8 (1959), 130-162.

Anwar, M A. *All-India Conference of Librarians, 1918: Chapter in the Library History of Indo-Pakistan.* Lahore, Amer Publications for the Deptt of Library Science, University of Punjab, 1980.

Ara, Matsuo. *Dargahs in medieval India: A historical study on the shrines of Sufi Saints in Delhi with reference to the relationship between the religious authority and the ruling power.* University of Tokyo: Institute of Oriental Culture, 197-

Arberry, A J. *India Office Library: A Historical Sketch.* London, India Office, 1967.

Arnold, Thomas. *Legacy of Islam.* Oxford, O U P, 1931.

Arnold T W, and A Grohmann. *Islamic Book.* Delhi, Munshiram, 1981.

Asheim, Lester E, "University Libraries in Developing Countries", in *Reader in Comparative Librarianship*. Ed. D J Foskett. Englewood, Information Handling Services, 1976. pp.197-203.

Asher, C E Blanshard. *Patronage of Sher Shah: A Study of Form and Meaning in 16th-Century Indo-Islamic Century Architecture.* Volumes I and II. PhD Dissertation. University of Minnesota, 1984. (see also DAI 45/05A, p.1226).

Asia Society. *Art of Mughal India: Painting and Precious Objects, with an intro. text and catalogue notes by Stuart C Welch.* New York, Arno Press, 1976.

Augustine, C A. and G Devarajan. Public Library System in India. New Delhi, Ess Ess Pub. 1990.

Aziz, Sh. Abdul. *Imperial Library of the Mughals*. Delhi, Idara Adabiyat, 1974.

Babu Ram (Lala). "Principal Woolner's Dream on the Phenomenal Growth of the Panjab University Library", *Modern Librarian*, 4 (1933-1934),41-53.

Babur, Zaheeruddin Muhammad. *Baburnama or Tuzuk-e-Baburi or Waqiat-e-Baburi or Babariyat.* Tr. A Beveridge. London, 1921.

Badauni. *Muntakhabat-ut-Twarikh*. Delhi, Idara Adabiyat, 1965.

Banerjee, B C, "Dewey Pleases Pakistan", *Indian Librarian*, 22:4

(1968), 203-204.

Barani, Ziauddin. *Tarikh-e-Firuz Shahi.* Tr. H M Elliot. Delhi, Idara Adabiyat, 1960.

Barua, B P. "Raja Rammohun Ray Library Foundation - Objectives and Implementation", in *Souvenir.* Calcutta, Bengal Library Assn., 1988. pp. 18-24.

Barua, S P, "Early Buddhist Monastic Libraries", *Indian Librarian*, 27 (Sept. 1972), 71-75.

Basham, A L. *Cultural History of India.* Oxford, Clarendon Press, 1975.

Bashiruddin, S and S Sajjad Hussain. *Intezam-e-Kutub Khana.* Delhi, Maktaba-e-Jamia, 1940.

Bavakutty, M. "Libraries and library science education in Kerala", in Souvenir. Calcutta, Bengal Library Assn., 1988, pp. 78-83.

——. Libraries in higher education. New Delhi, Ess Ess Pub. 1991.

Bawa, Gurupratap Singh. *United States Information Agency Organization and Operations in India.* M A Thesis. American University, 1964. (see also DAI 02/03,p. 7).

Bernier, F. *Travels in the Mughal Empire, 1656-1668.* Tr. A Constable. London, O U P, 1891.

Bernier and Kavindracharya at the Mughal Court. Poona, Oriental Research Institute. December, 1945.

Bhanu, D, "Libraries and their Management in Mughal India", *Journal of Indian History,* 31 (1953), 157-173.

——. "Libraries of the Mughal Rulers", *Library Herald*, 14: 3 & 4 (1972), 89-96.

Bharadwaj, B L, "Indian Librarianship in Perspective", *Indian Librarian*, 21: 4 (March 1967), 199-202.

Bhargava, G D, " Public Libraries in India - A Review", *Indian Librarian*, 18: 3 (Dec 1963), 144-150.

Bhatia, Sant Ram,"Contribution of the Punjab to the Indian Library Movement", in *Library Science Today*. Ed. P N Kaula. New York Asia, 1965. pp. 379-386.

——. "History of Libraries and Library movement in the Punjab", *Modern Librarian* 6 (1935-1936), 87-97.

——. "Indian Book League", *Modern Librarian*, 15 (1945), 63.

——. "Indian Librarian in the Changing World", *Modern Librarian*, 15 (1945), 47-51.

——. "Training for librarianship", *Modern Librarian*, 4 (1933-1934), 109-113.

Bhattacharyya, Haridas. Ed. *Cultural Heritage of India*. vol.4. Calcutta, Ramakrishna Mission, 1956.

Biggot, Stuart. *Some Ancient Cities of India*. London, O U P, 1945.

Bilgrami, Mir Gulam Ali Azad. *Maathir-ul-Kiram*. Delhi, Idara Adabiyat, 1961.

Biswas A K, "Libraries in Buddhist Monasteries", *Indian Librarian*, 17 (Sept. 1962), 104-128.

Biswas, Kanti, "Education: Union *vis-a-vis* State Governments", in *Souvenir*. Calcutta, Bengal Library Assn., 1988, pp. 25-28.

Blake, Stephen Paul. *Dar-ul-Khilafat-i-Shahjahanabad: The Padshahi Shahar in Mughal India,1556-1739*. Ph D Dissertation. University of Chicago, 1974. (see also DAI ADD X 1978).

Borden, W A. "Baroda, India, and its Libraries", *Library Journal*, 38 (1913), 659-663.

Bose, Anima. *American Missionaries' Involvement in Higher Education in India in the Nineteenth Century*. Ph D Dissertation. University of Kansas, 1971. (see also DAI 32/04A, p.2019).

Boulton, N Elizabeth. *Early Chinese Buddhist Travel Records as a Literary Genre*. Volumes I and II. PhD Dissertation. Georgetown Univ. 1982. (see also DAI 43/09A, p.2995).

Buhler, *Indian Paleography*. Calcutta, Bagchi, 1945.

Buragohain, Alaka, "Library situation in the state of Assam: A status report", in *Souvenir*. Calcutta, Bengal Library Assn., 1988, pp. 39-43.

Carr, Stephen. *Archaeology and Monumental Remains of Delhi*. London, O U P, 1876.

Chakrabarti, S N, "Some Problems of Book Production in India", *Indian Librarian*, 21 (Dec 1966), 107-122.

Chakravarty, Prabir, "Development of library service in Tripura", in *Souvenir*. Calcutta, Bengal Library Assn., 1988, pp. 125-128.

Chand, Mahindra Pratap, "Muslim Names and their Rendering in Cataloguing", *Indian Librarian*, 26 (Sept 1971), 95-99.

Chandel, A S and P K Mitra, "Library services in Meghalaya", in *Souvenir*. Calcutta, Bengal Library Assn., 1988, pp. 100-104.

Chandler, George. *Libraries in the East*. London, Seminar Press, 1971.

Chandrashekaran, K. *Library Science in India*. Madras, Madras Library Association, 1953.

Chatterjee, Sunil Kumar "Carey Library, Serampore College: A National Heritage", in *Handbook of Libraries*, Archives and Information Centres. New Delhi, Aditya, 1991, pp. 128-137.

Chaudhuri, Nirad C. *Continent of Circle: Being an Essay on the Peoples of India*. New York, O U P, 1966.

Child, Gordon. *New Light on the most Ancient East*. London, Routledge and Paul, 1952.

Chitale, T B, "Review of Library Profession in India", *Herald of Library Science*, 10 (Jan 1971), 42-54.

Chopra, P N. *Society and Culture in Mughal Age*. New Delhi, Ashajanak, 1976.

Commissariat, M S. *Mandelso's Travels in Western India*. Oxford, O U P, 1931.

Cultural Heritage of India. 3 vols. Calcutta, Ramakrishna Centenary Memorial Committee, 1937.

Dahl, Suend. *History of the Book*. London, 1945.

Dar, M Ibrahim. *Literary and Cultural Activities in Gujarat Under the Khiljis and the Sultanate*. Bombay, The author, 1960.

Das Gupta. *Jaina System of Education*. Calcutta, Mukherjee, 1969.

Das Gupta, A K, "How Learned were the Mughals: Reflections on Muslim Libraries in India", *Library History*, 10 (Jul 1975), 241-254.

Das Radhagovinda, "Libraries in Medieval India", *Herald of Library Science*, 3: 2-3, (1964), 126-130.

Dutta, Ajit Kumar, "Andaman and Nicobar Islands: Marching towards modernised public library system", in *Souvenir*. Calcutta, Bengal Library Assn., 1988, pp. 29-32.

Datta, B K, "Early Monastic Libraries and Other Institutional Libraries in India", *Library History Review*, 1 (1974), 18-42.

——. "India's Contribution to the Art of Early Printing", *Indian Librarian*, 17 (Dec 1962), 160-161.

——. *Libraries and Librarianship of Ancient and Medieval India*. Delhi, Atma Ram, 1970.

Dutta, D N. *Short History of Libraries with Special Reference to India, Indian Libraries and Their Uses*. Calcutta, World Press, 1975.

Datta, R, "India Office Library: Its History, Resources, and Functions", *Library Quarterly*, 36 (1966), 99-148.

Davids, T W Rhys. *Buddhist India*. New York, Putnam, 1903.

Davis, Donald G, "Status of Library History in India: A Report of an Informal Survey and a Selective Bibliographic Essay", *Journal of Library and Information Science*, 14:2, (Dec 1989), 98-114.

——. "Indian Library History: A Bibliographic Essay on Major English-Language printed Works", *South Asia Library Notes and*

Queries, No. 26 (Fall-Winter 1989-1990), 17-23.

Denning, M B. *Mosaics from India; Talks about India, its Peoples, Religions and Customs*. New York, Young People's Missionary Movement, 1902.

Deshpande, K S. "Library Movement in the Mysore State", *Indian Librarian*, 17 (1962), 1-18.

Devahuti, D. *Harsha: A Political Study*. Oxford, Clarendon Press, 1970.

Devapriam, Emma. *Influence of Western Art on Mughal Painting*. Ph.D Dissertation. Case Western Reserve Univ. 1972. (see also DAI 33/09A, p.5067)

Dhyani, Pushpa. *Classification Schemes and Indian Libraries*. New Delhi, Metropolitan, 1983.

Diehl, K S. *Primary Sources for 16th-19th Century Studies in Bengal, Orissa and Bihar Libraries*. Calcutta, American Institute of Indian Studies, 1971.

——. "Lucknow Printers", in *Comparative Librarianship*. Ed. N N Gidwani. Delhi, Vikas, 1973. pp. 115-128.

Dutt, N M. *Baroda and its Libraries*. Baroda, Central Library, 1928.

——. "History of Indian Libraries from Earliest Times to the Present Day", *Modern Librarian*, 2 (1932), 69-76.

——. "Library Movement in India", *Hindustan Review*, 54 (1930), 57-64.

Ettinghausen, R, "Near Eastern book covers and their influence on European bindings: a report on the exhibition 'History of Book-binding' at the Baltimore Museum of Art, 1957-58", *Ars Orientalis* 3 (1959), 113-131.

Fazle Kabir M. *Libraries of Bengal, 1700-1947: The Story of Bengali Renaissance*. New Delhi, Promilla, 1989.

Firishta, Muhammad. *Tarikh-i-Firishta*. Tr. J Briggs.

Fryer, John. *Travels in India in the 17th Century (1672-1681)*. London, Trubner, 1873.

Fusfeld, W Edward. *Shaping of Sufi Leadership: The Naqshbandiyya Mujaddidiyya, 1750 to 1920*. Ph D Dissertation. University of Pennsylvania, 1981. (see also DAI 42/06A, p.2807).

Ganguly, D C. *History of Paramara Dynasty*. Delhi, Gian, 1933.

Gardner, K B. "A Persian bookbinding of the sixteenth century", *Brit. Museum Qly.*, 29 (1964-65), 10-11.

George, K M. *Indian Libraries: Trends and Perspectives*. Hyderabad, Orient Longman, 1985.

Gidwani, N N. *Comparative Librarianship: Essays in Honour of Professor D N Marshall*. Delhi, Vikas, 1972.

Giles, H A. *Travels of Fa-Hien*. Cambridge, Cambridge Univ Press, 1923.

Gowen, Herbert H. *History of Indian Literature; From Vedic Times to the Present Day*. Delhi, Seema, 1975.

Goyal, S P. *Indian Librarianship: Essays in Honour of S R Bhatia*. Delhi, Scientific Book, 1973.

Granthalaya Sarvasamu. Vijayawada, Andhra Pradesh Library Association, Vol. 1, 1915.

Gupta, A B Sen, "National Library Buildings (of India): Old and New", *Lucknow Librarian*, 2: 4 (March 1964), 189-201.

Gupta B M. Ed. *Handbook of Libraries, Archives and Information Centres in India*. v.1-13 (-). 1985-1993 (-). New Delhi, Aditya.

Haider, S I, "Bibliographical Heritage of Muslims", *International Library Review*, 29 (1979), 207-218.

Harvey J F, "Libraries in Bombay", *Indian Librarian*, 28 (1973-1974), 129-136.

——. *Comparative and International Library Science*. Metuchen, Scarecrow, 1977.

Harvey, J F and S A Musavi, "Tehran Mosque Libraries and a Comparison with American Christian Church Libraries", *International Library Review*, 13 (1981), 385-395.

Herald of Library Science. v1-; 1962-. Banaras Hindu University, Varanasi.

Hessell, Alfred. *History of Libraries*. New Brunswick, Scarecrow. 1955. pp.30-31.

Hidayat Hosain, "Library of Tipu Sultan", *Islamic Culture*, 14 (1940). 139-167.

"Historical Museum-cum-Archives of the Deccan College", *Bull. of the Deccan College*, 30 (1971), 141-142.

Howell, E B. *Handbook to Agra and Taj*. London, Unwin, 1940.

Horrocks, Norman, National Organizations", in *Comparative and International Library Science*. Ed. J F Harvey. Metuchen, Scarecrow, 1977. pp.48-62.

Hoskote, Vasanti N. "Library movement in South Kanara: Historical survey", *Timeless Fellowship*, 3 & 4 (1966-67), 159-177.

Hossain, Serwar, "Akbar - The Great Library Administrator", in *Handbooks of Libraries*. New Delhi, Aditya, 1991. vol.9. pp. 209-212.

Hui-Li. *Life of Hieun Tsang*. Peiking, Chinese Buddhist Association, 1959.

Hussain, Ghulam. *Siyar-ul-Mutakhirin*. Tr. Sayyid G H Khan. Delhi, Idara Adabiyat, 1949.

Husain, M S. *Audio-Visual Library Methods*. Aligarh, Aligarh Muslim University, 1965.

——. *Audio-Visual Librarianship (A Select Bibliography of Articles, Books, Documents and Pamphlets published during 1961-1966)*. Aligarh, Aligarh Muslim University, 1965.

——. *Libraries and the Audio-Visual Programmes*. Aligarh, Aligarh Muslim University, 1966.

Husain, Mahmud. *Of Libraries and Librarians*. Karachi, University Library, 1974.

IASLIC Bulletin v1-; 1956-. Calcutta, IASLIC.

Ijari, S R. "March of libraries in Karnataka", in *Souvenir*. Calcutta, Bengal Library Assn., 1988, pp. 71-77.

Ikram, S M. *Muslim Civilization in India*. New York, Columbia Univ. Press, 1964.

ILA Bulletin (continuation of *Library Bulletin* 1942-1946; *Abgila* 1949-1953) v1-; 1965-. Delhi, Indian Library Association.

Imamuddin, S M. *Some Leading Muslim Libraries of the World*. Dhaka, Islamic Foundation, 1983.

Inamdar, N B and A W Shakira, "Management of Libraries in the State of Hyderabad: An Overview", *On Development in Administration Under H E H The Nizam VII.*, Eds. Shameem Aleem and M A Aleem. Hyderabad, The editor, 1984.

Indian Librarian. v1-; 1946-. Jalandhar City, Sant Ram Bhatia.

Indian Library Journal 1-10; 1924-1934. Vijayawada, All India Public Libraries Association.

Iqbalnama-i-Jahangiri. Translated into Urdu by Maulvi Muhammad Zakriya. Hyderabad, Translation Bureau, 1928.

I-Tsing. *Record of Buddhist Religion as Proclaimed in India and Malay Archipelago (AD 671-695)*. Tr. Takakusa. Oxford, O U P, 1896.

Jaffar, S M. *Rise and Fall of the Ghaznavids*. Delhi, Idara Adabiyat, 1972.

——. *Some Critical Aspects of Muslim Rule in India*. Delhi, Idara Adabiyat, 1972.

Jahangir, Nooruddin. *Tuzuk-i-Jahangiri*. Delhi, Idara Adabiyat, 1955.

James, H R. *Education and Statesmanship in India, 1797-1910*. London, Longman Green, 1911.

Jha V.S. Chairman. National Library Review Committee. Report. 1968.

Johnson, D C, "German Influences on the Development of Research Libraries in Nineteenth Century Bombay", *Journal of Library History,* 21 (1986), 215-277.

Joshi, P M, "Special Research Institute (and Library) of Medieval India", in *Comparative Librarianship.* Ed. N N Gidwani. Delhi, Vikas, 1973. pp.85-112.

Kabir, M, "Libraries and Academies During the Buwaihid Period, A C. 946-1055, *Islamic Culture*; 33 (1959) ??

Kabir, Humayun. *Indian Heritage.* Bombay, Asia, 1955.

Kalia, D R "Data on public libraries in India", *CLIS Observer* 1-2 Jan-Jun, 1994, 3-11.

Karaka, Dosabhai Framji. *History of the Parsis including Their Manners, Customs, Religion, and Present Position.* 2 vols. London, Macmillan, 1884.

Kaser, David, "Library Development in Asia", *Encyclopedia Americana.* v.17. New York, American Corp. 1984. p.324.

Kaula, Namita, "Indian Library Movement: A Chronology (1910-1977)", *Herald of Library Science,* 16 (1977), 108-130.

Kaula, P N *Indian Library Literature.* Delhi, Delhi Library Association, 1956.

———. *Library Science Today: Ranganathan Festschrift.* New York, Asia, 1965.

———. "Notes and News", *Herald of Library Science,* 15 (1976), 71, 75-76, 173, 387.

———. "Notes and News", *Herald of Library Science,* 16 (1977), 71, 73, 77-78.

———. "Notes and News", *Herald of Library Science,* 20 (1981), 113,119.

———. "Notes and News", *Herald of Library Science,* 22 (1984), 102-103. (Includes "Library profession then and now", lecture delivered at Mithila Univ., Darbhanga on 14 April, 1983).

———. "Notes and News", *Herald of Library Science,* 23 (1984), 235.

———. "Notes and News", *Herald of Library Science,* 25 (1986), 108, 119.

———. "Notes and News", *Herald of Library Science,* 26 (1987), 119-120, 141, 276.

———. "Notes and News", *Herald of Library Science,* 27 (1988), 276-277, 281.

———. "Notes and News", *Herald of Library Science,* 28 (1989), 267.

———. "Recent Developments of Libraries in India", *Library World,*

66:779 (May 1965), 276-278.

——. *Library Movement in India*. Delhi, Delhi Library Association, 1958.

Kautilya. *Arthashastra*. Tr. Shomasastry. Calcutta, Bagchi, 1965.

Kerala Granthasala Sangam. *Silver Jubilee: Twenty Five years of Growth, 1945-1970*. Trivandrum, The author, 1970.

Kesavan, B S, " Editorial", *Annals of Library Science and Documentation*, 15 (1968), 53-55.

——. Book in India: a compilation. Delhi, National Book Trust, 1986.

——. *History of Printing and Publishing in India: A Story of Cultural Re-awakening*. Delhi, National Book Trust, 1985. (Vol.1-)

——. *India's National Library*. Calcutta, The National Library, 1961.

Khan, Gulab, "Islamic Studies Libraries in India", *Handbook of Libraries, Archives, and Information Centres in India*, ed. B M Gupta, *et al*. Delhi, Information Industry Publications, 1984-85.

Khan, M S, "Early History of Bengali Printing", *Library Quarterly*, 32 (Jan 1962), 51-61.

Khan, Mubarak Ali. The Court of Great Mughals based on persian sources. *Bochum*: 1976. (Ph.D Thesis, University of Bochum).

Khan, Muhammad Saqi Mustaid. *Maathir-i-Alamgiri*. Tr. Henry Vansittart. Delhi, Idara Adabiyat, 1962.

Khan, Rahmat Ali, "Grand court of the Khan Khanan", *Lalit Kala* No.21, 27-35.

Khosla, Raj, K. *Men of Library Science and Libraries in India*. Delhi, Premier, 1967.

Khuda Bakhsh, S "Renaissance of Islam", *Islamic Culture*, 4 (1930), 297.

——. "Islamic Libraries", *Nineteenth Century*, 52 (1902), 125-139.

——. "Islamic Libraries", *Khuda Bakhsh Library Journal*, 6:6 (1972), 1-16.

Khurshid, Anis, "Growth of Libraries in India", *International Library Review*, 4 (1972), 21-65.

Konnur, M B. *Transnational Library Relations: The Indo-American Experience*. New Delhi, Concept, 1990.

——. "Dr S R Ranganathan and American Librarianship", in *Dimensions of Library and Information Science: Kaula Festchrift*. Ed. Velga Venkatappaiah. New Delhi, Concept, 1990.

Kothari, L S. Chairman. Education Commission. Report. New Delhi, Publication Div. 1968.

Kozlowski, G Charles. *Muslim Endowments and Society in British*

India. Ph D Dissertation. University of Minnesota, 1980. (DAI 41/11A, p.4801).

Krzys, Richard, "Library Historiography", *Encyclopedia of Library and Information Science.* v.15. New York Dekker, 1975. p.308.

Krzys, Richard and Mohammed Aman, "Middle Eastern Librarianship: Its Background-Emergence and Development", in *World Librarianship: A Comparative Study*, by Richard Krzys and Gaston Litton. New York, Dekker, 1983. pp.59-62.

Kudalkar, J S. *Baroda Library Movement: A Short Account of the Origin and Growth of the Central Library Department of the Baroda State.* Baroda, Central Library, 1928.

Kumar, Girija. *Library Development in India.* Delhi, Vikas, 1986.

Kumar, Narinder, "Manuscriptology and Manuscript Libraries in India", in *Library and Information Science, Current Trends in India.* Eds. P K Gupta and U Pawan. Jaipur, RBSA Publishers, 1986.

Kumar, P S G. *Indian Library Chronology.* New Delhi, Metropolitan. 1977.

———. *Research in Library and Information Science in India.* New Delhi, Concept, 1987.

Kumar, P Vijay. *Library Literature in Telugu, 1915-1981.* Ed Velaga Venkatappaiah. Guntur, Navodaya Publishers, 1981.

Labhaya, Ram, "Punjab Public Library", *Modern Librarian*, 15 (1945), 59-60.

Lahori, Mulla Abdul Hamid. *Badshahnama.* Delhi, B R Publishing Corp. 1975.

Lakshminarayana, K. *Pracheena Bharatiya Granthalaya Charitra.* Pamarru, Itihasa Parisodhaka Mala, 1946.

Lara, Manrique de. *Mughals.* Delhi, D K Publishers, 1984.

Law, B C, "Antiquity of Libraries in India", *Modern Librarian*, 1 (1949), 3-7.

Law, N N. *Promotion of Learning in India During the Mohammedan Rule.* London, Longmans, 1916.

———. *Promotion of Learning in India by the Early European Settlers up to About 1800 A D.* London, Longmans and Green, 1915. *Librarians in India and Pakistan: Commemorative Volume, 1890-1949.* Delhi, D K Publishers. 1969.

Levey, M, *et al.* "Some notes on the chemical technology in an eleventh century Arabic work on bookbinding", *Isis* 47 (1956), 239-243.

Lianzama, C. "History and development of library movement of

Mizoram state", in *Souvenir*. Calcutta, Bengal Library Assn., 1988. pp. 105-106.

Library Herald. v1-; 1958/59-. Delhi, Delhi Library Association.

Library History v1-; 1973-. Calcutta, K K Roy Pvt Ltd.

Library Miscellany. 1912-1919. Baroda, State Library Department.

Lipsius, Justus. *Brief Outline of the History of Libraries*. Chicago, 1907.

"A Little-known Bengal (Secretariat) Library", *Statesman*, 18 Oct. 1983.

Lockyer, Dora. Provision of Books and libraries by the East India Company in India, 1611-1858. FLA Thesis, 1977.

Ludington, Flora B, "American Contribution to Foreign Library Establishment and Rehabilitation", *Library Quarterly*, 24 (1954), 192-204.

Maasir-i-Rahimi. *Mulla Abdul Baqi*. 3 vols. Delhi, Metropolitan Book Co. 1985.

Mahajan, S G. *History of the Public Library Movement in Maharashtra*. Pune, Shubada-Saraswat Publication, 1984.

——. . "Library development in Maharashtra", in *Souvenir*. Calcutta, Bengal Library Assn. 1988. pp. 89-94.

Mahapatra, M. "Libraries and library movement in Orissa - An Overview", in Souvenir. Calcutta, Bengal Library Assn. 1988. p. 107-111.

Mahmood, Syed. *History of English Education in India*. Aligarh, Aligarh College Press, 1895.

Mahr, Theodore A. "Introduction to law and law libraries in India" Law Libr. J. 82 (1990), 91-128.

Majumdar, U. *India's National Library: Systematization and Modernization*. Calcutta, National Library, 1987.

Mandelso-Harris, Johann. *Travels*. v.2

Mangla P B. ed. *Library and Information Science Education in India: Papers and Recommendations of an All-India Seminar held at the Department of Library Science, during 3-8 October, 1977*. Delhi, Macmillan, 1981.

Mangla P B and others. *Fifty Years of Librarianship in India: Past, Present and Future*. Delhi, Indian Library Association, 1983.

Marshall, D N. *History of Libraries: Ancient and Medieval*. New Delhi, Oxford and I B H, 1983.

——. *Mughals in India: A Bibliographical Survey*. London, Mansell, 1985.

———. "Eight Conference of Indian Association of Special Libraries and Information Centres", in *Comparative Librarianship*. Ed. N N Gidwani. Delhi, Vikas, 1973. pp. 230-242.

Martin, *Miniature Paintings and Painters of Persia, India and Turkey*. Delhi, Motilal, 1970.

Mathews, Basil. *India Reveals Herself*. London, O U P, 1937.

Max Muller. *History of Ancient Sanskrit Literature as far as it Illustrates the Primitive Religion of the Brahmans*. New York, A M S Press, 1978.

Mehta, J C and N N Mohanty. *50 Years of Indian Library Association, 1933-1983*. New Delhi, Indian Library Association, 1983.

Melhotra. Chairman. University Grants Commissions' Committee on Revision of Pay Scales of Teachers in Universities and Colleges. New Delhi, U G C. 1986.

Miller, E Edgar. *Problem of Literacy in Central Provinces and Berrar, India*. PhD Dissertation. New York Univ. 1939. (DAI .LM S0/146).

Minhajus, Siraj. *Tabaqat-i-Nasiri*. Tr. Maj. Raverty. Delhi, Manoharlal, 1970.

Mishra, Jogesh. *History of Libraries and Librarianship in Modern India Since 1850*. Delhi, Atma Ram, 1979.

———. *et al.* "Library Movement in Bihar, Maharashtra, Madhya Pradesh and Punjab", *Herald of Library Science*, 3: 2-3 (1964), 185-206.

Mitra, Rajendralal. *History of the Society*. Part 1. Calcutta, Asiatic Society, 1885.

Modern Librarian. v1-16; 1930-1946. Lahore, Punjab Library Association.

Moreland, W H and Atul Chandra Chatterjee. *Short History of India*. New York, David McKay, 1957.

Mukerjee, A K. *Librarianship: Its Philosophy and History*. Bombay, Asia, 1966.

Mukerjee, S K. *Development of Libraries and Library Science in India*. Calcutta, World Press, 1969.

Mukerji, S N,"Education, History of" *Encyclopaedia Britannica*. Chicago, Encyclopaedia Britannica Inc. 1988. v.18.

Mukherji, B, "Presidential Address on Libraries Ancient and Modern", *IASLIC Bulletin*, 9 (1964), 166-170.

Murthy, M K. *Examination of Primary Sources in Indian Library Historiography*. 1974.

Mustaqi, Rizqullah. *Waqiat-i-Mustaqi*. Tr. H M Elliot. Delhi, Idara Adabiyat, 1979.

Nadvi, Abu Zaffar, "Libraries During the Muslim Rule in India", *Islamic Culture*, 19 (1945), 329-347; 20 (1946), 3-20.

Nadvi, Syed Sulaiman, "Literary Progress of the Hindus under Muslim Rule", *Islamic Culture*, 13 (1939), 412-426.

Nagar, M L. *Foundation of the Library Movement in India*. Ludhiana, India Library Institute and Bibliographical Centre, 1983.

———. *First American Library Pioneer in India*. 2nd ed.Ludhiana, Punjab, Indian Library Institute and Bibliographical Centre, 1983.

Nagaraj, M N. "Indian Association of Special Libraries and Information Centres", in *Souvenir*. Calcutta, Bengal Library Assn., 1988, pp. 12-17.

Nagaraj, M N and A K Ghosh. *National Library of India, 1903-1978*. Calcutta, National Library, 1978.

Nair, P R. *Library Movement in Kerala: The Need for Reform and Legislation*. Trivandrum, Trivandrum Writers Club, 1974.

Nair, R Raman. "Nature and use of Library History", Seminar Paper, *ILA Conference*, 1994 at Bangalore, Delhi, ILA, 1994, 1-13.

———. "Public library systems in ancient south India", *ILA Bulletin*, 27:1991.

National Informatics Centre: District Information System of National Informatics Centre. New Delhi. (n.d)

Narasimhan, S, "Classification of Oriental Libraries with the Case Studies of Four Regions", in *Ranganathan's Philosophy*. Ed. T S Rajagopalan. New Delhi, Vikas, 1986. pp. 228-237.

Noer, Count. *Akbar*. London, O U P, 1927.

Nashabi, H, "Three R's in the Mosque: The Pursuit of Learning as a Sacred Duty, *UNESCO Courier*, 30 (Dec 1977), 3-20.

National Library of India: Golden Jubilee Souvenir, Sunday, 1st February, 1953. Calcutta, National Library, 1953.

Nazir Ahmed, Shamsul Ulema. "Note on the Library of Abdur Rahim Khan-I-Khanan, the first Prime Minister of Emperor Akbar", *J.D.L (Calcutta University)*, 16 (1927), 58.

Neelameghan, A. *Development of Medical Societies and Medical Periodicals in India, 1730-1920*. Calcutta, IASLIC, 1963.

Neild, Susan Margaret. *Madras: The Growth of a Colonial City in India (1780-1840)*. PhD Dissertation. University of Chicago,1977. (see also DAI 38/03A,p.1581).

Nurullah, S and J P Naik. *History of Education in India During British Period*. New York Macmillan, 1943.

"Obituaries, K M Asadullah", *Indian Librarian*, 4 (1949), 116-122.

Ohdedar, A K. *Growth of the Library in the Modern India: 1498-1836*. Calcutta, World Press, 1966.

———. "Libraries in Muslim India", *Modern Librarian*, 15 (1945), 57-59.

———. "Library development in Calcutta, 1700-1900" *IASLIC Bull.* 37 (1992), 1-14

Ojha, P N. *North Indian Social Life During Mughal Period*. Delhi, Oriental, 1975.

Oldenburg, Veena Talwar. *Peril, Pestilence and Perfidy: The Making of Colonial Lucknow, 1856-1877*. Ph D Dissertation. University of Illinois at Urbana Champaign, 1979. (DAI 41/02A,p. 759)

Oliver, Robert. *Communication and Culture in Ancient India and China.* Syracuse, NY. Syracuse Univ. Press, 1971.

Ovington, *Voyage to Surat*. Delhi, D K Publishers, 1869.

Palmer, B I, "Madras Library Movement, 1895-1945", *Modern Librarian*, 15 (1945), 51-56.

Panda, B D. *History of Library Development*. New Delhi, Anmol, 1992.

Pandya, T R. *Education in Baroda*. Bombay, Manecjee Nowrogee, 1915 (Based on a doctoral thesis submitted to Columbia University, NY).

Parulkar, R V. *Literacy in India.* Calcutta, Macmillan, 1939.

Pathak, V and L S Ramaiah. *Bibliography of Research in Library and Information Science*. Gurgaon, Indian Documentation Service, 1986.

Patil, D R "Gupta inscriptions and Puranic traditions", *Bull of the Deccan College Res Inst.* 2 (1940), 148-165.

Patwardhan, Chintamani. *History of Education in Medieval India.* Poona, Anyabbhashan, 1939.

Prasad, Anirudh. *Libraries in Medieval India.* Ph.D Thesis Bhagalpur University, 1977.

———. "Libraries in Medieval India", *Library Herald*, 20 (1982). 155-59.

Prasad, Ishwari. *Life and Times of Humayun*. Bombay, Longman, 1955.

Prasher, R G. *Indian Library Literature*. New Delhi, Today & Tomorrow, 1971.

Priolkar, A K. *Printing Press in India*. Bombay, Marathi Samshodhana Mandala, 1958.

———. "Indian Incunabula", in *Comparative Librarianship*. Ed. N N Gidwani. Delhi, Vikas, 1973. pp. 129-135.

Puri, B N. *Cities of Ancient India*. Meerut, Meenakshi Prakashan, 1966.

Qaisar, Ahsan Jan. *Indian Response to European Technology and Culture, (A D 1498-1707)*. Delhi, O U P, 1982.

Qandhari, Arif. *Tarikh-i-Akbari*. Delhi, Munshiram, 1969.

Qureshi, M A. *Muslim Education and Learning in Gujarat, 1297-1758*. Baroda, M S University, 1972.

Raj, Janak, "Library movement in Haryana", in Souvenir. Calcutta, Bengal Library Assn, 1988. pp. 66-70.

Rajgopalan, T S "Trends and Perspectives in Indian Librarianship", *Presidential Address, ILA Conference, 1987*.

Rajbee, Mahmood, "Problem of Manuscripts in India", *Indian Librarian*, 23 (June 1968), 56-60.

Raju, A A N. *History of the Library Movement in Andhra Pradesh, 1900-1956*. Delhi, Ajanta, 1988.

Ramakrishna Rao, K, "Library Development in India", *Library Quarterly*, 31:2 (April 1961), 135-153.

———. "Preparation of Librarians in India", *Library Quarterly*, 33 (1963), 242-252.

Ramanayya, I Venkata, "Library Movement in Kerala", *Modern Librarian*, 15 (1945), 61-62.

Ranganathan, S R, "On Library History of India", quoted in *Herald of Library Science*, 12 (1973), 208.

———. "University Library Then and Now", *Library Herald*, 6 (July-Oct. 1963), 61-69.

———. *National Library Grid of Public Library System based on Library Acts*. Ed P N Kaula. Banaras Hindu University, Varanasi, The editor, 1972.

———. *Public Library System: India, Sri Lanka, U K and USA*– Comparative Library Legislation. Bangalore, Sharda Ranganathan Endowment for Library Science, 1972

———. *Library Tour 1948: Europe and America: Impressions and Reflections*. Delhi, Indian Library Association,

Ravichandra Rao, I K. *Quantitative Methods for Library and Information Science*. New York, Wiley, 1983.

Ray, A C, "Promotion of Learning and Culture Through the Library in

India", *Indian Librarian*, 16 (Mar 1962), 215-218.

Ray, K, "Library and Art of Penmanship", *Education in Medieval India*. Delhi, B R Publishing Corporation, 1984.

Richer, J. *History of Mission in India*. Delhi, Munshiram, 1908.

Rodrigues, Pia De Menezes, "Library movement in Goa", in *Souvenir*. Calcutta, Bengal Library Assn. 1988. pp. 57-61.

Roy, Arun, " Bengal Library Association", in *Souvenir*. Calcutta, Bengal Library Assn. 1988. pp. 149-152.

Roychoudhury, Makhanlal, "Akbar was literate", *Indian Historical Quarterly*, 32 (1956), 81-89.

Roychaudhury, Prabhir, "Public library development in West Bengal: A review", in *Souvenir*. Calcutta, Bengal Library Assn. 1988. pp. 135-148.

Sachau, E C. *Alberuni's India*. London, O U P, 1904.

Sadhu, S N and B N Saraf. *Library Legislation in India: A Historical and Comparative Study*. New Delhi, Sagar, 1967.

Saha, Ramkrishna, "Library Movement in West Bengal", in *Souvenir*. Calcutta, Bengal Library Assn. 1988. pp. 153-155.

Sahai, Yaduendra, "Pothikhana of Jaipur", in *Handbook of Libraries*. New Delhi, Aditya, 1991. vol. 9. pp. 108-111.

Saini, M L, "Manuscript Literature in Indian Languages", *ILA Bulletin*, 5 (Jan-Mar 1969), 6-21.

Saletore, B A. *India's Diplomatic Relations with the East*. Bombay, Popular, 1960.

Sankalia, Hasmukh D. *University of Nalanda*. Madras, Paul, 1934.

Sarkar, Jadunath. *Anecdotes of Aurengzeb and Historical*. Delhi, D K Publishers. 1970.

———. *Fall of the Mughal Empire*. Delhi, Munshiram, 1950. .

———. "English and Their Gifts to India", in *The Introduction to Civilization of India, Emergence of India and Pakistan into Modern World.* Chicago, Univ. Chicago Press, 1957.

Saryngjee, Sahay. *History of Libraries in Ancient India Down to 1200 AD*. Ph.D Thesis, Bhagalpur University, 1977

Sastri, M L R C, "Library in Islam", *Bengal Past and Present*, 61 (1941), 65-70.

Satthianadhan,S. *History of Education in the Madras Presidency*. Madras, Srinivasa Varadhachari, 1891.

Saxena, K K, "Libraries in Mughal India", *Orissa Historical Research Journal*, 16 (1967), 61-67.

Schimmel, Annamerie. *Islamic Literatures of India.* Harrosowitz, Osbaden, 1973.

Sen N B. *Development of Libraries in New India.* New Delhi, New Book Society, 1965.

———. *Progress of Libraries in Free India.* New Delhi, New Book Society of India, 1967

Sengupta, Benoyendra, "Librarianship in India, Profession and Practice", *Journal of Library Science*, 6 (1963), 51-53.

———. "Libraries and Library Movement in India", *Indian Librarian*, 15:1 (Jun 1960), 9-15.

Shah, P C. "Libraries in Gujarat", in *Souvenir.* Calcutta, Bengal Library Assn. 1988. pp. 62-65.

Sharma, C D. "Library movement in Rajasthan", in *Souvenir.* Calcutta, Bengal Library Assn. 1988. pp.115-124.

Sharma, J S. *Substance of Library Science.* New Delhi, Asia, 1965.

Sharma, Om Prakash, "History of the Development of the University Libraries in India - Appraisal", *Indian Librarian*, 19:3 (Dec 1964), 128-143.

———. "Development of Library Education in India: An Historical Survey", *Library Association Record*, 67:10 (Nov, 1965), 388-394.

———. "Literature of the History of Library Movement in India", *Herald of Library Science*, 7 (1968), 10-18.

———. *Forces Behind the Public Library Movement, 1858-1892.* Ph D Dissertation. University of Chicago, 1970.

Sharma, Pandey S K. Libraries and Society. 2d ed. New Delhi, Ess Ess Publishers, 1992

Sharma, Ravindra Nath, "Indian Library Association", *Encyclopedia of Library and information Science.* v.38. New York, Dekker, 1987. pp. 230-235.

———. *Indian Academic Libraries and Dr. S R Ranganathan: A Critical Study.* Delhi, Sterling, 1986.

———. *Indian Librarianship: Perspectives and New Prospects.* New Delhi, Kalyani, 1981.

Sharma, Ram. *Bibliography of Moghul India.* Bombay, Karnatak Publishing House, 1970.

Shastri, A, "Book Activity in Ancient India", *Indian Librarian*, 6 (June 1951), 16-18.

Shastri, Raghunandan. *Book Activity in Ancient India.* Calcutta, Bagchi, 1951.

Shirazi, Rafiuddin Ibrahim. *Tazkirat-ul-Muluk*. Delhi, Munshiram, 1955.

Shetty, Umapathy K. *American Books for Library Science Programmes in Developing Countries with Special Reference to India*. Tiptur, Sudarsana Prakashana, 1972.

———. *Standards for Teachers College Libraries in the State of Karnataka, India*. Ph D Dissertation. University of Pittsburgh, 1975. (see also DAI 36/04A,p. 1882).

Shriven, M Nixon II. *Centralized R&D: Cotton Trade Association Laboratories in Britain and India, 1923-1939*. Ph D Dissertation. University of Pennsylvania, 1978. (see also DAI 39/07A, p.4406).

Shukla, C P, "Development of University Libraries in India", *Library World*, 63:741 (Mar 1962), 235-242.

Siddiqui, I M, "Libraries in the Mughal Period: A Study", *International Library Movement*, 7 (1985), 146-148.

Singh, N Girdhari, "Development of Libraries in Manipur", in *Souvenir*. Calcutta, Bengal Library Assn. 1988. pp. 95-99.

Singh, Sewa. *Indian Library Literature, 1971-1980: An Annotated Bibliographic Guide*. New Delhi, Today and Tomorrow, 1986.

———. *Indian Library Literature, 1981-1985: An Annotated Bibliographic Guide*. New Delhi, Ess Ess Publications, 1988.

Singhal, Arvind and Everrett M Rogers. *India's Information Revolution*. New Delhi, Sage, 1989.

Sleeman, William. *Rambles and Reflections of an Indian Official*. London, 1844. II.

Smith, Vincent. *Akbar the Great Moghul, 1542-1605*. Delhi, S.Chand, 1966.

———. *Moghul Architecture of Fatehpur Sikri*. Delhi, S Chand, 1956.

———. *Oxford History of India from Earliest Times to the End of 1911*. New York, OUP, 1923.

———. "Treasure of Akbar", *JRAS*, (April 1915), 231.

Srivastava, Rochna, *et al*. "Library movement in Uttar Pradesh: A state of the art", in *Souvenir*. Calcutta, Bengal Library Assn. 1988. pp. 129-134.

Stewart, Charles. *Descriptive Catalogue of the Oriental Library of the Late Tipu Sultan of Mysore* Cambridge, Cambridge Univ. Press, 1809.

Strickland, W and T W M Marshall. *Catholic Missions in Southern India*. New York, A M S Press, 1985.

Sufi, G M D. *Al-Minhaj*. Lahore, Ashraf, 1941. (A doctoral thesis on

Education of Muslims in India, submitted to University of Paris in 1935).

Swamy, K S K. "Royal library at Bijapur", *Islamic Culture*, 8 (1934), 115-119.

Taher, Mohamed, "American Studies in India", in *Handbook of Libraries, Archives and Information Centres in India.* Ed B M Gupta. v.8. Delhi, Aditya, 1990. pp.230-240.

———. "American Studies Research Centre, Hyderabad", in *Handbook of Libraries, Archives and Information Centres in India.* Ed B M Gupta. v.8. Delhi, Aditya, 1990. pp.165-174.

———. "India", in *Encyclopedia of Library History*. Ed. W A Weigand and D G Davis. New York, Garland, 1994.

———. "Libraries as Instruments of Socio-Economic Development", *Hindu* (March 20, 1990), 19.

———. "Madrasa Libraries in India: A Case Study of Nadvatul Ulama, Lucknow", in *Handbook of Libraries, Archives and Information Centres in India.* Ed B M Gupta. v.9. Delhi, Aditya (1991).

———. "Mosque Libraries: Bibliographical Essay", *Libraries and Culture*, (1990), (1992)

———. "Role of Libraries in Promotion of Reading Habits", *Paper presented in the Seminar held at Hyderabad Book Fair, 17 January, 1990.*

———. "Salar Jung Museum and Library: Its Growth and Development as a Liberal University", in *Handbook of Libraries, Archives and Information Centres in India.* Ed B M Gupta. v.9. Delhi, Aditya, (1991)

———. "School Libraries: An Investment for Future" *Indian Book Chronicle*, (1990).

———. "State Central Library, Andhra Pradesh: A Centennial Review (1891-1990)", in *Handbook of Libraries.* Ed. B M Gupta. Delhi, Aditya, (1991).

Taher, Mohamed and A Majeed Pangal, "Bibliographical Control of Islamic Literature in India: Perspectives", *Islamic Culture*, 58 (1984), 161-169.

Taher, Mohamed and M A K Fatimy, "Mosque Library: A Case Study", *ILA Bulletin*, 22 (Apr-Sep, 1984), 38-42.

Taher, Mohamed and M Vishnu Kumar, "Collection Development and Evaluation of the American Studies Research Centre, Hyderabad", *Collection Management*, (1990),

Taher, Mohamed, *et al.* "Dargah Libraries in India: A Comparative

Study", *International Library Review*, 18 (1986), 337-346.

———. "Education for Oriental Librarianship: A Proposal", in *National Seminar on Hundred Years of Library Education and Its Future*. Nagpur, 1987.

———. "Madrasa Libraries in India", *International Library Review*, 21 (1989), 83-98.

Tamil Nadu, Public Libraries (Department of). *Know Your Connemara (State Central) Public Library*. Madras, The author, 1972.

Tarapor, Mahrukh. *Art and Empire: The Discovery of India in Art and Literature, 1851-1947*.PhD Dissertation. Harvard Univ. 1977. (see also DAI ADD X1978)

Thapar, Romila. *Ancient Indian Social History, Some Interpretations*. New Delhi, Orient Longman, 1978.

———. "India", *Encyclopaedia Britannica*. Chicago, Encyclopaedia Britannica Inc. 1988. v.21.

Thompson, J W. *Ancient Libraries*. Connecticut, Anchor, Hamden, 1962.

———. *Medieval Library*. New York, Hafner, 1965.

Trehan, G L, "Dewey Conquers Library India", *Herald of Library Science*, 15 (1976), 295-301.

———. *Learning and Libraries in the Ancient India: A Study*. Chandigarh, Library and Literature House, 1975.

———. *Modern Public Library Movement and Library Legislation for Punjab*. Chandigarh, Library Literature House, 1967.

———. "Library development in Punjab", in Souvenir. Calcutta, Bengal Library Assn. 1988. pp. 112-114.

Usmani, S A and Z R Khan, "Oriental Libraries in India", *Perspectives in Library and Information Science*, Ed. S N Agarwal, *et al*. Lucknow, Print House, 1982.

Vann, Sarah K "Dewey Abroad: The Field Survey of 1964", *Library Resources and Technical Services*, 11 (1967), 61-71.

Vashishth, C P, "Indian Library Association", in *Souvenir*. Calcutta, Bengal Library Assn. 1988. pp.1-11.

———. "Libraries in Delhi: A scenario", in *Souvenir*. Calcutta, Bengal Library Assn. 1988. pp.48-56.

Venkatappaiah, V. *Granthalaya Darshani*. Eluru, Sanchalana Sahiti, 1968.

———. *March of Library Science; Kaula Festschrift*. New Delhi, Vikas, 1979.

Vidyabhushana, S C. *History of Indian Logic*. Calcutta, University of

Calcutta, 1921. p.146.

Wadikar, A L. "Library scene in Madhya Pradesh", in *Souvenir*. Calcutta, Bengal Library Assn. 1988. pp. 84-88.

Waknis, T D, "Public Libraries in India (Janta Libraries)", *Indian Librarian*, 24:3 (Dec 1968), 101-105.

Wali, M D and B K Kaul, "Library Development in Kashmir", *Herald of Library Science* 8:4 (Oct 1969), 298-308.

Wali Mohammed. *Directory of Libraries in the United Provinces of Agra and Oudh.* 1937.

Wasserman, Paul. *Librarian and the Machine, Observations on the Applications of Machines in Administration of College and University Libraries*. Detroit, Gale, 1965.

Wood, Peter. *Vassal State in the Shadow of Empire: Palmer's Hyderabad, 1799-1867*. Ph D Dissertation. University of Wisconsin,1981. (see also DAI 42/03A, p.1276).

Zellner, Aubrey A. *History of Education in the Lower Ganges River Area of India from 1858-1948*. Ph D Dissertation. University of Iowa, 1949.

Ziauddin, M. *Monograph on Muslim Calligraphy*. Calcutta, Viswa Bharathi. 1980.

Zubair, Mohammed. *Islami Kutub Khana.* Delhi, Nadvatul Musannifeen, 1966.

———. *Islami Kutub Khane*. Karachi, Ec. Em. Said, 1978.

KEYWORD INDEX

CICIL LIST

CONCEPTS IN COMMUNICATION, INFORMATICS & LIBRARIANSHIP

(CICIL)

General Editor: **S.P. AGRAWAL**

CICIL-1 Development of Library Services in India: Social Science Information
S.P. Agrawal Rs. 150

CICIL-2 Development of Documentation in India: Social Science Information
S.P. Agrawal Rs. 250

CICIL-3 UNESCO and Social Sciences: Retrospect and Prospect
S.P. Agrawal and **J.C. Aggarwal** Rs. 250

CICIL-4 INDIANA : A Bibliography of Bibliographical Sources
M.K. Jain Rs. 200

CICIL-5 Dimensions of Library and Information Science: Kaula Festschrift
V. Venkatappaiah (Eds.) Rs. 600

CICIL-6 Book Numbers: Some Indian Methods
M.P. Satija and **S.P. Agrawal** Rs. 100

CICIL-7 National Policy for University Libraries in India: Problems and Perspectives
N.B. Inamdar and **L.S. Ramaiah** (Ed.) Rs. 250

CICIL-8 Media Utilisation for the Development of Women and Children
B.S. Thakur and **Binod C. Agrawal** Rs. 150

CICIL-9 Terrorism: An Annotated Bibliography
Susheela Bhan (Ed.) Rs. 275

CICIL-10 Transnational Library Relations: The Indo-American Experience
M.B. Konnur Rs. 175

CICIL-11 Geography of Marketing and Commercial Activities in India (Documentation on Research Information)
R.S. Dixit Rs. 130

CICIL-12 Information India 1988: Global View
S.P. Agrawal and **J.C. Aggarwal** Rs. 200

CICIL-13 Women's Education in India: Historical Review, Present Status and Perspective Plan
S.P. Agrawal and **J.C. Aggarwal** Rs. 360

CICIL-14 Cultural Communication in India: Role and Impact of Phonograms
J.M. Ojha Rs. 220

CICIL-15 Second Historical Survey of Educational Development in India: Select Documents 1985-1989
S.P. Agrawal and **J.C. Aggarwal** Rs. 490

CICIL-16 Documentation Encyclopaedia of UNESCO and Education
J.C. Aggarwal and **S.P. Agrawal** Rs. 800 (set of 2 parts)

CICIL-17 Attitude Towards Information: A Study of Post-Graduate Teachers and Researchers in Social Sciences
N.G. Satish (in press)

CICIL-18 Librarianship and Bureaucratic Organisation: A Study in the Sociology of Library Profession in India
P.K. Jayaswal Rs. 175

CICIL-19 Literature Search
K.A. Isaac Rs. 150

CICIL-20 Child Education in India: Index to Scholarly Writings in Indian Educational Journals and Newspapers since independence
S.P. Agrawal and **Naresh Kanta** Rs. 100

CICIL-21 Lok Sabha and Vidhan Sabha Elections in India 1989 & 1990: Process and Results with Comparative Study of Manifestos
S.P. Agrawal and **J.C. Aggarwal** Rs. 250

CICIL-22 Islamic Studies in India: A Survey of Human, Institutional and Documentary Sources
Mohamed Taher Rs. 180

CICIL-23 Panchayati Raj: An Annotated Bibliography
N.B. Inamdar, N.G. Satish and **Anil Takalkar** 290

CICIL-24 Information India 1989-90: Global View
S.P. Agrawal and **J.C. Aggarwal** Rs. 500

CICIL-25 First Handbook of Psychological and Social Instruments
Udai Pareek and **T. Venkateswara Rao** Rs. 500

CICIL-26 Educational and Social Uplift of Backward Classes: At What Cost and How? Mandal Commission and After
S.P. Agrawal and **J.C. Aggarwal** Rs. 275

CICIL-27 Mass Media and New Horizons: Impact of TV & Video an Urban Milieu
H.R. Trivedi Rs. 180

CICIL-28 Indian Writings on Education : An Indicator to Indian Educational Journals Grouped by Subject Deseriptors 1979 to 1986 (in two parts)
S.P. Agarwal Rs. 900 (per set)

CICIL-29 Nation in Crisis
S.P. Agrawal and **J.C. Aggarwal** Rs. 200

CICIL-30 Information India 1990-91: Global View
S.P. Agrawal and **J.C. Aggarwal** Rs. 500

CICIL-31 Development of University Libraries in India after Independence
O.P. Gupta Rs. 270

CICIL-32 Handbook on Child : With Historical Background
Pramila Pandit Barooah Rs. 320

CICIL-33 Weaker Section in Indian Society : Undiscovered Past, Uncertain Present and Unpredictable Future : Index to Writings in Indian Scholarly Journals and 10 National Newspapers Classified under 1500 Descriptors 1886-1990
S.P. Agrawal and **Rajeev Kumar Sharma** Rs. 600

CICIL-34 Communication Informatics and Librarianship in India : An Introductory Guide to Publications Based on a Survey of Libraries in Capital City of India
S.P. Agrawal and **Pushpa Rani Sharma** Rs. 720

CICIL-35 Problems of Collection Development in Special Libraries
M.S. Sridhar Rs. 225

CICIL-36 National Information Resources for Social Sciences in India : Mobilisation Dispersal and International Enhancement
S.P. Agrawal Rs. 225

CICIL-37 Modern History of Punjab : A Look Back into Ancient Peaceful Punjab Focusing Confrontation and Failures Leading to Present Punjab Problem, and a Peep Ahead : Relevant Select Documents
J.C. Aggarwal and **S.P. Agrawal** Rs. 400

CICIL-38 India Information Sources : Economics and Business
Kyllikki Ruokonen and **Manohar Lal** Rs.

CICIL-39 Educational Planning in India : With a Slant to Educational Financing and Administration, Vol. 1, Reports of Committees and Commissions, Five Year Plans, Statistical Tables
J.C. Aggarwal and **S.P. Agrawal** Rs. 650

CICIL-40 Integrated Library System : Two Case Studies : Latin America and India
Maria Luiza Rigo Pasquarelli, Rosaly Favero Krzyanowski, Ines Maria M. Imperatriz and S.P. Agrawal Rs. 160

CICIL-41 Social Science Information in India: Effort towards Bibliographical Control
S.D. Vyas Rs. 300

CICIL-42 Higher Education in India Since Independence: U.G.C. and Its Approach
O.P. Gupta Rs. 360

CICIL-43 Government and Politics in India: A Bibliographical Study of Contemporary Scenario Chronicling Rajiv Gandhi Era
S.P. Agrawal and **Rajeev Kumar Sharma** Rs. 500

CICIL-44 Second Handbook of Psychological and Social Instruments
D.M. Pestonjee Rs. 300

CICIL-45 Development/Digression Diary of India; 3D Companion Volume to Information India: 1990-91
S.P. Agrawal Rs. 200

CICIL-46 Development/Digression Diary of India; 3D Companion Volume to Information India: 1991-92
S.P. Agrawal Rs. 300

CICIL-47 Information India 1991-92: Global View
S.P. Agrawal and **J.C. Aggarwal** Rs. 500

CICIL-48 Committees and Commissions in India 1974, A Concept's Project, Compiled by a team of professionals guided by **Virender Kumar** (Vol. 12) Rs. 450

CICIL-49 Committees and Commissions in India 1975, A Concept's Project, Compiled by a team of professionals guided by **Virender Kumar** (Vol. 13) Rs. 450

CICIL-50 Committees and Commissions in India 1976, A Concept's Project, Compiled by a team of professionals guided **Virender Kumar** (Vol. 14) Rs. 450

CICIL-51 Committees and Commissions in India 1977, A Concept's Project, Compiled by a team of professionals guided by **Virender Kumar** (Vol. 15) (in four parts) Rs. 450 each

CICIL-52 Committees and Commissions in India 1978, A Concept's Project, Compiled by a team of professionals guided by **Virender Kumar** (Vol. 16) (in two parts) Rs. 450 each

CCL-53 Subject Guide to Communication, Informatics and Librarianship in India (Based on a Survey of Library Holdings in Capital City of India)
S.P. Agrawal and **Pushpa Rani Sharma** Rs. 400

CCL-54 Restructurring of Library and Information Science Curriculum
A. Tejomurty Rs. 250

CCL-55 Committees and Commissions in India 1979, A Concept's Project, Compiled by a team of professionals guided by **Virender Kumar** (Vol. 17) (in two parts) Rs. 450 each

CCL-56 Committees and Commissions in India 1980, A Concept's Project, Compiled by a team of professionals guided by **Virender Kumar** (Vol. 18) (in two parts) Rs. 450 each

CCL-57 Third Historical Survey of Educational Development in India
S.P. Agrawal and **J.C. Aggarwal** Rs. 700

CCIL-58 Model Library Legislation
Velaga Venkatappaiah Rs. 400

CCIL-59 Indian Library and Information Science Literature (1990-91)
Sewa Singh Rs. 525

CCIL-60 Librarianship and Library Science in India
Mohamed Taher abd **Donald Gordon Davis, Jr.** Rs. 350